*Just Like
Bob Zimmerman's Blues*
DYLAN
In Minnesota

Dave Engel

River City Memoirs - Mesabi, Rudolph, Wis.

Copyright © 1997 by Dave Engel
River City Memoirs-Mesabi, Rudolph, WI 54475

All rights reserved. Reproduction in whole or in part of any portion in any form without permission is prohibited.

First Edition

*Library of Congress Cataloging-in-Publication Data 96-071974
ISBN: 0-942495-61-6*

Printed and distributed by
Amherst Press, PO Box 296, Amherst WI 54406

Unlike the typical Dylanologist, Dave Engel lives and breathes the north country. The Wisconsin native has published numerous history-based books in the *River City Memoirs* series, including *Shanagolden* and *The North Woods Journal of Charles C. Hamilton*. He is the founder of *Mid-State Poetry Towers* and *Hepcat's Revenge*.

Turning a corner in 1965, Dave first heard "Subterranean Homesick Blues" by "Bobby Dye-lan" on the car radio. The experience completely changed Dave's life. *Not really.* Dave's first Dylanography was spurned a quarter-century ago. But he never lost the faith, not even in the Christian period. *Self Portrait; Saved; Under the Red Sky; World Gone Wrong.* Will *you* swear on the Bible you bought *Empire Burlesque?* Now, after umpteen-million Dylan books by others, Dave has, in a truly existential act, written this unique homage to person and place. *Man wants $11 bills? You only got ten.*

American music bucked the Mississippi upstream from New Orleans to St. Louis and Davenport, flared east to Chicago, then zigzagged north toward Hibbing, where it coalesced with polka bands, *Your Hit Parade*, Faron Young and Bobby Vee, into the phenomenon of Robert Zimmerman. This is an immigrant's tale and a wicked messenger's; scholars will consult *Just Like Bob Zimmerman's Blues* for many years to help explicate Dylan and the genre he created.

Toby Thompson, author of Positively Main Street

Cover: Howard Street, Hibbing, looking west, c. 1959. *IRRC*

till I heard the sound
A the iron ore cars rollin' down...
I'd shyly wave t' the throttle man
An' count the cars as they rolled past
Bob Dylan, 1963

Aubin Studio

Ore train heading east through Hibbing.

Acknowledgments

Toby Thompson, whose epigush, *Positively Main Street*, remains an enduring testament. Norman Arendt, for gifts; Paul Aubin, who took the pictures; Ed and Judy Beckers, "mi casa es su casa"; Robert Des Jarlais, the adventurous boy; Roberta Schloesser, "I have some names"; Barry Singer, "I think you'll be excited by this." Those who shared: John Bucklen—soul; Sally Engel—LaserJet & lagniappe; Larry Fabbro—*Hematite;* Rick Kangas—a dream; Robert J. Karon—youth forever; Lynda Knudsen—trust; Jim Nuhlicek—friendship; William Pagel—devotion. My wife, Kathy, without whom this would be a blank sheet of bleached pulp.

& Kathy Adams, Denise Adams (State of Minn.), Hebert Aldrich, Zachary Baker (Yivo Institute), David Beckers, Bert & Sue Bergeron, James Beron, Claudia Bodway, John Bushey, Pat Cadigan, Colbert S. Cartwright, Echo Casey, Chicago Public Library, David Christenson (Zimmy's Downtown Bar & Grill), Florian Chmielewski, WLMH Clark, Isadore Crystal, Rabbi E. Daniel Danson, Johnny Dark, The Depot (Duluth), John Dougherty, Douglas County Courthouse, Duluth *News Tribune*, Bobby DuPah, Monte Edwardson, Jill Elzinga (McMillan Memorial Library), Angelica Engel, Gary Engel, Elissa Engel, Jessica Engel (Chisholm Senior Citizens Polka Club), Kenneth Engel, Deb Fena (Iron Range Research Center), Donna French, Greg Frey, Robert Frisk, Larry Furlong, Conrad Gabrielson, Joe Gallant, Earle Garber, Pat Gargano, Bud Gazelka, Lynn Gigliotti (Hibbing High School Library), Neil Gillis, Bruce Golob (Camp Herzl), Nancy Gooding, Dominic & Doris Grillo, Jerry Grillo, Warren Grillo, George C. Haidos, James L. Hansen (State Hist. Society of Wis.), Dale Hanson, Rev. Kenneth Hanson, Hibbing High School, Hibbing Historical Society, LeRoy & Bette Hoikkala, Justin Isherwood, Alan D. Johnson, Dennis Johnson, Don Johnson (Duluth Public Library), Odin Johnson, Richard Johnson, David Karakash, Elizabeth Kenyon (Chisholm Public Library), Joseph Korman (Fairlawn Museum), Dan & Diana Kossoff, William Lah, Lew Latto, William Lawlor, Jenny Ledeen, Frances Lopides, Angel Marolt, Casey Martin, Mick & Laurie McCuistion *(On the Tracks)*, Barbara McGowan, Patricia Maus (N.E. Minn. Hist. Center), Ugo Mechesney, Frank Mehle, Charles Miller, Terry Moore (Hibbing Public Library), David Morton, Gary E. Myers, Charles Nara, Nancy Neumann (Sioux City Public Library), James Nehiba, Ed Nelson (IRRC), Gene Nicolelli, Steve Nielsen (Minn. Hist. Soc.), Dennis Nylen, Tom O'Hearn, Jr., Jim Oldsberg, Jacqueline O'Reilly, Benedict Orlando, Dee Dee Paolo, Ruth Pavich, Tom Paxton, Kenneth Pederson, George Peterson, Kevin Proffitt (Am. Jewish Archives), Jim Propotnick, Judy Radovich (Homer Bar), Mark A. Raider (Am. Jewish Hist. Soc.), Lynette Randy, Nancy Riesgraf (Hibbing Public Library), Barbara M.J. Samarzia (St. Louis County Courthouse), Mark Scarborough, Beth Schaeffer (McMillan), Linda Schloff (Jewish Hist. Soc. of the Upper Midwest), Robert Sedlock, Joanne M. Sher, Julie Smith (IRRC), Charles & Roberta Spanbauer, Hebert Stern, George Stoupe, Thom Strick, Ron & Sharon Taddei, Ione Tomasetti, Bobby Vee, Jon Walstrom (MHS), Richard Wissolik, Hebert Wojcik, Charlotte Wright, Mary Yeager, Al Zdon

There are others but that's our little secret.

To Government Weirdo and President Crazy
Who traveled every trail.

1996 by President Crazy, age 6

Minnesota
1950
Minnesota Historical Society

Contents

Chapter 1   **3,000 Hebrews** (Superior/Hibbing)...................11
Chapter 2   **The One-Legged Street Singer** (Duluth)....... 29
Chapter 3   **King Hematite** (First Grade)......................... 49
Chapter 4   **Positively Howard Street** (Second Grade)...... 59
Chapter 5   **Agudath Achim** (Third Grade)....................... 69
Chapter 6   **The Political World** (Fourth Grade) 77
Chapter 7   **Over the Rainbow** (Fifth Grade).................... 83
Chapter 8   **North Country Fair** (Sixth Grade).................95
Chapter 9   **The Garmaker Syndrome** (Seventh Grade)..... 103
Chapter 10   **Blackboard Jungle** (Eighth Grade).................115
Chapter 11   **Rebel Without A Cause** (Freshman)............... 129
Chapter 12   **Daddy Cool** (Sophomore)............................... 143
Chapter 13   **Golden Chords/Glissendorf** (Junior).............. 163
Chapter 14   **Elston Gunn** (Senior)......................................193
Bibliography... 211
Index.. 215

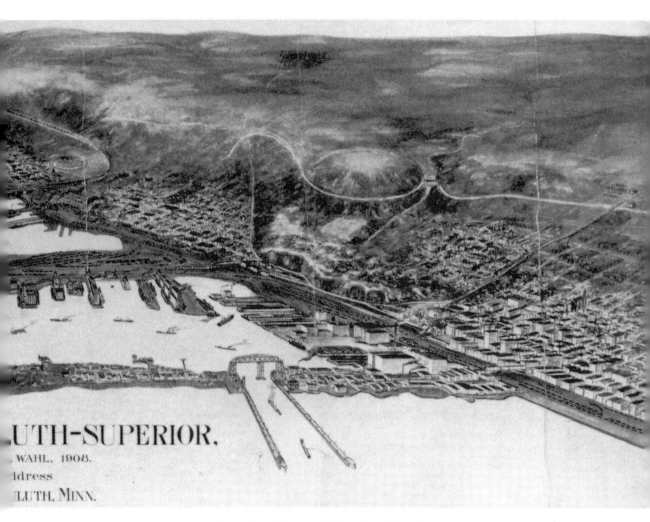

Douglas County Historical Society

Superior, Wis.
Connors Point, bottom left
Douglas County Historical Society

Chapter One
Superior/Hibbing
1893-1924

3000 Hebrews

My so-called Jewish roots are in Egypt. They went down there with Joseph, and they came back out with Moses, you know, the guy that killed the Egyptian, married an Ethiopian girl and brought the law down from the mountain. The same Moses whose staff turned into a serpent. The same person who killed three thousand Hebrews for getting down, stripping off their clothes and dancing around a golden calf. These are my roots. Jacob had four wives and 13 children, who fathered an entire people. These are my roots too.
<u>Minneapolis City Pages</u>, *1983*

Grandma's home, he hushes—and pries open the window. *We can't let her find us up here.* Pushes the girl out. *I gotta go t' the library!* he yells, hurries down the stairs. *Gotta go.* Grabs some books and slams the door. *Bye.* Sneaks around the side of the house to Echo. Blonde on blonde, baby-smooth, free spirit, soul mate, wrong-side-of-tracks, motorcycle Madonna—Echo is *there* for Bobby this spring afternoon in 1957. Echo is *there* at 7th Avenue and 25th Street, in broad daylight, hanging by her manicured fingernails from the sun porch over the garage roof. Her skirt's up around her waist and Bobby's below waiting to catch her, she hopes. She guesses the whole wide world is watching.

In the flat-roofed stucco house on the corner are three second-story bedrooms: one at the head of the stairs for Bobby's parents (Abe and Beatty Zimmerman); a second down the hall on the right for the boys (Robert Allen and David Benjamin); and, on the left, a bedroom for the grandmother, *Florence Sara Stone*, 64, twelve years widowed. She's a typical, middle-class grandmother, living with her daughter's middle-class family in their middle-class American home in a middle-class neighborhood in the middle-class American town of Hibbing, in Minnesota, the most middle-class state, in the midst of the most middle-class decade of America's middle-class 20th Century. *Vive la bourgeoisie.*

Yet Florence, like so many of her neighbors on the Mesabi Iron Range, speaks with an accent of long ago and far away.

AGUDATH ACHIM

Roots, man—we're talking about Jewish roots. Check up on Elijah the prophet. He could make rain. Isaiah the prophet, even Jeremiah—see if their brethren didn't want to bust their brains for telling it right like it is, yeah—these are my roots, I suppose. Am I looking for them? Well, I don't know. I ain't looking for them in

synagogues with six pointed Egyptian stars shining down from every window, I can tell you that much.
  Minneapolis City Pages, 1983

"Tell me about your grandma, Bobby."
   There's nothin' t' tell.
   There's nothin' to tell about Grandma Stone. Well, yeah, her father, Bobby's great-grandfather, is 87, if being old means anything. Otherwise, there's nothin' to tell about Great-Grandpa Edelstein. *Benjamin Harold Edelstein.* He likes to be called "B.H." but signed his 1916 naturalization papers, "Boruch"—which happens to be Hebrew for "blessed," much as "Edelstein" is German for "precious stone." Ben Precious Stone. *So what? Some words have meanings.*

You have to be born somewhere and his place was Kovno, Lithuania. Boruch is a Jew and Jews lived in Kovno four hundred years and more. If you have to be born somewhere, better that it be somewhere else. Attacked by Cossacks, Poles and Russians in turn, Jews flee into the night, only to return time and again because you have to live some place. In the 1800s, the reforms of Czar Alexander II allow the Kovno Ashkenazi to breathe freely for a while.

In 1881, when Boruch is eleven, a terrorist bomb kills the "good czar." While Alexander III fiddles, freelance mobs commit vandalism, rape and murder against Jews. So what? *There's nothin' t' tell about the pogroms.* Or the government persecution that follows, in which conscripted males are often never heard from again. Besides, everyday life is overcrowded, shabby and destitute. Yet, between 1800 and 1900, world Jewish population *increases* from 2.5 to 10.6 million, mostly in the area to which they are confined—the "Pale of Settlement" that includes Lithuania, White Russia and the Ukraine.

So what if Boruch marries *Lybba Jaffe*, daughter of Aaron and Fannie Jaffe. *The family is common in Kovno and most people do get married.*

Born in 1892 to Boruch and Lybba is *Fage*, to be known as Florence. The Edelstein's home is the *shtetl* or village of Vilkomir, said to be a stronghold for Jewish zealots. An 1897 census counts 7,287 Jews in Vilkomir, comprising 53 percent of the population. The shtetl is considerably farther north than Minnesota and Wisconsin, for which many of Boruch's friends have departed.

By law, Jews cannot leave the Pale of Settlement unless they abandon Russia entirely. In less than 25 years, more than a third of the region's Jews say *guten tog*. The majority settle in New York City. Among the states, tenth on the list of destinations is Minnesota.

By 1900, a million Jews reside in America; by 1910, the number is two million; by 1914, three million. Beginning by peddling and rag-picking, many rise quickly to white collar occupations, professions and business ownership. The happy result is described by historian S.M. Dubnow, in 1918: "the poor, down-trodden, faint-hearted inhabitant of the infamous Pale, with the Damocles sword of brutal mob rule dangling constantly over his head ... transformed ... into a free American Jew who holds his head proudly, whom no one would dare to offend, and who has become a citizen in the full sense of the word."

So what? A lotta people go from one place to another.

Boruch, Lybba, and four children depart, in 1902, aboard the "Tunisia." From Liverpool, England, they pass through St. John, New Brunswick, and Montreal, Quebec, to enter the U.S. at Sault St. Marie, Michigan, on Christmas Eve. They settle among relatives at Superior, Wis. With proper dispatch, B.H. renounces Nicholas II, "Emperor of All the Russians."

In quick succession come brothers and sisters, of whom Boruch is second oldest: Chana Reva or *Ann*, Samuel, Morris, Roy L., Etta, Lena, Rose and Sarah. With other Lithuanian Jews, the Edelsteins settle the flat, industrial "north end," called West Superior. In the shadow of grain elevators and shipyards, Boruch's brother, Samuel, immediately establishes a furniture and stove dealership.

With the arrival of their parents, David and Ida (daughter of Yehuda Aren and Rachel Berkovitz a.k.a. Weinberg), the family is rebuilt in the new north. Looking quite ancient in his long beard, David Edelstein, who does not speak English, attempts to teach his grandchildren Hebrew. If someone must perpetuate the holy rituals, it might as well be him.

THE KEY IS FRANK

"Faith is the key!" said the first king. "No, froth is the key!" said the second, "You're both wrong," said the third, "the key is Frank!"
<u>John Wesley Harding</u> cover notes, 1968

January, 1892, Florence Edelstein is born at Vilkomir, Russia. On another cold side of the world, Frank Hibbing clears a road west from Mountain Iron, Minn., where iron ore had been discovered the previous year. After twenty miles, the crew sets up camp on land Frank has leased.

At the late break of winter dawn, Frank emerges from his tent, shakes frost from his whiskers and utters the Iron Range's most enduring quotation: "I believe there is iron under me. My bones feel rusty and chilly."

As Frank's yeomen scrape with picks and shovels, it is not long before— Gesundheit!—they have tickled the largest exploitable body of iron ore in the world. The ensuing boom town is named "Hibbing" after its finder, planner and benefactor.

But who is this namesake, Frank Hibbing? Locals say he was born at Kirchboitzen, Hanover, Germany, in 1856, as Franz Dietrich von Ahlen; that he came to America at age 18, taking the name Hibbing after his Episcopal, English-born mother, who died when he was an infant.

Yet, in 1885, when he marries Barbara Lutz, of the Stevens Point, Wis., brewing family, he says his parents are H.D. and Catherine Hibbing; not von Ahlen. Later, his death certificate says he, Frank Hibbing, was born in Holland, not Germany. Kirchboitzen Kirchenbuchern name "Diederich Hibbing," born Dec. 14, 1855, of "unclear ancestry," and "Dietrich Heinrich Ahlden," born Dec. 6, 1855. Ship's logs supposedly say the two emigrated together June 8, 1872, and changed or exchanged names.

At Stevens Point, What's-His-Name loses three fingers in a sawmill accident and fails the study of law due to his poor English. Later, as a timber cruiser, he becomes adept at finding ore. In 1885, he helps lay out Bessemer, Michigan, for mine developer Dan Merritt and moves to Duluth in 1887.

After his big dig west of Mountain Iron, he leases large tracts of land, using the cash of A.S. Trimble, of Duluth, since he is virtually penniless himself. He forms the Lake Superior Iron Co., which is almost immediately absorbed by the New York and Missabe Iron Co. Pretty soon it's a Rockefeller subsidiary and then United States Steel Corp. What's-His-Name is reputedly a millionaire.

An in-law, Michael Lutz, is among the first residents of "Hibbing" but the man for whom the Iron Ore Capital is named never actually lives there. "Capt. Hibbing" resides at 1830 East Superior Street, Duluth, in a modest two-story house near the lake, and keeps office hours downtown at the Lyceum Building.

He is sitting on top of the world—until something goes awry with his appendix. After an operation, he's told peritonitis has set in and he has but a few hours to live. The "millionaire" calls for his bookkeeper, dictates a few last business deals and cashes in his checks at 11:15 p.m., July 30, 1897. The Benevolent and Protective Order Of Elks throws one in a long line of largest funerals ever seen in the city as they convey the remains to Forest Hills Cemetery.

Besides his wife, Barbara, among the bereaved is Anna Marie, a nine-year-old adopted daughter, whose lineage is attributed to a "brother-in-law." Probate papers enumerate values in real property of a mere $25,000, consisting of lots in Duluth and Hibbing and timber and mining lands in Minnesota.

At the time of his death, the eponymous old pioneer, according to most accounts, is about 40 years old.

KING HEMATITE

There is a lot of Indian Spirit. The earth there is unusual, filled with ore. So there is something happening that is hard to define. There's a magnetic attraction there, maybe thousands and thousands of years ago some planet bumped into the land there. There is a great spiritual quality throughout the Mid West. Very subtle, very strong and that is where I grew up.
    Playboy, 1978

80 acres are set aside in 1893 for the town site—far enough south, Frank Hibbing figures, that the settlement won't be disturbed for a while. By the end of the first year, someone counts three hotels, five saloons, three food stores, three real estate dealers, two meat markets and other shops—serving 326 inhabitants. Southern European and Finnish miners share the boardwalks of Pine Street with lumberjacks from nearby camps.

Almost immediately, plagues test the town. With the only water drawn from the village well, a typhoid epidemic ensues. Locusts devour everything green, including paper money. An unrelated national financial panic threatens. The 1894 Hinckley fire sparks unfounded hysteria.

None of it matters. Every Cousin Jack and Brother Job can keel over dead and he'll be replaced in a New York minute. In Hibbing, drawn by ferrous magnetism, accumulate the pioneers: peddlers, minstrels, podiatrists, preachers, nimrods, drunks and drones looking to make a buck. A man such as R.D. Birdie can disembark with 35 cents in his pocket and a pack of cigars on his back to become one of Hibbing's first promoters. James Dillon, a "dray man," can charge $1 per move and expect to have things named after him some day.

By 1900, Hibbing is so prosperous that, seeking to dispose of a substantial sum raised for charity, a committee can find only three needy widows in the entire village. The democratic wealth is quickly gentrified—by churches: Methodist, Catholic, Episcopal, Finnish Lutheran, Presbyterian—by the first high school graduation, the 1903 class of two—by, in 1907, the Carnegie public library with arched, stained-glass ceiling and breathtaking murals. Not to mention a public Comfort Station, two municipal potato warehouses, a municipal barn and marketplace and a city day nursery on Pine Street.

Athletics already abound: basketball in 1895; high school sports 1906-07; a girls basketball team in 1910. Baseball, boxing, wrestling, curling and horse racing. For other entertainment there are theaters: Power's—a vaudeville house that also shows films; Peoples'—the first real picture house, built December 1, 1906. Soon, the Bijou, Lyric and Victory.

In 1910, Hibbing's population of 8,800 entitles it to fifth place among the state's municipalities, with sewers, municipal lighting plant, fire department, the largest grade school building north of the Twin Cities and a superb high school.

After a few years, local writer Sandford Howard describes a chain of iron mines, mountains of ore dumps, a network of railroad beds and hundreds of noisy locomotives. Of the many parks that provide free wood and fireplaces, Bennett is the best. Its zoo holds monkeys, deer, buffalo and birds. There are organizations such as Boy Scouts, YWCA, American Legion and National Guard and an excellent concert band. For a nominal monthly co-payment, the Oliver Mining Co. sends its ill or injured employees to Rood, one of three hospitals.

From Europe, encouraged by labor agents, come immigrants. The flow of Italians fleeing high taxes, overpopulation and agricultural crises crests in 1907. Next, Slavs, Czechs, Serbs and Slovenes, leaving economic and political turmoil. The multitudes of peasants, Jews and political dissidents from the USSR, Baltic States and Finland peak in 1913. Add Germans, Scandinavians, Greeks, English and Celts to total more than 40 nationalities, speaking a variety of languages and dialects, all bound for the town named after What's-His-Name: Eebeen, H'bink, H'binga. With 75 percent of foreign birth, the Iron Range acquires an ethnic variety usually found only in the most cosmopolitan centers. "Remember when the mark of a miner was his handle-bar mustache, and the pick and shovel was a major dirt-moving combination?" prompts the Hibbing *Tribune*. "The long frame boarding houses were the homes of these mining pioneers who spoke a babel of European languages and the swinging doors of a saloon were the entrance to the club."

An alert of sorts is sounded as the city is found to be underlaid with rich iron ore and mines begin to encroach upon the business section. The Oliver Mining Co. has leased the mineral rights under Hibbing. In 1918 it begins buying surface rights. That year, the first building is moved south to Central Addition, a subdivision owned by Oliver, in a suburb called Alice.

EDELSTEIN

contrary t rumors, I am very proud of where I'm from an also of the many blood streams that run in my roots.
   To Emergency Civil Liberties Committee, 1963

Did I ever tell ya I got my nose from the Indian blood in my veins? Well, that's the truth, hey. Got an uncle who's a Sioux.
   (1961) <u>Bob Dylan</u>, pub. 1971

Boruch Edelstein does not stay in Superior, Wis. From the boreal forests seventy-five miles north, comes the call of native opportunity. The iron mines are going great guns and each new boom town has a major hunger for merchandise and services. B.H. moves up to twelve-year-old Hibbing in 1904. After the birth of Jennie in June 1905, the rest of the family follows.

Already, there are Hebrew brethren on the Mesabi Range—in Tower, Eveleth, Virginia and Chisholm. Kitzville Location is named for Jacob Kitz, a Jew. On Hibbing's Pine Street, Charles Hallock operates a clothing store. He is soon joined by the Sachs brothers' Fair Store. Other early Jewish arrivals are Max Greenblatt, Max Rogalsky and Nathan Nides. Simon Sapero, with sons Moe and Abe, opens a ready-to-wear store in nearby Chisholm.

Boruch, now called Benjamin, does as did his brother, Samuel, in Superior; he finds a market for furniture and cast-iron stoves. Soon, he enters the emerging silent movie and vaudeville theater business with the Victory in downtown Hibbing. His sons, Max and Julius, join him in the Garden Theatre at Alice. Benjamin's daughters also help out in the business as the family home follows the moving city from North Hibbing to Brooklyn neighborhood to new Hibbing.

By now, B.H. can speak English with only a trace of an accent. Though to the world, he's a little Yiddish guy taking tickets, his word at home is law. An old-country patriarch, he's stubborn and opinionated. An officer in the Hibbing synagogue, he might question the meaning of life but dutifully reads the Talmud, prays every day and keeps the Sabbath. His kosher home bustles on Jewish holidays. When the family sits down to any Shabbat dinner, there are most likely a dozen family members plus relatives and guests.

On one such occasion, so the story goes, the house is crowded as usual; nevertheless, a traveling salesman is invited to stay for dinner. *Think nothing of it. You'll do the same for us some time.*

The salesman takes a place of honor next to B.H. Served first, he accepts the platter of stuffed chicken neck casings called *helzel*. As the rest wait hungrily for their turn, he consumes the entire contents, smiling and complimenting. *Wonderful!*

Later, the family laughs about the salesman *who ate all the helzel.*

Of ten Edelstein children, four are born in Lithuania: Florence (1892), Goldie (1896), Julius (1896) and Rose (1899). Two are born in Superior: Samuel (1903) and Jennie (June 8, 1905); and four more in Hibbing: Max (1906), Mike (1908), Ethel (1911) and Sylvia (1912).

The other girls resemble Lybba, but short, dark-eyed Florence takes after B.H. In her youth, she is said to be "unconventionally pretty," her dark hair worn loosely to the side. Her family finds her witty, warm and compassionate. She is one of those clever cooks who can concoct a meal for ten from one chicken. A favorite old-country treat is ground lung meat rolled in dough and called "Lungenmundah."

Don't ask me nothin' about Grandma. There's nothin' t' tell.

SUPERIOR

I pity the poor immigrant
Who tramples through the mud
Who fills his mouth with laughing
and who builds his town with blood.
  "I Pity the Poor Immigrant," 1968

Superior, Wisconsin. 1885. Iron ore. Millions of tons by rail from the Gogebic and Vermilion ranges, shipped on the Great Lakes to the steel cities of mid-America. And grain. Billions of bushels from the Great Plains, shipped to mill cities in Michigan and east.

Superior, tough, flat-chested little sister of Duluth, Minnesota, inclined to saloons and whorehouses—by the turn of the century, second in Wisconsin only to Milwaukee in population. Along with thousands of Swedes, Finns and Poles, scores of newly-arrived Jews find their way along the harbor, pushing peddlers' carts among grain elevators, ore docks, scrap iron docks, warehouses, coke ovens, coal cranes and freight cars embarking for Chicago and Pittsburgh and Cleveland.

Most Jews of Superior have come *from* Vilkomir, Lithuania, to escape the czar's regime and *to* Superior because of a relative. Consider the Kaners. The old man, *Shabsie Solomon Kaner*, comes in 1888; couple years later, sends for his wife and kids. One by one, manages to get four or five of his brothers over; before long some of *them* go out and get married and pretty soon there are twenty-five or more families of Kaners around. Likewise, so many Sabses, Sabsies, Shapsies and Shabsies, one is called "Shabsie Downtown," another, "Shabsie Connors Point." To confuse matters worse, a fair number of *Shabsies* are called *Sam*. So they call the one on John Avenue, "Sam the John Kaner." And so on.

Some say you can tell old-country Jews a mile off, real bearded greenhorns picking iron or selling fish. *Hilstein, Holzberg, Lasky, Lurye, Siegel, Nides, Kaner, Averbrook, Karon, Cohen, Popkin.* They dress and talk strange, foreign, backwards, Yiddish. *Sheenies!* Some Swedish or Finnish kids fling snowballs and curses. *Kikes!*

Orthodox Agudas Achim congregation, "the Hebrew Brotherhood," begins worship in 1890 at Shabsie the Sam Kaner's at John and Second Street. In 1892, a Connors Point schoolhouse is moved to Sixth Street and Banks Avenue for a synagogue. But some of the high-toned Germanic Jews with businesses on Tower Avenue prefer not to associate with peddlers and start their own synagogue.

SOLEMOVITZ

I took the Dylan because I have an uncle named Dillon. I changed the spelling but only because it looked better. I've read some of Dylan Thomas's stuff, and it's not the same as mine. We're different.

What about your family?

Well, I just don't have any family, I'm all alone.

<u>Chicago Daily News</u>, 1965

There's nothin' t' tell about Solemovitz, the Jew peddler. Just another Shabsie. The peddlers call him Shabsie Collis-Pointee. Or Sam. *Sam Connors Point.* Born in 1853 to Abraham and Mary "Salamovitz," he's one of the first Lithuanian Jews to arrive at Superior—in 1888 or 89, about the same time as his in-laws, the Kaners. After five years, he brings his wife, "Bessie," and family, including Ben, born in September, 1883.

Shabsie Collis-Pointee.

The 1893 Superior city directory calls him *Robert Solomowitch*. He's a peddler, this Samuel or Robert, residing at 482 Main Street, Connor's Point, Superior. *You can call me Bob.* It's the same address used by one of Superior's four Samuel Kaners, also a peddler. Solemovitz's younger sister, Kate, marries Shabsie Kaner; his sister Chana marries Oser Shabsie Kaner.

The 1900 census records Solemovitz as a literate, dry goods peddler and homeowner. His 43-year-old wife, *Bessie*, cannot read, write, nor speak English. Their children are: *Rosy*, 13, in school; *Eddy*, in school and *Ida*, 16, a servant. Son Ben has worked several years as a clerk for both Azriel Averbrook and Mark & Karon. In 1900, he is penciled in "at Rochester," a "dry goods peddler." Ben has been a merchant all his young life. In order to sell things, he will continue to make his way into the wilderness.

NORTH COUNTRY FAIR

I don't have much of a Jewish background. I'm not a patriot to any creed. I believe in all of them and none of them. A devout Christian or Moslem can be just as effective as a devout Jew.

<u>Playboy</u>, 1978

There's nothin' t' tell. Dock workers across the pond see the old Jew peddler leave the shack before dawn. A little later, the mother trudges toward the mainland. Now maybe the pretty little daughter will show herself with some washing. *So what?*

It's 10 a.m., Sept. 24, 1906, an ordinary Monday. But wait! Instead of the girl, it's a fish peddler crossing the front yard who suddenly falls to his knees, fervent Yiddish gushing forth. *Got in himmel! The breast of her dress red with blood...*

The fish peddler rushes from shack to shack along Main Street, the lone thoroughfare of the peninsula that is Connors Point. Neighbors and dock workers quickly gather around.

Can it be pretty little Ida Solemovitz? A Finn milkman searches the rooms next door for bachelor John Young's old but still-working telephone. When Police Chief McKinnon arrives, he looks at Ida. *Show me to Young*, he says.

In the back room of his dwelling, Young's body is found against a wall, his head blown apart by a gun shot, a shining .32 caliber revolver nearby.

The bodies of Ida and John are loaded on McKinnon's wagon and driven to the coroner's office. The mother is summoned. *Oi!* The father rushes in. *Ida!*

The distraught father, Sam Solemovitz, confesses *John Young* had wanted to marry his daughter. From Young's pocket, the coroner pulls a crumpled, handwritten note. "In 1900 I came to West Superior. I treat everybody white and everybody treats me white in the city. I have lived two years on the point. In June 1906, Ida told me to ask her father if we could wed. I asked her father and he did not say yes or no.

"Then after that every time I would go up town she would tell me I would be sorry for it, going up town every night with other girls. Her mother makes my bread for me.

"Ida come to my room last week. She told me she would put poison in my bread and poison me if I went with other girls.

"She said to me, 'John I will die with you. *I want for you to die among the Jews like Christ.*'

"Then I said to her, 'my dear, don't have the like in your mind.'

"Then I laughed. I was up again it. The Jews shall remember me... Ida told me they killed Christ. Put both of us down in one place as we met and had to part. We loved each other. She made me do this. Goodbye."

Ida has *never* been intimate with her murderer, Sam says. Young is *meshugeh*, he says. Crazy! At home, Sam sits forever in his chair, a dead man weeping. Sorrow like this, never has a father felt.

Neighbors explain that Young, an unemployed former worker for the Great Northern railroad shops, had lived in the adjoining rooms for three years or more and was a frequent visitor at the Solemovitz home, doing odd jobs in return for cooking and sewing from Mrs. Solemovitz and the girl.

Young was not handsome, "decidedly the opposite," in the opinion of the *Superior Telegram*. "His face lacks the look of average intelligence." Young's sister, May McDonald, testifies that, while composing his farewell note Young asked her how to spell "Ida."

"I guess I will turn Jew," he told her.

"You might as well," his sister said, "You are with them most of the time."

An investigation finds the kitchen in a wild state of disorder. *I guess I will turn Jew*. Police figure Young asked Ida to marry him. *You might as well*. Upon her refusal, Young fired point blank into the girl's breast and she ran out the back door.

In the newspaper, the murder-suicide is called one of the most horrible tragedies to happen in Superior, the result of a hopeless love affair—a Scotchman and Christian falling in love with a *Jewess* whose parents consider marriage to a non-Jew a virtual death.

Young's last note says he wants to be buried beside his lady love. *Impossible!* After a funeral at home, Ida is buried in the Hebrew cemetery.

The *Superior Telegram* : "It is said by friends of the dead girl that a lover in Russia was about to come to America to wed her next month and that it was this fact that impelled Young to take her life and his own. It is said that Young was madly infatuated with the girl and a difference of opinion is apparent as to whether the girl reciprocated his love. The parents of the girl profess to be ignorant of the lover in Russia."

The surviving Solemovitzes move from Connors Point to 1514 4th Street, Superior proper. Within a year, Ida's mother, Bessie, dies of a broken heart. She is buried near her daughter in the wind-blown hills way south of town.

BEN STONE'S DREAM

Captain Arab he started
Writing up some deeds
He said, 'Let's set up a fort
And start buying the place with beads'
   "Bob Dylan's 115th Dream," 1965

There's nothin' t' tell. Benjamin David Solemovitz has disappeared from Superior and the world. But hallelujah! He's not dead but reborn. He makes his way into the great American hinterland as an offspring of the earth itself. *Mr. Stone*. He has no history, *Mr. Stone*. No nationality, no accent, no *vitz*. His wife will be *Mrs. Stone*. Their children will be just plain *Stones*.

His township of opportunity is 75 miles north of Superior on the Iron Range of Minnesota. His home will be Hibbing, a mining town grown from 2,500 in 1900 to 8,800 in 1910; of those, 219 are Jewish.

It is a land of opportunity. At mines' edge are village-like "locations." Utica, Albany, Agnew, Harold, French, Finn, Sellers, McKinley, Morris, Monroe, Morton, Brooklyn, Nelson, Nassau, Webb, Laura, Leetonia, Penobscot, Penobscot Hill, Glen, Kerr, Pillsbury, Carson Lake, Hartley, Frazer, Clark, Kitzville, Lavina and Pool. Some have no organization; streets no more than wagon trails between houses and around rocks. Others are company towns, rows of simple frame houses in platted blocks.

In 1900, within the deep woods west of Hibbing, Corrigan and McKinney steel of Cleveland open Stevenson location. In the city of Brainerd, Crow Wing County, Minn., Benjamin D. Stone, 17, lives on Laurel Street, a partner with Edwin Levant, an 18-year-old junk dealer, who, like Ben, was born in Russia.

In 1909, short, light-skinned, overtly authoritative, but surely still shaken by his sister's slaying, Ben Stone, 26, takes a position as a clerk for Abraham Friedman in downtown Hibbing. Soon, he meets Florence Edelstein, a dry goods "saleslady." Her father, Ben H. Edelstein, 38, runs a furniture store. Florence lives at home with Goldie, Julian, Rosa, Sam, Jennie, Maxie, Mike, B.H., her mother Lybba, 40, and 21-year-old Sam Jaffe, a wagon driver for the store.

In 1911, Ben Stone and 19-year-old Florence Edelstein are married. Their first child, born in 1912, is Vernon.

The next year, Ben and Florence open a general store at Stevenson, population maybe at most half a thousand. Three more children are born: Beatrice R. (June 16, 1915); Lewis (1918) and Irene (1923).

In 1926, they add a store in nearby Leetonia location. Within a year, the Stevenson structure is leveled by fire.

Rebuilding is not worth the trouble. Stevenson is rapidly being vacated as the mine that spawned the village consumes its reason for being. The Stones continue with the Leetonia store until 1932 when they move to Howard Street and 1st Avenue in the new downtown of South Hibbing. They offer miners' families sturdy, unpretentious clothing and other "dry goods" at reasonable prices. When times are hard, they do their best to accommodate unemployed miners.

Ben's father, Shabsie "Sam" Solemovitz, is able to save enough as a teamster and laborer to buy several lots on the north side of Superior—not far from the old Connors Point neighborhood. In 1909, he remarries: to a recent Russian immigrant, May Levinson, who brings along her sons, Roy, Bennie and Sam.

Florence's grandmother, Ida Edelstein, 69, 615 1/2 Baxter Avenue, Superior, dies Aug. 18, 1922, of tuberculosis. In the Jewish tradition, arrangements are made by the burial society. Her son, Roy Edelstein, acts as "undertaker."

Florence's grandfather, David Edelstein, 73, 421 John Avenue, Superior, passes away Aug. 6, 1924, of heart failure. Again, there is a gathering in the hills and the sound of shovels chopping into America to build an immigrant's last home.

Above: International Workers of the World in North Hibbing, probably early 1900s. *IRRC* • Below: Hibbing, 1893. *IRRC*

Road from Hibbing to Stevenson
1904
Mesabi Pioneer

Above: Moving the Hibbing Hotel from North Hibbing to South Hibbing, 1921. *IRRC* • Below: Looking west on Howard Street. *IRRC*

Above: Hibbing High School, completed early 1920s. *IRRC* • Below: Androy Hotel, Howard Street. *Aubin Studio*

Howard Street, looking west, c. 1940.

1932 Hematite

Beatrice Stone

Chapter Two
Duluth
1907-1947

The One-Legged Street Singer

Years later, when I'd recorded a few albums, <u>then</u> I started seeing it in places: 'Bob Dylan's a Jew,' stuff like that. I said, 'Jesus, I never knew that.' But they kept harping on it; it seemed like it was <u>important</u> for people to <u>say</u> that—like they'd say 'the one-legged street singer,' or something. So after a period of time, I thought, 'Well, gee, maybe I'll look into that.'
<u>Rolling Stone</u>, **1984**

"So what is your destination?"
America.
Very good, gentlemen with beards, but you *are* standing *in* America, at Ellis Island, New York City. Congratulations. You have arrived at the *goldeneh medina*, where the streets are paved with gold.
"Why not try Minnesota?"
Minnesota.
Why not try it? They say Minnesota resembles the homeland. And, if *Minnesota* needs workers for lumber and shipping, surely it needs those who make their living selling items to lumber men and shipping men.
Why not Minnesota?
Why couldn't a couple of ambitious Lithuanian Jews find a place there? *You can make a livelihood in Duluth*, on Lake Superior—a fine, cold, big lake that reminds some of the Baltic.
Why not Duluth?
Why not? One of the Jews is a Torah-bearing *shochet*—ritual slaughterer. Fish from Lake Superior will enable him to maintain *kashrut,* the kosher diet.
So the two immigrants, after another tedious journey, find themselves among a busy community at the western extreme of the big lake. Yes, they can purchase fresh fish at the docks and peddle door to door, saving enough of their earnings to send for wife, son, daughter, mother, father, brother, nephew, uncle, cousin, countryman and neighbor. From Russia and Lithuania, in the 1880s and 1890s, come Kenner, Karon, Kaner, Klatzky, Klein, Loeb, Levis, Goldish, Golden, Abramson, Edelman, Oswald, Oreckovsky, Polinsky, Shapiro, Salks, Josephs, Salnovitz, Hammel.
It would be a mild overstatement to say all the newcomers are called "Sabse," "Shapsie," or "Shabsie" like their compatriots in Superior, Wis. But don't forget "Shabsie the Geller" with his red beard; "Shabsie the Schwartzer" with the black beard and "Shabsie by the Bridge." But of all the Shabsies, if you say Shabsie, you're talking about tall, goateed Shabsie Karon.

"Who's the president?" asks a judge and a newcomer from Russia answers, "Shabsie Karon." Hebrew brothers are told, "Go see Shabsie—at 20 East 2nd Street, across from Central High School." He's an example of what a Jew can do in America. A Jew come from Kovno to America can start as a peddler and soon bring his family. The newcomers live at first like in the old country: a cow, chickens, a garden, pot-belly stove, kerosene lamps, a privy. Father learns English at night school, starts a scrap metal business. Pretty soon: running water, gas heat, electricity and a bathroom. Time for roller skating, ice-skating, sleigh rides, dances and parties.

Karon joins other Orthodox Jews in supporting the *mikveh*, a bath house for ritual cleansing; and *Chavra Kadisha*, the burial society. Prayer meetings move from his house—to rented rooms—to Adas Israel synagogue on 3rd Street.

More Russian than Lithuanian is Tifereth Israel, the 1898 "4th Street shul," incorporated by Goldstein, Polinsky, Cohen, Surovsky, and Oreckovsky. Its first rabbi is Odessa-born Joseph Shapiro. By the time the temple is built in 1923, Tifereth Israel is Duluth's largest Orthodox house of worship. In the early years, old-country faces prevail: bearded peddlers seated near the Holy Ark. A few years pass and the sons of fishmongers shave their cheeks and celebrate 20th century Duluth.

ZIGMAN

I don't know how they got a German name coming from Russia. Maybe they got their name coming off the boat or something. To make a big deal over somebody's name, you're liable to make a big deal about any little thing.

Playboy, 1978

I don't know how Jewish I am. See, with these blue eyes, which are Russian. Y'know, back in the 1700's, 1800's, I know I have different blood in me...Cossack blood...From the questions I asked of my old family, and the answers that I've been given, I know there's Russian blood in me...It comes from Odessa...In Odessa mostly everyone has the colour of my eyes.

New Musical Express, 1978

Zigman: his Hebrew name is Zisel, "Zisa," a Yiddish "sweetie pie." *Zigman Zimmerman:* German for "room man," or "carpenter." Zigman Zimmerman's forebears probably traveled the Pale of Settlement by way of Lithuania to Odessa, where Jewish merchants retained German ways.

It is believed a man can live like God in Odessa.

Odessa, by Zigman's 1875 birth, has grown from a remote seaport to the most modern and international of Russian cities. It is viewed by many as a denizen of predators preoccupied with pleasure over traditional values and religion. In adulthood, *Zigman* is not, by trade, a *Zimmer-man*; he is a *Schumacher*. They say he operates a shoe "factory."

Seven miles around Odessa burn the fires of hell.
But to tell the truth, only with difficulty can a Jew live like God in Odessa. Throughout Zigman's childhood, the community is harried by anti-Semitic mobs. His teenage years suffer student protests, peasant revolts, worker strikes, a war with Japan and attempts at revolution.

In 1905, under czar Nicholas II, occurs one of the worst *pogroms*. No wonder that, in 1906, 31-year-old Zigman heads for the territories. With a few thousand of the millions of Jews to come to America, Zigman finds himself, by way of New York City, on the frosty frontier of Minnesota.

Seven miles around Duluth burn the furnaces of progress. A good choice at a good time, Duluth is an Odessa without enslavement, a bustling port linking the Mesabi iron range with eastern manufacturing centers. With the rise of open pit mining, the "Zenith City" balloons from 80 in 1860 to 33,000 in 1890; to 53,000 in 1900. New people getting rich in a free land: *A Jew can live like a God in Duluth.*

Like most newcomers, Zigman adopts the trade of peddler. Like many Jews, he lives in the central hillside, originally subdivided as "Ashtabula Heights." Above is the "Barg," a poor section of Russian and Polish fish peddlers and garbage collectors along 9th Street. Immediately below is downtown Superior Street where Jews own some of the finest businesses.

Zigman is not the first *Zimmerman* to push the peddler's cart in Duluth: "Samuel" Zimmerman makes the rounds in 1904, but the man of that name liberates himself as *Samuel Friedman.*

By 1910, Zigman sends for his wife and family. Come by way of Ellis Island are his Odessa-born wife, Anna *Chana Greenstein* Zimmerman, about 30 years of age, and their children: *Maurice*, 8; *Minnie*, 6; *Paul*, 4; and *Jake*, a nominal "1."

With other Russian and Polish Jews, the family attends, but is not prominent in, Tifereth Israel, the "4th Street Shul."

The 1911 Duluth city directory lists *Ziske* Zimmerman, a peddler, at 22 1/2 West 1st Street—apartments above a modest brick commercial building. The next year, the peddler at the same address is listed as *Joseph Zimmerman*. Mr. Zimmerman's official first name takes a while to settle on "Zigman."

ABRAM

Duluth's an iron ore shipping town in Minnesota
It's built up on a rocky cliff that runs into Lake Superior
I was born there—my father was born there—
   "My Life in a Stolen Moment," 1962

My father was a very active man, but he was stricken very early by an attack of polio. The illness put an end to all his dreams I believe. He could hardly walk...my grandfather had come over from Russia in the 1920s. He was a peddler and made shoes. He had 7 sons and one daughter, well, my father never had the time to go to college. He used to do odd jobs to bring home some money to his mother.
   <u>L'Expresse,</u> 1978

My father had to sweat...In this earthly body he didn't transcend the pain.
   No Direction Home, 1986

First born in America is Abram H., Oct. 19, 1911. The father, Zigman, a "traveling salesman," is now 35; his wife, "Annie," says she is 33. With five children in the small apartment at 22 1/2 West 1st Street, no wonder the newest is quiet and observant.

By the birth of Max in 1914, the family has moved to a house at 221 Lake Avenue North. In 1917, Zigmond H. Zimmerman terms himself a "solicitor" for Prudential Life Insurance Co. The next year, he is a "clerk" for that firm.

With the entry of the United States into World War I, in 1918, aliens must go down to the government offices and register. Mrs. Zigman Zimmerman, calling herself a "dressmaker," says she speaks "a little English." Her alien children are Minnie, 14; Morris, 16; and Paul, 12. Her American children are Jake, 8; "Abraham," 6; and Max, 5.

Did any member of the family serve a foreign government in the present war?
Yes. Uncle Wolfe Zimmerman, a soldier in the Russian Army.

Wolfe's brother, Zigman, registers separately from Anna and the kids, telling government clerks he is in the "insurance business," that he owns no real estate; his only investment is a $50 Liberty Bond. He can read but not write English.

In 1918, Zigman is called again, this time for the draft, giving his birth date as Dec. 25, 1875. Of medium height and build, his eyes are blue and his hair, brown. Having learned more English, he works as a dry goods clerk at the "1st Street Dept. Store" or "Fair Store" for another Jewish immigrant, Froike "Frank" Labovitz.

In the early 1920s, "Zigmund," with the help of fellow Jew Jacob Crystal, opens a family shoe store downtown at 19 North 1st Avenue West. Better suited as salesman than businessman, he doesn't make a go of it. His wife, *Annie*, "takes in" sewing. A typical, uneducated Yiddisher mama, she sweeps down the path of righteousness—cooking, cleaning, scrimping and saving. All for the children, who in their time contribute to the family. Mechanically-inclined, *Morris*, 18, repairs railway equipment; in 1922, he advances to train car inspector. He also clerks for his father's store when there is a store. *Minnie* or "*Mirian*," is a stenographer for the Duluth Herald; *Paul*, a clerk and packer for Manhattan Woolen Mills.

Abe attends Liberty School on 1st Avenue East and 3rd Street. Diligent and business-minded, by age seven, he's shining shoes and selling papers to help the family with his earnings. Later, he attends the imposing Washington Junior High and then Central High School, both a few blocks from home. Central, a massive brownstone landmark with its 300-foot tower, is considered one of the finest high schools in the nation. In 1925, it graduates a class of 500. Abe, a good, basic student, is more at home working than playing and keeps pretty much to himself.

In 1925, the family moves from Lake Avenue North to 725 East 3rd Street—a two-story house among a row of two-story houses. "Zigmund" brings the failing shoe-sales business home but it doesn't work out and he returns to clerking.

Even for hardworking Abram, the social life of young Jewish Duluth includes skating, tobogganing, going to movies and a enjoying a kosher bologna sandwich at Crystal's Corner Deli. Now and then, a dozen boys and girls pack into a parent's truck and drive up to the rich mining towns of the Iron Range to meet other Jewish kids. Dating a *goy* gal—you might do it for fun; but for a relationship, you take out a nice Jewish girl. You don't want your mother coming down to the rink and finding you skating with a *shiksa*.

In summer, the Jewish "Iron Rangers," of Hibbing, Chisholm and Virginia, come down to the Zionist picnic to be regaled by personalities from New York City: a speaker, a cantor, Yiddish theater, Workmen's Circle, socialists and union organizers. The young enjoy games and races.

When Abe graduates in 1929, the Duluth Central yearbook, *Zenith*, credits his involvement in History Club, Commercial Club, Class Basketball and Athletic Association. "Abe is no foe to arduous work/He never has been known to shirk." With the onset of the Depression, shirkless Abe is one of the lucky ones: he has a job. From Standard Oil messenger boy, he graduates to clerk.

American Zionist Association is a Jewish boys' and young men's organization sponsored by B'nai B'rith. In 1930, Abe's AZA basketball team wins a Minneapolis tournament. Joining a team photo are Abe and his brother, Paul, "coach." Listed as forward and captain, Abe looks young, short and slight in build.

Abe golfs at Lester and Enger parks but not, of course, at the anti-Semitic country club. He plays handball with friends at the YMCA near the high school and wins medals in tournaments. He plays baseball; some say, "semi-pro."

In July 1931, the Nu-Epsilon-Phi fraternity sponsors a dance at the Boat Club ballroom. Among those helping with preparations are Sam Friedman, Norman Goldfarb, Joseph Goldfine, Harry Kossoff, Gerald Kenner and Abe Zimmerman.

Abe and his family live at 626 East 5th Street in the small Krause apartment building. With four grown children working, it can't be too long before somebody gets married and moves out.

BEATRICE

When I was growing up in the fifties, the thirties to me didn't even exist. I couldn't even imagine them, in any kind of way. I don't suspect anybody growing up now is gonna even understand what the sixties were all about, any more than I could the thirties or twenties.
20/20, 1985

Meanwhile, up on the Iron Range, Beatrice Stone, in 1932, graduates from Hibbing High School. She is vivacious, petite, pretty and aggressive. At fourteen, her father asks if she wants him to teach her to drive his big Essex automobile. "You don't have to teach me," she says and drives off on the road to Duluth.

To the Hibbing girls, Duluth is a great big beautiful city with numerous synagogues and plenty of young Jewish fraternity men. At a New Year's Eve party, Beatty's aunt, only a few years older than she, introduces her to Abe Zimmerman. This is Steady Abe, *no foe to arduous work*, earning about $100 a month. "The right boy for you. Hang onto him!"

After they meet, Beatty (she says "beat-ee") is snowed in at Hibbing for the remainder of the winter. They get together only, Abe says puckishly, "weather permitting."

It isn't long before Beatty holds a "small family gathering" at the Hibbing home of her parents, Ben and Florence Stone, June 10, 1934—her wedding. With the visiting Rabbi Gusse officiating and Charlotte Gusse at the piano playing the Wedding March, the bride enters, lovely in a white ensemble trimmed with blue; she carries roses, Easter lilies and baby breath. Ethel Edelstein, an aunt of the bride, is maid of honor; Sylvia Edelstein, another aunt, bridesmaid. Both are attired in navy blue dresses. Paul Zimmerman, brother of the groom, is best man. Irene Stone, sister of the bride, sings, "I Love You Truly."

The bride and groom depart for a honeymoon in Chicago prior to moving in with Abe's mother and three brothers at 402 East 5th Street, Duluth.

What about Zigman?

Abe's father now maintains a separate address at 105 West 1st Street in the hotel-like Kinsley Apartments, near downtown and a few steps around the block from his death.

Monday, July 6, 1936.

Normally cold-blooded Duluth finds itself in peculiar straits. In the worst heat wave of its 75 years, the temperature tops 100 degrees F for the first time. If you're going to die before your three-score and ten, this is a likely afternoon. One little girl bakes to death in a parked car. On 2nd Avenue West, between Superior Street and 1st Street, a 58-year-old immigrant shoe peddler drops dead on the sidewalk of "coronary sclerosis." According to Jewish custom, Zigman Zimmerman is quickly buried in Tifereth Israel Cemetery out on Howard Gnesen Road.

Abe and Beatty continue to live at the 402 East 5th apartment with the rest of the family. Maurice becomes a serviceman for General Appliance Co. Paul, as did his father before him, enrolls as a special agent for Prudential Life Insurance Co. Beatrice also works, as a saleswoman at a downtown clothing store.

To her friends, Beatty's outgoing personality dominates any situation. Abe, his wry sense of humor subdued by large family gatherings, is said to disappear into the wallpaper. One of Beatty's specialties is matchmaking. *Like in any religion, we see to our own.*

In 1938, Anna, Max, Paul, Abe and Beatrice move to Apartment A in a four-unit brick building at 308 East 5th Street.

On April 19, 1938, a few Duluthians find their way across the Interstate Bridge, landing on Connors Point and continuing into Superior, Wis., for the funeral of Beatrice Zimmerman's grandfather, Shabsie "Sam" Solemovitz, 84.

Loyalty to management may account for his rise through a 75-employee office to junior supervisor, and in 1941, to supervisor. Avoiding CIO involvement, Abe's employer, Standard Oil, forms a company union; Abe is elected leader. He also belongs to Golden Circle, an executive group whose members "can do no wrong." Following his latest promotion, he and Beatty move several blocks to 503 East 3rd Street, Apartment 201, leaving Anna, Max and Paul at 310 East 5th Street.

Abe and Beatty need more space. Their seven years of marriage have been enjoyed during the Depression. With the return of prosperity, comes the big news; they're going to have a baby.

The Zimmermans move somewhat higher on the urban hillside, renting the second floor of a frame house at 519 3rd Avenue East. It's a thoroughly Jewish property, owned by the Overmans and formerly occupied by the Goldfines. Within a couple blocks are grocery stores, schools, a Polish Catholic church, Adas Israel synagogue, Tifereth Israel synagogue, St. Mary's hospital, Nettleton elementary school, Washington Junior High and Central High School. Down the hill, is bustling, downtown Duluth. Beyond, the waterfront.

The apartment is reached by a long, dark stairway. At the front, a pocket door can be closed to isolate the living room from the dining room. A central hallway extends toward the rear. On the left are a dining room, bathroom and white-trimmed kitchen with built-in wooden cupboards. On the right: two bedrooms and a walk-in pantry. Out the back, a small porch overlooks the alley.

Off the living room is a porch high above 3rd Avenue East from which can be seen ore boats against the horizon, almost imperceptibly moving. The porch faces north, and on a good percentage of days, enjoys a bracing wind from the lake, often rendering the temperature twenty degrees lower than inland.

ZENITH CITY

The town I was born in holds no memories/but for the honkin' foghorns/the rainy mist/an' the rocky cliffs/I have carried no feelings/up past the Lake Superior hills

"11 Outlined Epitaphs," 1964

Thought I'd shaken the wonder and the phantoms of my youth Rainy days on the Great Lakes, walkin' the hills of old Duluth

"Something There Is About You," 1973

Duluth—where Baudelaire lived & Goya cashed in his chips, where Joshua brought the house down!

<u>Planet Waves</u> *album jacket, 1974*

In 1941, they still call it Zenith City: Duluth, the biggest city on Lake Superior and third-largest in Minnesota. Yet its 100,000 is down 10,000 from its actual apex in 1929, the year Abe Zimmerman graduated from high school.

A 1938 WPA handbook describes Duluth as a scenic strip running twenty miles along steep bluffs lining the shore of Lake Superior. The harbor is second in total net shipping tonnage only to New York—and that in a shipping season of eight months. Thirty-eight steamship companies operate out of Duluth, including two passenger lines. Thousands of vessels pass in and out per day, many stopping at one of seven iron ore docks.

A 1941 survey by Joseph Papo counts 827 Jewish family units comprising 2,633 persons; 903 foreign born, 79 percent from Russia and Lithuania. Most are "white collar" employees and owners of businesses. Because of a common Eastern European origin, class distinctions are not sharp.

"There is no serious, open anti-semitism in the community and the relationship with the non-Jews is friendly," opines Papo. "During the Brotherhood Week, the Temple Men's Club arranges a special meeting to which the members invite non-Jewish men. These meetings have succeeded in generating a better understanding and good will among Protestants, Catholics and Jews."

About forty percent of the Jewish families are affiliated with the synagogue. The old, more devout group that speaks and reads Yiddish is dying out. The young tend to lack dedication to religious rituals. Most have a vague belief in Zionism that does not translate into active work, except for Hadassah fund raising. Only during the High Holidays are the four houses of worship well attended.

"Duluth is off the beaten path for lecturers and speakers, and the educational and cultural life of the Jewish community suffers as a result," determines Papo. "Opportunities for Jewish education 15-30 years ago were very limited and as a result many of the Jewish parents today show little interest in Jewish education for their children."

In 1945, the membership of Tifereth Israel, formerly considered Orthodox, votes to change to the middle-of-the-road Conservative mode, making living in modern America more comfortable.

BOBBY

I didn't create Bob Dylan. Bob Dylan has always been here...always was. When I was a child, there was Bob Dylan. And before I was born, there was Bob Dylan...Sometimes your parents don't even know who you are. No one knows but you.
   Dylan, pub. 1984

My being a Gemini explains a lot. It forces me to extremes.
   TV Guide, 1976

"A child born on this day may have many talents of a cultural nature, with music, poetry, literature and mysticism having strong appeal to its gentle soul." So say the stars for May 24, 1941, the day the first child of Abram and Beatrice Zimmerman is born at St. Mary's Hospital, Duluth, a few blocks from the family apartment. Dr. James R. Manley records, after a difficult labor, a 20.5-inch, 7-pound, 13-ounce baby boy, about as big as a good-sized lake trout.

The *News-Tribune* of May 24 is headlined VIOLENT ATTACK HURLED AT LAST NAZI FOOTHOLD—reporting the storming of a Nazi-held airport by the Allied defenders of Crete. While aviator hero Charles Lindbergh does his part to keep the U.S. *out* of war, others say that, if we can beat *the enemy within*, meaning Lindbergh and his kind, we can surely beat Hitler.

The newspaper also reports that Duluth is abloom with peonies, two weeks earlier than the previous year. Also flowering—artificial flowers reminiscent of the previous "Great War." May 24 is "Poppy Day."

"Got a piece of change, Buddy, for a poppy?" You *should* buy a poppy, says the newspaper, whether you are for or against entering the current war.

Concern is expressed for the Jews of Europe. Rabbi Burton E. Levinson tells listeners at the ethnically-German Temple Emanuel synagogue that, as art, literature and medicine grow from the depth of religious inspiration, only religion can bring "peace, justice, mercy for the human race." In an annual Jewish Welfare Federation campaign, speeches at the Covenant Club consider, "Can the Jew Survive?"

For Duluth at large, Don McNeill, master of ceremonies of the NBC Breakfast Club, brings "the most popular variety show on the air" to the Duluth Armory.

An entertainment column in the *News Tribune* ridicules a recent trend of music. "The so-called hill-billy songs, so nostalgic and real, are not always as authentic as they sound. Many hill-billy singers and players heard nowadays never saw a hill, never knew a moonshiner and never went a-feuding." Blind Lemon Jefferson, for example, called the greatest blues singer of all time, had been discovered deep in the heart of Dallas.

The birth certificate is filed May 28, coinciding with the circumcision ceremony. *Brit milah*, or *bris*, signifies God's covenant with Abraham (and thus, Abram with his son). The operation is performed by a religiously-schooled *mohel* in the presence of relatives and congregation members; a big party follows.

The names chosen for this first son are popular and American-sounding: "Robert Allen." He is called *Bobby* or *Bobby Allen*. His Hebrew name is understood to be Shabtai Zisel ben Avraham, combining the names of maternal great-grandfather "Shabtai" Solemovitz and paternal grandfather, Zigman, "Zisel" Zimmerman. "Ben" signifies "son of," and his father's name is certainly Abram.

The parents attach colored ribbons to the baby's golden curls and pose him for the camera. Beatty tells her blue-eyed son, *you are so beautiful you should have been a girl.*

On December 7, when Bobby is seven months old, Japan devastates the U.S. naval base at Pearl Harbor, Hawaii, and America abruptly enters the war. The first years of Bobby's life are colored by the worry of adults and rationing of sugar, rubber, gasoline, meat, coffee and dairy products. While Abe's "essential" job with Standard Oil exempts him from military service, brothers and sisters go to war and cousins perish. Reports persist that Jews are persecuted in great numbers. Waiting to hear of relatives in Germany, Poland, Russia and Lithuania, Duluthians raise money enough that at least a few families can be brought to sanctuary. Because of the mutual concern for the Hebrew brotherhood, local barriers between German and eastern-European Jews fall.

In 1941, Abe's brothers, Maurice and Paul Zimmerman, purchase the Micka Electric business up north in Hibbing, where Maurice had worked as an electrician for Ed Micka. With iron mining going great guns, the Ore Capital's wartime boom should only accelerate and the Zimmerman fortunes along with it.

Hibbing also happens to be the home town of Beatty Zimmerman. There, on Sept. 5, 1942, her grandmother, Lybba Edelstein, 72, Lithuanian immigrant and wife of theater-owner B.H. Edelstein, dies.

"One of the best known Jewish welfare leaders," and an "ardent worker in the local synagogue," "her advice and counsel was sought often," according to the

Hibbing *Daily Tribune* obituary. She had lived in old North Hibbing, then moved to the Brooklyn neighborhood and only recently had found a home in new South Hibbing. Her final resting place is the Hebrew cemetery in Superior, Wis., where she had landed a half-century earlier.

Ten children survive: Mrs. Goldie Rutstein, Mrs. Ben Stone, Mrs. Louis Deutsch (Virginia, Minn.), Mrs. Jennie Agranoff (Sioux City, Iowa), Sam, Julius, and Max (Hibbing), Michael (Wisconsin), Mrs. Hyman Divine (St. Paul) and Mrs. M. Goldberg (Superior).

Early in the war, Barbara McGowan, a Hibbing friend, moves to Duluth, where Beatty's sister, Irene, also lives. Irene stops by one day while Barbara sits on the swing with her two young children. Barbara asks Irene, "How are Beatty and the baby?"

Honest to God, that kid is going to grow up not even knowing the nursery rhymes right, Irene says, *because Beatty makes up her own words to the verses.*

The kid is a born performer. Seated on his father's desk, he talks and sings into a dictation recorder. Abe teases secretaries by inserting Bobby's performance between dictated invoices.

On May 17, 1945, a week before Bobby's fourth birthday, there comes the death in Hibbing of another old pioneer—Ben Stone, Beatty's father. According to the death certificate, the cause is "respiratory embarrassment" and cirrhosis of the liver. The obituary notes that Benjamin David Stone had owned a downtown Hibbing clothing store. Was a member of B'nai B'rith and the Elks. Is survived by his wife, Florence; daughters Mrs. A. Zimmerman, Duluth, and Irene Stone, a physical therapist in the army hospital at Galesburg, Ill.; sons, Cpl. Vernon Stone in the Philippines and Sgt. Lewis Stone in New Guinea with the medical corps.

The only grandchild of Ben Stone is Beatty's boy, Robert Allen Zimmerman.

The burial, once again, is at Superior, Wis. *That's where your mother's family is buried. And here, on Connors Point, your mother's aunt, Grandpa Stone's sister, Ida, was...*

No, Connors Point is *not* mentioned as the Zimmerman vehicle crosses the Interstate Bridge on the way to the cemetery south of Superior. *There's nothin t' say.* Nothing to say about "Solemovitz," which, the death certificate attests, is Ben Stone's father's surname. In the north country spring, a new grave is consecrated: *God will create the world anew.*

A second son, David Benjamin, is born in February, 1946.

On Mothers Day in mid-May 1946, there is a party at which a lot of guests are getting up to perform. They call on the little fella, curly-headed Bobby, who promises to sing for Grandma Zimmerman, but only *if everybody in this room will keep quiet.* He performs "Some Sunday Morning," a current favorite by Helen Forrest and Dick Haymes. The applause is so enthusiastic, he encores with Johnny Mercer's "Accentuate the Positive."

A few weeks later, at Beatty's sister Irene's June 9 wedding reception at the Covenant Club, Beatty dresses Robert in a white suit. An uncle offers to pay him to sing but the lad demurs. Abe argues that Bobby should sing because all those people came to hear him. If he *does* sing, they won't pester him any more. Afterward, he accepts $25 from an uncle, but is credited with saying, *Mummy, I'm going to give the money back.*

Abe reports that people laugh with delight at hearing the boy; that Bobby is an unusually lovable child others will go out of their way to talk to and to touch. As the only relative who seems to doubt Bobby is going to be famous some day, Abe doesn't make too much of the boy's *talent.* Any child could learn a song from the radio if he heard it enough times. With so much attention directed at the little entertainer, Bobby's parents wonder how he remains unspoiled.

Duluth is his father's world and Abe surely shows off the sights.

Look, Bobby—the towering waterfront smokestacks of steel mills and cement plants; the half-mile long iron ore docks and giant grain elevators.

Look!

Abe's alma maters, a few blocks from the house: Washington Junior High and, kitty-corner, Central High School with its giant clock high in the clouds.

The teachers college. *It's a decent school to get started. Maybe you'll go here some day.*

The Armory on the north lake front. *Some famous people have played there. Maybe you'll see one some day.*

Minnesota Point—a thin crescent of land held to the mainland by the visual symbol of Duluth, the Aerial Lift Bridge. Three deep blasts announce an approaching ore boat. The gates close and the roadway rises. *Look, Bobby!* There follows the rattle of opening hatches, a screech of winches, a shout from the deck, a rush of churning water and hundreds of gulls in the propeller's wake as the ship moves through the canal.

Duluth is a city with the north country close at the back of the neck. During short, intense summers, wildlife crowds down to back doors: porcupines and great horned owls; trilliums in patches like gardens; pines and birches with the scent of the forest. Rock steps, laced with wild flowers and strawberries. Spring-fed creeks plunging through gorges to the lake.

In autumn, seated between Mom and Dad in the front seat of the family car, Bobby travels Skyline Parkway. At Enger Park, he can climb the forty-foot observation tower to view the red sun blooming from the blue infinity of Lake Superior. *It's the largest body of fresh water in the world:* several hundred miles long, a couple-hundred miles wide and a million feet deep.

In winter, it's all frozen. Residents, when they must leave superheated rooms, rush from door to doorway between piles of snow, while trying not to slip on the icy slopes of every steep east-west thoroughfare, breathing great clouds of frost, wondering when, if ever, it will end. But truth to tell, it doesn't end. Any day of the year can be winter cold, wind whipping flags and jangling ghostly chains.

Any night, you can hear foghorns. Any day, you hear the waterfront babble of a seaport and the lilt of Yiddish-speaking Russians like Bobby's grandparents—along with Yugoslavs, French-Canadians, Poles, Germans, the few Negroes, the innumerable Italians and Scandinavians.

To a boy, it's the north country fair, even in the business section, where woolen-clad lumberjacks and Indians pass by. Canoes lashed to automobiles. Carcasses of deer are attached to many a running board. A black bear busts into the restaurant of Duluth's grandest hotel. He must have smelled the fish.

KINDERGARTEN
1946-1947

I got no father...I got no mother either.
   (1961) to union secretary (Absolutely Dylan, 1991)

I've had black leather jackets since I was five years old. I've been wearing black leather all my life.
   Nora Ephron Interview, 1965

Bobby refuses! It's his first day of school and he won't go without his father. So Abe walks him two blocks to Nettleton School at 1st Avenue and 6th Street. If Abe is embarrassed to be the only father present, little Bobby is surely more than a little intimidated by the big, red-brick building and the demanding strangers.

Escorting his son along 6th Street composes one of the father's last good walks. A few weeks later, Abe's personal Duluth, and that of his family, falls apart. In the midst of what has become an annual epidemic, he is stricken by infantile paralysis. He stays only a week in the hospital, because, he says, the facility is short of help and equipment. Instead, he recuperates at home for six months. Unable to use his legs, he has to be carried or must crawl with his arms up the long flight of steps to the second-floor apartment.

Abe continues to list his occupation as manager of the stock department for Standard Oil, though that job is little more than history by now. He gradually overcomes the paralysis but is left with one crippled leg and weakness in the other. Pain will be a good portion of Abe's lot in life.

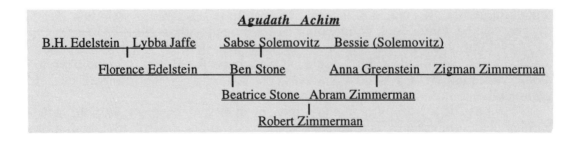

Jewish Historical Society of the Upper Midwest
Adas Israel Synagogue, Duluth, c. 1919

Duluth, c. 1915
Lake Superior Museum of Transportation

WEDNESDAY, JULY 8, 1936.   Duluth Herald *Minnesota Historical Society*

DULUTH DEATHS

(Funeral notices will be found on page 15, eighth column.)

Funeral Rites Held For Stroke Victim

Funeral services were held Tuesday afternoon at the Johnson mortuary for Zigman Zimmerman, 58, 402 East Fifth street, and interment was made in the Jewish cemetery, Woodland. Mr. Zimmerman, who had been a resident of Duluth for 28 years, died of a heart attack in Second avenue west Monday.

He is survived by his wife, a daughter, Mrs. L. J. Kenner, and five sons, Maurice, Paul, Jack, Abe and Max, all of Duluth.

Zigman Zimmerman.

Italian Planes Fly In Ethiop Reprisal

ROME, July 8.—(AP)—Italian military airplanes were reported today sent out to make "mass reprisals" against an Ethiopian district in which at least four Italian fliers were slain June 26.

Among those killed was Maj. Antonio Locatelli, famous pilot and a member of the Balbo mass flight to the United States in 1933.

The victims, occupying three airplanes, had been making an observation flight over the Wallega area. They landed in a district frequented by fierce and hostile tribesmen.

The natives attacked the group, destroyed the planes and killed at least four occupants.

A priest, the Rev. Father Barollo, a passenger, escaped and carried the news of the massacre to Addis Ababa.

QUITTING BUSINESS

To save the cost of packing and storing the balance of this stock of Men's Suits and Furnishings

All Prices Again Reduced!

An Assorted Lot Regular $25

Men's Suits

Sincerity Brand All High Grade Clothing

Final Reduction

$14.50

ADJUSTER'S SALES CO.
Cor. 2nd Ave. W. and First St.

Two Admit Assault On Joseph Gapco

Louis Ream, 28, and William Isaacson, 33, pleaded guilty this morning in district court to a second degree assault charge which grew out of the reported robbery and beating of Joseph Gapco last week.

They appeared before Judge Bert Fesler. Sentencing was deferred. Ream in municipal court yesterday was given an examination and then bound over to district court, while Isaacson waived examination when arraigned in city court.

Gapco, who said that the pair robbed him of $7 after beating him, was held as a material witness in the county jail.

Marvin Goldberg, charged with third degree burglary in connection with a break-in at the Swanstrom Clothing Co. store, West Duluth, several weeks ago, pleaded not guilty when arraigned before Judge Fesler.

Yesterday in municipal court John R. Flynn, 33, failed to appear for a hearing on a count of driving while intoxicated and forfeited $100 bail. An attachment was ordered for his arrest, however. Joseph H. Winter, 37, also charged with driving while intoxicated, was fined $100.

RIVER NEARS LOW RECORD.

ROCK ISLAND, Ill., July 8.—(AP)—The Mississippi river, which splashed over its banks into thousands of homes a few months ago, was nearing an all-time low stage yesterday. United States army engineers said only heavy rains could prevent a startling new record.

Increase Is Shown In Cotton Acreage

WASHINGTON, July 8.—(AP)—Cotton in cultivation July 1 was estimated today by the crop reporting board at 30,621,000 acres, or 109.8 per cent of the 27,888,000 in cultivation a year ago.

Trade in your old furniture. Liberal allowance now.

FRENCH – BASSETT & SCOTT CO.
Better Furniture. Duluth, Minnesota
502 WEST FIRST STREET

COMING TUESDAY, JULY 14th

Ted Weems and his ORCHESTRA

Famous the Nation Over

ADVANCE TICKET SALE, $1.00 PER PERSON. We pay tax.

Ticket sale starts July 10th Glass Block, The Amph. and Ringside. IN SUPERIOR—And Drug and People's Drug. You will 70c per couple by buying your tickets in advance at the above places.

The AMPH.

READ THE WANT ADS.

Our Newly Remodeled

SPALDING GRILL
AND
OAK DINING ROOM
ARE BOTH

Air Conditioned

72 Degrees Cool Always

SPALDING HOTEL

"SKYWRITING ACE" HERE THURSDAY

COL. ARTHUR C. GOEBEL, famed Hawaiian Flight Ace and Nationally Known Skywriter Will Demonstrate Plane-to-Car Radio Communication With Stunt Program Here

Weather Permitting **THURSDAY and FRIDAY** Weather Permitting

NORTHERN OIL COMPANY

DISTRIBUTORS PHILLIPS 66 PRODUCTS   DULUTH, MINN.

Above: Duluth's AZA basketball team after winning a 1930 Minneapolis tournament. Seated, from left: James Cherson, Ben Fischman, Louis King, Abe Zimmerman, forward and team captain. Back: Isadore Crystal, business manager, Marvin Goldstein, Max Cherson, Paul Zimmerman, coach. *Duluth Fellowship News* • Below: 1929 Duluth High School yearbook, *Zenith*. *Duluth Public Library*

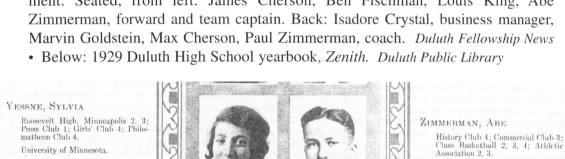

Duluth, 1940
Photo by Gallagher
Northeast Minnesota Historical Center

Left: Dylan Thomas, c.1943

Below: Identified as Beatrice and Robert Zimmerman, right.

Zimmy's Downtown Bar & Grill

Chapter Three
1st Grade
1947-1948

King Hematite

But Hibbing, Minnesota, was just not the right place for me to stay and live...The only thing you could do there was be a miner, and even that...was getting less and less. The people that lived there—they're nice people...they still stand out as being the least hung-up. The mines were just dying, that's all; but that's not their fault.
<u>*Playboy*</u>, *1966*

Bugs. To the boy peering over the edge, the figures are insects. The power shovels and ore trains are toys. Not that men or machinery are truly tiny. They just look that way, deep in the Hull-Rust-Mahoning iron ore mine—often called the biggest hole dug by man.

The boy's platform is precarious. Even while he peers into the abyss, the home town around him is consumed by the underworld that created it. First, there are tree-lined streets, sturdy houses and a modern downtown; then, structures disappear, one by one, until the plat is vacant. In the end, even the grid of streets and sidewalks crumbles into huge shovels and everything real is trundled away.

North Hibbing is where great-grandparents Edelstein lived, and Grandma Stone and Mother too, the boy hears, as Mother drives the car south on Third Avenue.

Lucky if they don't take the cemetery!

Lucky! Speaking from the passenger's seat, the boy's father, Abe Zimmerman, seems to know something about fortune—though he has no stake in the necropolis on the cusp; his family will be interred elsewhere.

That's Bennett Park, Bobby, says Mother. *It's not like it was—but it's nice.*

It's still a good place to play ball, says Abe. *Maybe we'll get a catcher's mitt.*

But *will* Abe train the boy to trip deftly across dreamy, green fields? Maybe not. After Bobby's kindergarten year, they have traveled from Abe's home, the world port of Duluth (pop. 100,000), to the mining town of Hibbing (pop. 18,000), where Mother grew up. The move is compelled by the disease of infantile paralysis, or "polio," that has crippled Abe.

In a new Hibbing, built further south of the mine, the Zimmerman uncles have been running Micka (MIKE-ah) Electric for six years. Maurice and Paul will continue electrical work. Abe will join the firm as secretary-treasurer. With all the postwar building activity, there should be enough income for three families.

The Hibbing *Daily Tribune* heralds the grand opening of "ultra modern" Micka Electric Co., June 6, 1947. "Everybody's coming to see the one and only BENDIX, the modern home laundry that washes AUTOMATICALLY."

Waiter, there's no chicken in my chicken soup. In his ads, Uncle Morey hopes to amuse with canned humor. *So what? We don't have horse meat in our horse radish do we?*

"The satisfied customers of Micka Electric Co. can tell you of the swell service they dish up."

THE POLITICAL WORLD

We live in a political world...where courage is a thing of the past...wisdom is thrown into jail...peace is not welcome at all...
  "Political World," 1989

World War II is recalled with each dead soldier shipped home for reburial in Hibbing's Maple Hill Cemetery. Now comes a *cold war*, with the United States and Soviet Union living in fear of mutual nuclear obliteration.— Looking to the skies, Hibbing sees not Russian bombers but interplanetary *flying saucers*. Hull-Rust mine foreman Vern Novak's vision of three large plate-like objects at about 10,000 feet is affirmed by tourists on the observation platform.— *Evidence of lost civilizations.* A sword hilt said to have been dropped in the 14th century is plowed up by Mike Pribich a short distance from Howard Street.

Mohandes K. Gandhi. The non-violent father of Indian independence is murdered by a Brahmin who opposes tolerance for all creeds and religions.— *Palestine*, partitioned by the United Nations to form Israel. Many Hibbing Jews, including Abe and Beatty Zimmerman, subscribe to the "Zionist" cause.

DFL. Hibbing remains a one-industry, union town. Miners vote in a bloc for Democratic Farm Labor party founders Hubert Humphrey, John Blatnick and Orville Freeman. The leftist climate is the residue of bloody strikes in the days of the International Workers of the World. Miners demanded an eight-hour day; companies imported gunmen and scabs. On Highway 37 east of Hibbing, you can still see the Mesaba camp for young Communists. Not far away is the childhood home of party leader Gus Hall, the former Arvo Halberg, a Finnish miner's son.

KING HEMATITE

You've seen that great ugly hole in the ground, where that open-pit mine was. They actually think, up there, that it is beautiful. They think it is a scenery place.
  <u>No Direction Home</u>, pub. 1986

"A man who says he has seen America but has never gazed on the Hibbing pit is merely deluding himself," writes Stewart Holbrook in *Charm*. "The pit has sheer beauty too, this amphitheater carved out of solid iron by countless immigrants. In the bright sun of a Minnesota morning, the terraces mount one above the other like crimson-lined benches."

To promote Hibbing as *Iron Ore Capital of the World*, the King Hematite Jubilee, a 4th of July celebration, is inaugurated. The three-day festival includes carnivals, parades, athletic contests, fireworks and pageantry. It is hoped King Hematite will achieve a legendary status, like gigantic lumberjack Paul Bunyan.

If Hematite is sovereign, the Oliver Iron Mining Co. has enthroned him. The subsidiary of U.S. Steel is the world's largest iron ore-producing company, with 2,800 employees in the Hibbing district—more than any time since the 1920s.

Hopeful plans call for an even bigger output of ore. Yet depletion and abandonment of the Mesabi have been predicted for years. Oliver president R.J. Elstad bluntly informs the Chamber of Commerce the newborn monarch actually gasps on his deathbed. "Most of you have probably observed daily the mining of the great Hull-Rust open pit. You have noticed that the 'ribs' of the mine are now showing and that *the greatest of all iron ore mines is nearing the end of its life.*"

In compensation, Elstad describes studies underway in Oliver's Duluth laboratory. Taconite, a low grade iron ore intermixed with hard rock, has been unprofitable to mine, but new methods make it the hope of the future, he says.

POSITIVELY HOWARD STREET

There's no place I feel closer to now, or get the feeling that I'm part of, except maybe New York; but I'm not a New Yorker. I'm North Dakota-Minnesota-Midwestern. I'm that color. I speak that way. I'm from someplace called Iron Range. My brains and feelings have come from there. I wouldn't amputate on a drowning man; nobody from out there would.
Playboy, 1972

"So where *is* Hibbing?" asks the program, *Meet the Stars,* from Chicago's WGN radio station. The guest, Kirsten Kenyon, soprano in *The Song of Norway,* retorts that her home town should be recognized as home to: the Greyhound bus system; the third largest high school in the U.S.; the first 'glass' schoolhouse in America and the biggest open pit iron mine in the world.

To Kirsten and many others in Minnesota, the "Iron Ore Capital of the World" is a municipal showcase. Mining taxes have provided parks, libraries, public buildings and schools at virtually no cost to the public. As a social critic had remarked sarcastically, *Why shouldn't these towns have everything they want? If we don't get it, it will go to New York to buy cigars for the damn capitalists down there. All we'll have left anyway is big holes in the ground.* The village office bears a resemblance to Independence Hall. The rainbow-roofed War Service Memorial Building covers an entire block and contains a First Settlers room, servicemen's quarters, kitchens, meeting rooms, bowling alleys, a curling club, the Little Theater and a 5,000-seat arena for ice hockey, ice skating, dances and conventions.

When the boy arrives from Duluth, he finds two towns: one busy being born and one busy "dying." He soon hears how, in 1919, the Oliver Mining Co. wanted ore under Pine Street and began moving buildings a mile south to "Alice," the "New" or "South" Hibbing. The process, dormant, along with mining, in the Depression of the 1930s, is renewed in the 1940s. Houses are often towed with furniture and occupants in place. When Dr. Fred Carstens climbs into a house on wheels in Old Hibbing and delivers a baby next morning in New Hibbing, he has to walk back a mile to get his car. Even churches trundle along, their spires, pews and decorations intact. Christ Memorial Church is moved stone by stone and reassembled. Stray graves are scooped up with steam shovels and the occupants given new resting places.

In the old town, a boy can ride his bike through near-abandoned streets with signs still in place. He can see sidewalks leading across a yard to the slab where a house had yesterday stood. He can pluck crab apples from trees planted by pioneers. The boy can see, like the Parthenae of a ruined acropolis, the abandoned Oliver Mining Company shops and offices and, in its last days, the big school his mother had attended. He can walk by the grand old courthouse or visit the still-functioning 1916 Main Library with its unforgettable stairways, pillars, murals, and ornamental lions.

He soon learns how the moving of the village provides another kind of fame. To transport workers from New South Hibbing to the mines of North Hibbing, "Bus Andy" Anderson establishes the first motor bus route outside New York City; it becomes the famous "Greyhound" line.

Post World War II New Hibbing is riding a second crest of the wave that started in the 1920s when it was built. Gas stations, stores, restaurants, theaters, banks and office buildings line Howard Street and continue down First Avenue. Radio station WMFG broadcasts from the heights of the elegant Androy Hotel (although ore deposits can interfere with reception). The Hibbing *Daily Tribune* provides news, information and comment. The St. Louis County Fair brings crowds every summer.

Hibbing is home to what a WPA guide calls "the most lavish school system in the world." The "largest and most costly" high school building contains two gymnasiums, a swimming pool, workshops, offices and a suite of rooms for the school dentist, doctor and nurses. An 1,800-seat auditorium is accented by ornate imported chandeliers and a remarkable pipe organ. Teachers are paid high salaries for teaching small classes.

The houses of Hibbing, as surveyed by WPA writers, include spacious mansions of mine executives; comfortable residences of higher-salaried mine employees and business-and-professional men; neat houses and gardens of established miners; and the typical shacks of "swarming neighborhoods." Yet, marvels the WPA writer, even the smallest "cottage" is equipped with electricity, water, plumbing, gas and municipal heat; the family can stroll to its own community center for games, dances, lectures and music. Children are offered summer park programs, annual Christmas parties and a community-sponsored Halloween party that brings thousands of youngsters to the Memorial Arena. Many youth return the favors. Rather than treat themselves to a banquet, members of the Junior Chamber of Commerce Teen-Age Canteen purchase safety tape and apply it to thousands of bikes.

An urgent need arises for 800 new dwellings to house a population increase of 2,000 since 1940. Many families live, like the Zimmermans, doubled up in homes with friends or relatives. The average Hibbing family can afford to build when the material becomes available—with an effective buying power after taxes of $4,219, compared to the national average of $3,640.

The Ore Capital's response to the annual threat of polio includes a March of Dimes charity ball and a teen dance at the Sons of Italy Hall. "Hibbing people acted the way they always do in an emergency," says George Fisher, *Tribune* editor, "cut red tape and started in."

When your dad is crippled, you watch newsreels with special interest. Here are moving pictures of boys your age, paralyzed by the plague of 1948, and imprisoned for what must be an eternity in massive metal tubes called iron lungs.

GARMAKER SYNDROME

Coached by Mario Retica and spearheaded by Milan Knezovich, the Hibbing High School Bluejackets take third place in the state basketball tournament.

OVER THE RAINBOW

Hibbing's got schools, churches, grocery stores an' a jail
It's got high school football games and a movie house
Hibbing's got souped up cars runnin' full blast on a Friday night
Hibbing's got corner bars with polka bands.

"My Life in a Stolen Moment," 1962

Into Hibbing come the entertainers: the Ink Spots, first black act to play numerous venues throughout the nation; Harry James and his big swing band; "popular young violinist" Isaac Stern. To Power Field on Dupont Road comes Clyde Beatty's circus. *Out* from the Range travels lesser talent. "The Solidaires," Betty Lou Minkler's quartet from Buhl, auditions for the Arthur Godfrey Hour radio program.

Hibbing has four movie theaters, all owned at least in part by the Edelstein Amusement Co.: the double-matinee *Gopher* on Howard Street, the high-class *State* on Howard, the *Homer* on 1st Avenue and, as of Feb. 1, 1947, the Lybba, a 600-seat facility on 1st. The Lybba shows a first-run picture every Sunday and a second run of "outstanding" movies mid-week, closing with a double feature of action movies on Saturday. A special feature is an insulated "cry room," meant for unruly infants. The theater is named after Lybba Edelstein (1870-1942), wife of Hibbing's "pioneer showman," B.H. Edelstein.

Lybba Edelstein's daughter is Florence Edelstein Stone; Florence's daughter is Beatty Stone Zimmerman; Beatty's oldest son is Robert Allen Zimmerman. Bobby's a lucky lad; he can get into the movies free.

NORTH COUNTRY FAIR

Well, if you're travelin' in the north country fair,/Where the winds hit heavy on the borderline,/Remember me to one who lives there./She was once a true love of mine.

"Girl of the North Country," 1963

Beginning in late October or early November, a typical Hibbing winter hangs on through April, with no guarantees for May. Mid-winter temperatures linger between 20 degrees F and minus 20, with lows to minus 55. Young Minnesotans shovel the driveway clear of snow and shoot some buckets. For the less robust, winter can be deadly. A 42-year-old Brooklyn woman is found near her back steps, frozen in a snow drift.

If May is "spring," the season is a startling moment of transition. Mountains of snow disintegrate into rivers that, here at the continental divide, run to several seas.

Beginning in June, summer is short, sweet and swarming with mosquitoes. Residents, many of whom are "Minnesota cabin" owners, enjoy a month or two of swimming in clear lakes and water-filled former mines. This in a climate where summer night-time temperatures often dip into the forties and a 90-degree day causes some excitement.

Hibbing's heaviest rainfall as yet recorded arrives Sept. 10, 1947. Nine inches of rain overnight cover the ground floors of many houses. On the streets of Brooklyn neighborhood, boats replace automobiles for transport. A 14-year-old boy swims through his back yard to phone for help from the neighbor's house.

Due to a scarcity of berries in the area, considerable damage had been done the previous year by bears. As predicted, in August 1947, they again go on the prowl.

Out at Dillon Road by Maple Hill, Stanley Mehle spots *ursus* about to attack some *bovinae*. Not having a gun at hand, he starts his truck to make it backfire. This frightens "ol' bruin" away from the calves and summons Joe Mrkonjich, who arrives with a 30.06. Three shots kill the 500-pound beast, one of the largest seen lately.

AGUDATH ACHIM

Did you ever grow up thinking about the fact that you were Jewish?

No, I didn't. I've never felt Jewish. I don't really consider myself Jewish or non-Jewish. I don't have much of a Jewish background.

Playboy, 1978

Shapiro and Stein drug; Sapero dress shop; Feldman's and Herberger's department stores; Hallock's, Sach's, Stone's and Friedman's clothing stores; Sher and Mackoff insurance; Stein law office; Edelstein theaters; Banen finance; Daneiko office supplies; Zimmerman's Micka Electric; Jolowsky's junkyard. All Jewish-owned businesses on or near Howard Street. And almost all Jews are businessmen, such as the recently-deceased B.M. Lippman, 71, founder of Lippman Dept. Store, who was active in Chamber of Commerce, B'nai B'rith, Kiwanis, Elks and Odd Fellows, retiring to California seven years before his death.

Agudath Achim (Ah-GOOD-ith AHK-um, meaning "fellowship of brothers"), originally met in the Workers Hall in North Hibbing. When the town moved, the congregation bought the Swedish Evangelical Emanuel Lutheran church from Oliver Mining Co. and moved it to 2nd Avenue West, making sure the building did not arrive with the cross still on the steeple.

With 50 or more families and 125 persons attending services, the synagogue is active. Yet, more often than not, it has no local clergy. The spring weddings of Sara Hallock and Betty Ann Margulis are conducted by rabbis from Duluth—and are attended by, among others, Mrs. Abe "Beatty" Zimmerman. About the same time, Abe Zimmerman is elected secretary and Beatty's brother, Lewis Stone, an officer, of the B'nai B'rith Iron Range Lodge.

Following the lead of Duluth and Superior, the local congregation is "orthodox evolving toward conservative." Businessmen observe prime shopping hours on Friday evening rather than the profitless Sabbath proscriptions.

Almost every family has a Chanukah Menorah, ceremonial candles, Kiddish cups and other objects brought from Europe. On September 13, the *Tribune* notes that Rosh Hashanah, the Jewish New Year, will be commemorated by "residents of the Hebrew faith." Ten days later, the High Holidays end with the "most solemn" of Jewish holidays: Yom Kippur, the *Day of Atonement.* The children of Agudath Achim are often brought to the synagogue, especially at holidays. Following the requisite services, there's likely to be a bingo party.

A well-traveled Hibbing anecdote tells of a Passover meal, held on a Friday night at the home of the Feldmans, owners of the Howard Street department store.

"I gotta go back to the store."
"What's the problem, Herman?"
"I left the safe open."
"Why are you worried? *We're all here.*"

Agudath Achim is big enough to bring the 1947 Minnesota-Wisconsin B'nai B'rith convention to the Androy Hotel. The principal speaker, Ben Goldman, of the Anti-Defamation League, declares anti-Semitism at a low ebb nationally. In Hibbing it is subdued. Others agree. *If you want an ethnic group, you might mention the Bohunks or Italians.* There is no outright persecution, though there is the occasional offhand insult. *The sheenies'll skin ya.* The Mesaba Country Club follows the routine anti-Semitic policy.

Most Hibbingites respect the successful businessmen of Howard Street who are also, in some cases, close friends. Daughters of druggist Louis Stein learn to "cook Italian" from Mrs. Dougherty next door, a good Catholic; she enforces Jewish rules. *You know it's not right for you girls to come over and eat bacon. Your mother wouldn't like it.* Over time, kids of different religions mix more and more. *Why would we feel any different just because they didn't go to our church?* Though still discouraged by both sides, some Jews marry Catholics.

BOBBY

Well, we had...a big extended family. My grandfather had about 17 kids on the one side, and on the other side about 13 kids. So there was always a lot of family-type people around.
<u>Duluth News-Tribune</u>, 1986

We slept in the living room of my grandma's house for about a year or two. I slept on a roll-a-way bed, that's all I remember.
<u>Biograph</u>, 1985

Actually, I was raised more by my grandmother. She was a fantastic lady. I loved her so much, and I miss her a lot.
   <u>Spin</u>, 1985

Grandma, someday I'm going to be very famous. You are never going to have to worry about anything.
   <u>No Direction Home</u>, pub, 1986

Grandma said, 'Boy, go and follow your heart
And you'll be fine at the end of the line.'
   "Going, Going, Gone," 1973

The older Zimmerman brothers, Maurice and Paul, pay attention to the community, raise their families, run an honest business. They stop on the sidewalk and say, "How are you?" The newest arrival, Abe, is a little more reserved.

Because of the housing shortage, Abe and his family—Beatty, Robert, and baby brother, David Benjamin—join Grandma Florence in one of the four "Alice Apartments," 2323 3rd Avenue East, just south of Alice School. With a second "Mom" for the boys, Beatty can go back to work—as a clerk at Feldman's.

Florence Stone and her son Lewis, "Label," own a clothing store a couple blocks away, at 1st Avenue and Howard Street in an old bank building; rubber boots and overshoes are displayed in the vault. It's a working man's shop and out-of-work miners are allowed credit when nobody else will help.

In the block are the Greeks who run the Delvic restaurant. Beatty and her sister, Irene Stone, have known the Haidos boys for a long time. George Haidos remembers Beatty helping him string his guitar. Naturally, when he comes to Hibbing, Abe Zimmerman dines often at the Delvic. The Haidoses move their business to the L&B Cafe on Howard Street and also begin to manage the Kay Hotel in the Micka building—for the owners, the Zimmerman brothers; naturally, Abe transfers his lunch to the L&B.

Home, at Grandma's, Bobby can hear a neighbor, "Chuckie Solberg," playing piano in another apartment.

The predominantly Italian neighborhood is typified by the corner grocery of Mrs. Paulucci who brews *Dago Red* for friends on the block; by the handsome young tennis pro and former neighborhood baby-sitter, Vince Bugliosi, whose family also owns a grocery; and by Vendetti's, where kids pick up beer for their fathers. Little Bobby Zimmerman is just a little different than the normal Blessed Sacrament Catholic kid on the block. He's not so much for sports, though he might join in games such as tag, hide-and-seek, duck duck goose or chasing the Island Farm Creamery horses. After dark, anyone who's around—the Antonelli girls, Sharon LeVoir, Larry Fabbro—run around under the street lights and up and down the alleys that divide every block.

Bobby attends first grade next door at Alice School. He thinks the ringing of the recess bell means *time to go home*. It takes a few extra trips to figure out how very long the school day is. A Christmas pageant presents songs by children of each grade. If Bobby goes along with it, so what? The Zimmerman brothers advertise heavily for the Gentile holidays.

In Hibbing, almost every family of substance owns a house. Abe and Beatty find theirs at 2425 7th Avenue East in the established Fairview Addition, a few blocks south of the high school and the Memorial Building. The two-story, wood framed, flat-roofed, stucco house is seemingly displaced in the snowy north, but examples of the same *Mediterranean Moderne* style can be found all over town. On the first floor, there is the usual kitchen, bathroom, dining room and living room—with a fireplace. Upstairs, a hallway connects three bedrooms.

There is not much yard space. The "fair view" looks southeast at rocky, gray and red "dumps" of excavated mining earth, resembling the mesas and buttes of a western landscape.

The former owner was Exhilda M. Madden, widow of Timothy J. Madden, who had died the previous October. When Madden built the house in 1939, he permitted an easement to Purity Baking Co. for a double garage behind the house. This bread "warehouse" is an exception in Fairview, a residential neighborhood, where peace is disturbed mainly by work on new houses added almost daily.

When the Zimmermans arrive, Hibbing is truly the Ore Capital in its prime, although other residents are already unemployed. Fortunately, the Zimmermans are busy being part and parcel of the economic boom.

Many residents resent poor and rich alike. Fortunately, the Zimmermans are neither poor nor rich and find no quarrel with either. Others, not so many, resent industrial exploitation. Fortunately for the Zimmermans, there's a good chance any dollar paid out by the mines will come their way.

Some hate barren hills and bottomless pits: fortunately, it's not that way on 7th Avenue, where trees are beginning to shade tranquil sidewalks and provide some shelter from the storms.

Some feel isolated by endless swamps bristling with bears and bugs. Fortunately, the Zimmermans have little interest in the prickly environs and spend most of their time on or near concrete. Many complain about the endless winter that precludes agriculture. Fortunately for them, the Zimmermans have a good furnace and wouldn't worry a whole lot about a rutabaga's well being.

Newcomers who "don't know anybody" are shut out by extended families and ethnic groups and may be virtually shunned at the same church for years before anyone extends a greeting. Fortunately, the Zimmermans belong to a clan; they find ready company with numerous relatives in a fairly large Jewish community.

Some find a town without pity, where "differences" are barely tolerated, if at all. Fortunately for them, the Zimmermans are *not* different; they share the general appearance and values of the majority.

Some complain that good bagels are hard to find. Fortunately, excellent baked goods can be had at the Sunrise Bakery. Not enough Jews in town to keep a rabbi? Every day, it seems, there's seven new people born.

Some curse the parking situation downtown. Unfortunately, Abe Zimmerman is one of them. He is ticketed three times in April for illegal parking.

Looking south from Howard Street, Androy Hotel, left.
Hibbing Historical Society

Chapter Four
2nd Grade
1948-49

Positively Howard Street

I see pictures of the '50s, the '60s and the '70s and I see there was a difference. But I don't think the human mind can comprehend the past and the future. They are both just illusions that can manipulate you into thinking there's some kind of change. But after you've been around awhile, they both seem unnatural.
   <u>On the Tracks</u>, *1995*

THE POLITICAL WORLD

PLAYBOY: Did you ever have the standard boyhood dream of growing up to be President?
DYLAN: No. When I was a boy, Harry Truman was President; who'd want to be Harry Truman?
   <u>Playboy</u>, *1966*

They rise from the dead, *but they're still dead*—the soldiers, retrieved from their first graves in battleground Europe. In July 1949, Robert H. Edelstein, Bobby Zimmerman's cousin, comes home to Minnesota.

Ku Klux Klan. From Alabama, Tennessee and Georgia, reports of lynching, flogging, cross burning, bombing and intimidation by a hooded gang: Negroes are the usual victims.

At the polls. Stuntz township, made up mostly of the "village" of Hibbing, votes, as always, solidly Democratic.

For President: Harry Truman: 7,316. Thomas Dewey: 2,688.
For U.S. Senator: Hubert Humphrey: 7,893. Joe Ball: 2,485.

KING HEMATITE

The iron ore poured
As the years passed the door,
The drag lines an' the shovels they was a-humming
   "North Country Blues," 1963

The North Hibbing *problem* has simmered in city councils for some time as the Hull-Rust mine consumes block after block of the old town. Remaining public property must be dealt with, not to mention 25 privately-owned parcels. When the Oliver Iron Mining Co. wants to vacate Third Avenue, a major thoroughfare, the village council objects. Condemnation and trades of property become hot issues.

By year's end, a mountain in the Venezuelan jungle begins yielding prodigious tons of ore for the steel mills of North America. The source is said to be ultimately greater than the *fabulous Mesabi range.*

POSITIVELY HOWARD STREET

Don't follow leaders/Watch the parking meters
"Subterranean Homesick Blues," 1965

Parking meters. Installed first in Hibbing, July 1949: a penny for 12 minutes and a nickel for an hour. The first violator gripes that a cop hid behind a lamppost until the red flag came up, then gave him a ticket.

Plenty of potential parkers need the places meters will fund. Besides jammed multi-family apartments, Hibbing is crowded with trailer houses, cabins and army surplus "Quonset huts." Materials have become available but labor costs are high and mortgages unpopular. Potential buyers will only pay $7,500 for a house when $8,000 is the minimum cost, explains Hibbing contractor Max Gray.

Polio. Following the annual epidemics come the accessories: braces, crutches, wheel chairs and iron lungs. It is common to have over 50 children and a half-dozen adults receiving treatment at Hibbing hospital. The first polio fatality in the area is a 19-year-old woman. On the 1949 March of Dimes board of directors is Bobby Zimmerman's great uncle, Max Edelstein: Bobby's father is still recovering from the disease.

Although there is no sure prevention, prudent mothers tell children to avoid crowds and polluted waters. Some fathers build sandboxes to occupy their children at home alone. Any headaches, sore throats, nausea, fevers, obscure pains and stiffness are watched nervously.

A child also learns to fear tuberculosis, the leading cause of death for those 15-44. St. Louis County, which includes Duluth and Hibbing, considers itself first in the world to attempt mass X-ray work with a mobile unit, at sites that include the Edelstein-owned Lybba Theater.

Human Reproduction. In April, 500 parents and teachers attend the first "Social Hygiene" class at the high school auditorium.

Frozen custard. A double dip, with the opening of the Dairy Queen on 169, just west of the highway "Y," and the Bridgeman Dairy Store on Howard Street.

THE GARMAKER SYNDROME

First annual. The Hibbing ski jumping tournament at Maple Hill in March. And the All-Nations basketball tournament featuring teams calling themselves *Swedes, Italians, West End Slavs, Fighting Finns, Fighting Irish, Brooklyn Slavs* and *Irish Shamrocks.*

Jack Dempsey, former heavyweight boxing champion, and Bronko Nagurski, football All-American from International Falls, visit Hibbing long enough to sign autographs and to receive a *King Hematite* honorarium.

OVER THE RAINBOW

SAM: So you heard this polka music in what—dance halls or something?
BOB: Yeah—no—taverns. Beer joints. They played it in all the taverns. You just walk down the street and hear that all the time. People'd come flyin' out into the street doin' the polka. Accordions could come flyin' out.
"BOB" in Esquire, 1987

4th of July—a good day to be a kid: free ice cream at Bennett Park; free cartoons at the Lybba. *Porky Pig, Daffy Duck, Tom and Jerry, Barney Bear, Goldielocks and the Three Bears, Mighty Mouse.* A parade down Howard street. Fireworks at the fairground. A teen dance. For adults, the 4th brings a bonanza of music and dancing: the Four Sharps at the Servicemen's Club; *the music you like* by *Joe Mlaker's Polkatiers*; *Frankie Smoltz and his orchestra* at the Club Band Box, Leetonia; a free dance at the Italian Hall with music by *Cippelones 6 Piece Rhythmaires*. At the Crystal Lounge of the Androy Hotel: *The Four Naturals*.

Like the community it represents, the Hibbing *Daily Tribune* enjoys its best days, even as it reports with some enthusiasm the advances of its rival, television. Numerous newspaper owners are also investors in the new medium. The number of stations in the United States has tripled; the number of sets has zoomed from 200,000 to 1 million. The average price of a television is $350. Because Bobby's parents own an appliance store, they can get one wholesale.

Reflecting the broad popularity of the idioms, *Billboard* magazine drops the term "hillbilly" for "country and western" and "race" for "rhythm and blues."

NORTH COUNTRY FAIR

SAM: Did you feel like you were cut off back then?
Bob: How d'ya mean?
SAM: I mean being up in the Far North like that. In the boondocks.
BOB: Nah, 'cause I didn't know anything else was goin' on.
"BOB" in "True Dylan," Esquire, 1987

Farmers expect bear raids "again this year" due to a scarcity of berries. A 310-pounder is shot as it prowls through garbage in the city of Grand Rapids, 30 miles from Hibbing. In August, a bear breakfasts on raspberries just outside a kitchen door in Auditor's Addition of Hibbing. "Following a typical feminine reaction under such circumstances," the housewife screams and ol' bruin wanders into nearby bushes.

AGUDATH ACHIM

The original "pioneer merchants" of South Hibbing are just now dying, such as Lithuanian native Hyman Bloom, 73, who ran a department store in North Hibbing and, later, the Boston Store on Howard Street. Bloom, a Jew, was for many years chairman of the downtown Christmas committee, "helping to provide cheer for needy families and children of Hibbing."

And Louis Stein, 56. Born in Russia, Stein in 1918 started the first drug store in South Hibbing. He belonged to Rotary, Elks, Odd Fellows, B'nai B'rith, Hibbing's Zionist organization and was past president of Agudath Achim.

Honors. Dr. Bertram Sachs, selected to head the 1949 Hibbing Jaycees.

A new rabbi, Joseph W. Wiesenberg, arrives in August 1949. The 35-year-old Czechoslovakian immigrant hopes to make the synagogue not just a religious but a cultural center. During *the bad time* in Germany and Czechoslovakia, Wiesenberg and his wife had escaped to London.

BOBBY

I don't really think in terms of growing up or not growing up... I've been doing what I've been doing since I was very small, so I have never known anything else. I have never had to quit my job to do this...So I don't think in terms of economics or status or what people think of me one way or the other.
   Playboy, 1978

HELLO FOLKS!
"I operate the Micka Electric company, remember? You and I have sweat many times over your broken down appliances in the last seven years. Remember, our electrical contracting and wiring . . . we wired your grandfather's house, your father's house, and can guarantee expert work on yours." The advertisement in the *Daily Tribune* pushes the new General Electric line. "Come in and have a listen. You will be amazed at the scratch free phonograph and wonderful tone."

Wishing you all the Season's Greetings from my associates and myself, I am,
Your trouble shooter,
Maurice (Morey) Zimmerman.

Another Micka ad concludes, *A Cheery Little Message to wish you MERRY CHRISTMAS.*

As electricians and appliance salesmen, the Zimmerman brothers are in the right place at the right time. In the flurry of development following the huge hematite harvest of recent years, they find themselves expanding rapidly. Maurice hires John Verne Carlson, formerly an insurance salesman, to assist Bobby's father, Abe, as an appliance salesman. To the service department are added John Costello, Leo Diachok and Gene Gabardi.

In nearby Nashwauk, Zimmerman-owned Micka opens a branch store, run by another brother, Max, who is elected president of the Nashwauk Parent-Teachers' Association.

Chanukah. When the Maccabees cast Syrian conquerors from the Temple in 165 B.C., candles were relighted, containing only enough purified oil for one day; somehow, they burned eight days. In modern homes, one candle is lighted the first night, two the second, and so on, until eight candles are burning. The happy, increasingly Christmas-like observance is accompanied by family gatherings, gifts, entertainment and the serving of latkes, a form of potato pancakes. Agudath Achim Sunday School presents a program in the Little Theater of the Memorial Building Taking part are Roger and Marilyn Alto, Robert Cohan, Barbara and Jean Edelstein, Shirley Feldman, Naomi Hallock, Sally Mae Jolowsky, Janey Lee Kamman, Barbara, Rochell and Sharon Ladin, Fredda Mackoff, Lori Milkes, James and Lynette Randy, Michael Roth, Diane and James Sher, Thomas Shuirman, Allan Spector, Nancy Stone and Robert Zimmerman.

In 1948 there is an extra Chanukah prayer for the modern Jews of Palestine as they fight "to preserve the same religious freedom that the Maccabees fought for so long ago. This dream is being realized in the new State of Israel."

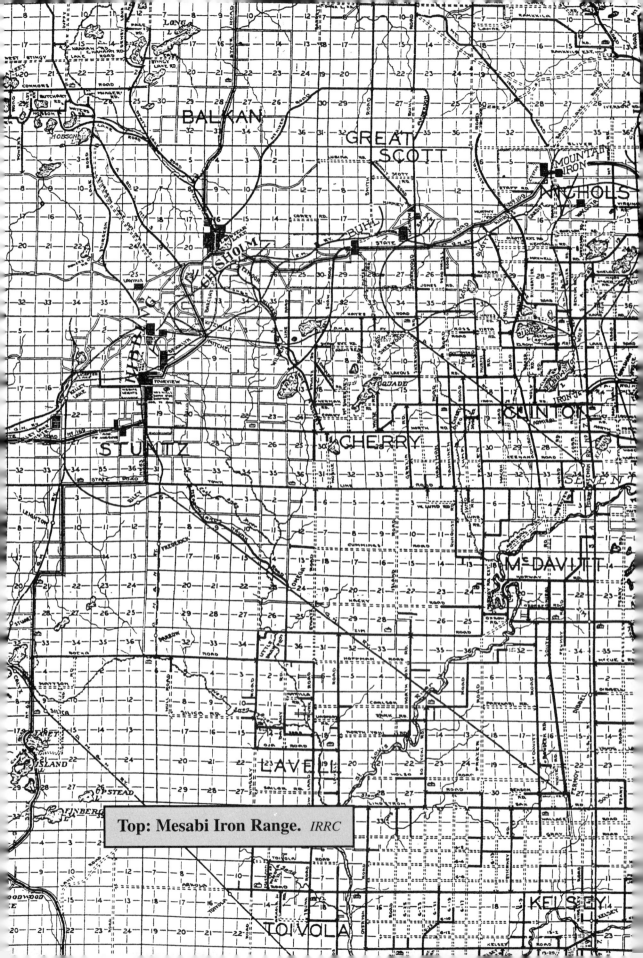

Top: Mesabi Iron Range. *IRRC*

Above: Frank Hibbing statue, Hibbing, dedicated 1941. *Aubin Studio* • Below: Hull-Rust-Mahoning mine, old Hibbing on the edge. *Aubin Studio*

Howard Street, looking west, 1940s, Androy Hotel, left. *Aubin Studio*

Herald Mine, 1909
Hibbing Historical Society

Chapter Five
3rd Grade
1949-50

Agudath Achim

When is the first time you ran away, as you put it?
I took off when I was in New Mexico...
How old were you then?
Uh, about seven, eight, something like that. For the most part my base has been in upper—way upper Minnesota—almost to the border. Can I mention the town? Hibbing, Minnesota—that's a mining town—lumber town. I was there off and on ever since I was seven to seventeen.

Billy James Interview, 1961

THE POLITICAL WORLD

Communism. Against its perceived menace in the mid-year of the 20th century, the U.S. works "full blast" to develop a hydrogen super bomb in the arms race with Russia. After incursions by Communist North Korea into capitalist South Korea, U.S. President Harry S Truman authorizes Gen. Douglas MacArthur to augment Air Force bombing and a Naval blockade with Army and Marine ground troops. The ensuing losses to the "invincible" U.S. military are shocking. On June 25, Communist "reds" from North Korea pour past the defenses of the stunned South Koreans. In waves, thousands of Chinese hurl themselves against the Allies. *Like locusts they pour out of Manchuria, and behind them lay millions more.* American troops race up from Japan in a "police action," hoping to put down the aggressors.

KING HEMATITE

People survived for 6000 years without having to work for slave wages for a person who comes down and...well, actually, it's just colonization. But see, I saw that stuff firsthand, because where I come from, they <u>really</u> got that deal good, with the ore.

<u>Rolling Stone</u>, 1984

Phil Stong in *Holiday* magazine, in July 1950, writes: "Hibbing's size and wealth derive largely from the Hull-Rust-Mahoning iron pit, which is *the biggest excavation ever made by man,* something over three miles long, a mile wide at some points, and 458 feet deep, as of January 1, 1949." *And getting bigger and deeper every day.*

Mesabi mining history spans only about sixty years, most of it as the nation's top producer. But two wars and the tremendous expansion of industry have nearly exhausted the high-grade ores. *There may be ten years' supply left, or twenty...*

With a minimum wage for common labor at $8.27 per day, labor relations are very good, according to Stong. "In the five Mesaba clinics, a miner is entitled to free accident care, paid for by the mining companies; he may also have Blue Cross service; and if he chooses to sign a contract with the clinic (he would be foolish not to) he may have, for a couple of dollars a month, complete medical care for his entire family, except for surgery." Because of the happy workers, the United Steel Workers union is more or less a social body, Stong says.

Not quite. In September 1949, a national strike for "free" pensions and insurance puts 12,000 iron miners in Minnesota, Michigan, Wisconsin and Missouri out of work. The effects of unemployment are vivid: men standing three rows deep in taverns, discussing the strike; pupils eating at the school rather than in more expensive downtown eating houses; "that frightful silence that hangs like a pall over the working areas of the mines," according to the *Tribune*. "In the mornings and at night, not a sign of smoke, no whistles, no trains moving, and no sounds from the Diesels. How we hate it!" Men and women head for the woods, seeking game for food.

A few weeks later, the situation worsens. "There are evidences every day that the continuation of the strike is knocking the props from under the economic life of Hibbing... One little grocery store owner told me that if the strike continues he would be forced to discontinue. Several Hibbing stores have discharged their extra help... A number of wives of miners are seeking jobs... some have taken manual labor tasks to tide the family over the depression period."

After two months, U.S. Steel settles the strike by agreeing to pensions and co-payments for insurance; the good times roll again.

Strike or not, the town that moved is on the move again. In 1918, the Oliver Iron Mining Co. bought and began transporting 185 houses and 20 business buildings from the "North Forty" in order to get at the iron ore beneath. The process continued until a 1934 agreement that buildings not be moved but be demolished to provide more employment for the building trades during the Depression. Moving resumed in 1942 with the war-induced housing shortage.

Newly-displaced residents of North Hibbing can purchase their buildings at $1 each. If they do so, moving and remodeling costs will add an average $4,500 to the total cost. In the first half of 1950, 56 moving permits are issued. For Hibbing, relocation becomes a way of life. Residents scarcely turn their heads when a two-story dwelling comes wheeling by at fifteen miles per hour, towed by large trucks with rubber-tired trailers.

As Hull-Rust devours Hibbing, it has become a litany. The future lies in lesser grade ores that can be improved before marketing. It's not a new idea. A taconite-extracting plant erected during World War I near Babbitt had closed in 1924.

"Taconite," explains the *Tribune*, derives from the Greek, meaning "to melt." Reference books say the word is taken from the Taconic mountains in Vermont.

POSITIVELY HOWARD STREET

I didn't leave home because of my curiosity to see what was going on elsewhere. I just wanted to get away...Hibbing was a vacuum. I just kept going because I was bored.

<u>*No Direction Home*</u>, pub. 1986

America enjoys the highest standard of living on earth; in Hibbing, the Woolworth store enjoys the biggest Saturday sales ever. The Ore Capital is no "Ghost town," asserts the *Tribune's* Fisher. What about construction, up 133 percent, compared to 1949? *Looks as though we are very much alive, doesn't it?* What about the new "el MOTEL COURT" on 2nd Avenue West—complete with wiring by Micka Electric?

What about Howard Street, as featured in Republic Steel's *Plant Towns* magazine? "Perhaps no other city in the United States has had a more important part in the building of this 20th Century America." The 16,000 citizens have enabled countless refrigerators, stoves, automobiles, trucks, buses, skyscrapers and suspension bridges to be produced. The Ore Capital is proud to call itself a town of prosperous middle-income families with 250 "business men" and 2,700 "salaried" persons, mainly in mining-related activities. Tax records for 1949 show only 33 persons making over $20,000. Likewise, few fall in the lowest group.

What about a busy Christmas, helped by the free show at the Jewish-owned State, Gopher or Lybba theaters—complete with a free box of Cracker Jack? The shopping season is inaugurated by Santa, when he switches on "brightway" mercury vapor lighting, touted as one of the most modern systems in the "Northwest."

What about some fun? Stong in *Holiday* says there is more to Minnesota than mining. The North is the world's biggest playground: "3,700,000 acres strung with chains of innumerable lakes." "Big cars streak up the roads of the Arrowhead, with shiny canoes on top, upside-down, and a fortune in fishing rods sticking out the back. Men stroll into the modest bars and lunch rooms of these little towns wearing a couple of hundred dollars' worth of Abercrombie & Fitch fishing finery."

What about vandalism? At the Lybba, lipstick defaces the walls of the ladies lounge. At another theater, seats are slashed with knives, a projection machine damaged and oil poured on upholstered chairs. *Wouldn't straight jail sentences be the remedy?*

What about the good kids? "Teenager family week" inspires a Hibbing girl, 17, to write to the newspaper. "Sally Teenager" is happy; she lives in a comfortable home with a Mom who is never too busy to listen and a Dad always fixing something. "Mom let us roughhouse on beds." Dad was always ready for a game of baseball.

Summer for Sally meant long, peaceful days at a lake cabin on the Canadian border. "What I remember best, though," she writes, "are the blustry winter evenings that we spent gathered around the piano as my mother accompanied us while we sang old songs."

THE GARMAKER SYNDROME

Vince Bugliosi, *a smooth stroking 10th grader*, seen in any season banging a ball against the Memorial building, brings the Region Seven singles tennis championship title to Hibbing High School.

OVER THE RAINBOW

"Disa bus it goes Seventh Avenue only." In his column, *Along the Iron Range*, *Tribune* editor George M. Fisher quotes da girl on "disa bus," who defines a celebrity as "a person who works all his life to become famous--and then goes around in dark glasses so no one will know who he is."

Da "Hibbing Girl Who Made Good," Kirsten Kenyon, appears at the high school auditorium. A "romantic lead" in the Broadway musical, *Song of Norway*, she is now on tour with Sigmund Romberg, "famous musical comedy composer."

"Hibbing's gift to the music world is as anxious to sing before her townspeople as they are to hear her," notes the *Tribune*. Kenyon hopes old friends will be in the audience because, "My view of them from the stage of the Hibbing high school auditorium might be the only opportunity I will have to see most of them."

The only training the "blonde lyric soprano" has received comes from Harry Davidson, who had moved to New York from Virginia, Minn. Her inspiration began with two uncles, George Naeseth, known as Newman the Great, "one of the nation's greatest mentalists and hypnotics," and Marius Naeseth, an actor. Her name is taken from Uncle Marius' stage name of *Robert Newman Kenyon,* itself chosen for his birthplace, Kenyon, Minn. *Kirsten*, a nod to Nordic ancestry, "goes well with Kenyon," she says. Daughter of the Hibbing chief of police, her original handle is Helen Naeseth.

A crowd of 1,900 listens with "rapt attention and great pride as the lovely blonde native daughter sang from the stage of the school, where . . . she was a student in the days when a musical career wasn't even contemplated by the lady of song." *One of the greatest musical treats ever offered in the Ore Capital in modern times,* according to the *Tribune*. For his part, orchestra leader Romberg, who had never seen white birch bark, takes home a scrap of Minnesota.

Another visiting celebrity is Terrance McReddy, *king of the bums*. His *Bums Ball*, sponsored by the Hibbing Youth Coordinating Council, is attended by 800 in the Memorial Building. The "once-popular" *hurdy-gurdy man*, Salvator Cansona, plays his music box at Herberger's Carnival Days, while a companion works the crowd. "The solemn-faced monkey puts on spectacles, smokes a pipe, accompanies the hurdy-gurdy music with the cymbals in an off beat, and, of course, wraps her hot little fist around a penny in a hurry," observes the *Tribune*, adding that children "nowadays" are better behaved than 30 years previous.

At the State Theater, Jim Molohon revives the "craze" of old-time amateur shows, sending the winners to Radio City, Minneapolis. The "College Capers" talent show, sponsored by the junior college and held at the high school auditorium, features *Hammed Up Hamlet,* the tambouritzans of Keewatin, *Shoe Shine Boogie Woogie* and a western skit with Ray Bugliosi.

As part of a national rage to hear the centuries-old instrument, William Kuntara, a Slovenian refugee now in Eveleth, displays his talents on the zither.

"Squeeze-box dancing," at a wedding west of Ely, is described by journalist Phil Stong as a "Range ritual." Long tables—quickly deserted. Young men and girls, "old men and old girls," who spin and dip and proudly tap the pine floor with their "stout and serviceable feet." Bride and groom vanish; by midnight the younger guests are gone. But six or seven pairs of plump, middle-aged women go on whirling. At the end, the band duo, not old, bearded folk musicians, as we half expect, but two trim, serious young men, tuck accordions into rain-proof covers as tenderly as if the instruments were babies.

"And this night—if not before—we could understand why the Mesabi juke boxes have at least three records by Frank Yankovich, and only an occasional one by Frank Sinatra, and why the window of the music store at Hibbing displayed six accordions, four harmonicas, and back in a corner, just one saxophone. The squeeze box is the national instrument of the Range, the one that best relaxes it after its mighty work."

NORTH COUNTRY FAIR

I was driving right straight into the sun, and I looked up into it even though I remember someone telling me a long time ago when I was a kid never to look straight at the sun...My dad or an uncle or somebody...I always believed that must be true or else why would an adult tell you something like that. And I never did look directly at the sun when I was a kid.

"BOB" in *Esquire*, 1987

A blizzard in mid-January drops the "mercury" to minus 30. The noon temperature: minus 24. Hilingoss Chevrolet offers to start any cars malfunctioning after the Hibbing-Eveleth hockey game at the Memorial Arena. The average local temperature for January 1950 is minus 5; average low, minus 15; average high, plus 5.

Seagulls seen in early April are supposed to promise spring—but not this year. Winter-weary residents review decreasing coal piles and increasing snow piles. "The weatherman has the Old Timer stopped this spring. He can only squirt a small spot of brown defiance into the prevailing whiteness from his cud of Peerless as he mutters to himself: I've lived here 60 years, man and boy, and I ain't never seen anything like this."

The April 12 low of plus 4 is the coldest on record for that date. The previous year, the high temperature for the same date had been 64 degrees. Ice is still 16-inches thick on the Sturgeon River north of Hibbing in mid-April. Northern Lights streaking across the sky seem to depict Old Man Winter hanging on with his wintry grasp.

When the snow finally begins to melt, the results are major floods and impassable roads. Not until the end of April does the first ore train load up at Hull-Rust to depart for Two Harbors. On May 3, six inches of snow fall overnight. Some blame the crazy weather on the A-bomb.

AGUDATH ACHIM

There weren't too many Jews in Hibbing, Minnesota. Most of them I was related to.
      Spin, 1985

Busy busy busy. At Agudath Achim synagogue, the Council of Jewish Women sponsors study groups, speakers, food fairs, arts and crafts, rummage sales, progressive dinners, festival dinners and luncheons—raising money to furnish the synagogue and to provide medical equipment to the needy. It publishes THE CALENDAR of birthdays, anniversaries, candle lighting times and holidays. *Woe be to those who forgot to congratulate friends on special days—it was all on the calendar.* The Council creates a Sunday School for 40 children, *so our children will know and be proud of the Jewish heritage.*

An addition to the synagogue—of classrooms and a rabbi's study—takes the name of the late civic leader and drug store owner, Louis Stein. In his memory, a "sick loan cupboard" containing medical supplies is donated by the Council. Among dedication speakers is the donor of electrical work and chairman of the building committee, Maurice Zimmerman, from Micka Electric. Dinner is served by the women of Hadassah, under the direction of Mrs. Abe Zimmerman, president.

When Stein's daughter, Leone Rae, marries Gerald Altman in Duluth's Tifereth Israel synagogue, Mrs. Zimmerman throws a "prenuptial entertainment."

Members of Hadassah also earn money for immigrants crowding into Israel from European Displaced Person camps by baby-sitting, baking, card parties and selling greeting cards. "Mrs. Abe Zimmerman, president of the local chapter, will report on the northwest regional conference held in Duluth," reports the *Tribune*. At the Androy, Hadassah honors Sarah Lewis of Chisholm, who founded the northeastern Minnesota group in 1919. Mrs. Zimmerman welcomes 100 delegates and presents Mrs. Lewis with funds to provide books for a new Hadassah-built medical school in Jerusalem.

In June, Abe Zimmerman is elected president of Louis Stein Lodge No. 793 of B'nai B'rith.

How about that "Max Edelstein Day" at the Androy? For Beatty Zimmerman's uncle, members of the Round Table explore the theme, "How Mild Can a Cigarette Be?" The choristers, directed by Gustie Ekola, Al Strand and Dr. Bertram Sachs, fill the lounge and coffee shop with the strains of "My Wild Irish Rose."

Another in a long list of "pioneers," Thomas Sachs, 65, who opened the Sachs clothing store in 1908, is buried at Superior, Wis.

To be religious means added responsibilities, new resolutions and a searching of soul. Rabbi Wiesenberg explains that Rosh Hashanah-Yom Kippur is the time of year when the Lord of Creation reviews his handiwork and passes judgment on it. It is also the only time some Jews set foot in the synagogue.

Young Judea. A group for Jewish youth on the Range between ages of 13 and 18 is organized at Hibbing. Young people will get together with other Range clubs for social activities, sports, debates and the like. A convention is to be held the following June at Camp Herzl, Webster, Wis.

BOBBY

A lot of people have trouble with their parents up until they're 50, 60, 70 years old. I never had that kind of problem with my parents ...I've been raised by people who feel that fathers, whether they're married or not, should be responsible for their children, that all sons should be taught a trade, and that parents should be punished for their children's crimes.
   <u>*Spin,*</u> *1985*

Because most Jewish parents value accomplishment, even the more exotic ambitions have a chance to be nurtured. Maybe the dancer will become a doctor; the bug collector a professor; the philatelist a philanthropist. With much expected, parents commonly are disappointed and children feel like failures. Likewise, much is given and a child may feel unable to repay the debt.

Order is accomplished by reasoning and explaining. The very verbal mother outdoes herself encouraging her children and worrying about them. Beatty says: wash your face and hands; brush your teeth; put your things away; do your homework; be polite; don't play rough with brother David; don't play with matches. Use a little common sense. And her ministrations seem to succeed. No one has ever called to say her boys are teasing dogs, throwing rocks or stealing. There is only high regard in the neighborhood for her sons!

Like most Jewish men in Hibbing, Abe is a solid citizen and a good provider. *We are more like friends,* says Abe. *We tell the boys they will have children of their own one day and they will want to be friends with them.* "Don't ask for anything unless you're prepared to take 'No' for an answer," he says—and gives them almost everything they want. He tells them, "Do things because you like us not because you're afraid of us," but becomes cross when the boys don't do what he wants them to. He gets Bobby into Boy Scouts but the boy's clearly not interested in working his way toward Webelos and, at first opportunity, drops out.

Like most Jewish parents, the Zimmermans are law-abiding. Unfortunately, court records show, Beatty is "arrested" at 11 a.m., June 3, for a parking offense and chooses to plead guilty.

Chet Crippa entertaining, 1950. *Holiday*

Chapter Six
4th Grade
1950-51

The Political World

Letters?...The ones that call you a sellout?
Yeah. Sellout, fink, Fascist, Red, everything in the book. I really dig those. And ones from old friends.
Like, 'You don't remember me but I was in the fourth grade with you?'
No, I never had any friends then.
    (1965) <u>Bob Dylan: The Early Years</u>, *1990*

THE POLITICAL WORLD

I'm just rooted back there in the '50s, and what's got me this far keeps me going...
    <u>*Newsweek*</u>, *1995*

Communism: In Korea, weary American soldiers retreat *to avoid massacre by the overwhelming Red horde.* President Harry Truman fires Gen. Douglas MacArthur for failing to support the United Nations strategy in the "police action." *Communism.* Residents of Las Vegas wait for a good view of the fifth atomic test in eleven days. The 5:48 a.m. flash is seen in Oakland, Calif., 450 miles away. The action is broadcast by the still-novel medium of television. *Communism.* Minus 7 degrees, January, 1951. The high school band, trying to keep mouthpieces from freezing to their lips, send Hibbing National Guardsmen off to Camp Rucker. "And I confess it didn't take long to detect not from the boys in colors, but from the bystanders that this war is far from being a popular one," writes *Tribune* editor George Fisher. *Communism.* In case of atomic bomb attack, Hibbing residents are warned to fill bathtubs with water while there's still pressure and to take the family to the basement until an "all clear" sounds. *Communism.* There's a red tinge in Hibbing, says Col. Ted Oberlander, civilian defense director. Indeed, Minnesota ranks ninth on the FBI list *as a haven for reds,* notes the *Tribune's* Fisher, without apology. The I.W.W. had long ago been active in the mines and everyone knows Communist Gus Hall was born just outside of town.

KING HEMATITE

a train line cuts the ground/showin' where the fathers an' mothers/of me an' my friends had picked/up an' moved from/north Hibbing/t' south Hibbing
    "11 Outlined Epitaphs," 1964

Oh yeah? George Fisher bets the "Great Mesaba Iron Range" will be shipping its riches long after "the experts" predict. Forty years now, someone has been predicting "fifteen more years," he says, *and we are still going strong.* Even as he speaks, nearby Carson Lake, a "location" at the Leetonia mine, is disappearing in "the restless moving process which has marked the history of the Hibbing area."

Within five years, 106 houses have been relocated, mostly from North Hibbing to Home Acres and Aviators Addition. By the end of 1950, all that is left of what was once the Mesabi Range's largest community, is 40 acres projecting into the Hull-Rust-Sellers-Mahoning-Buffalo-Scranton pit.

POSITIVELY HOWARD STREET

I didn't change my name in honor of Dylan Thomas. That's just a story. I've done more for Dylan Thomas than he's ever done for me. Look how many kids are probably reading his poetry now because they heard that story.

Saturday Evening Post, 1966

Do you say Dylan or Dye-lan?
Oh, I say Dylan. Dyelan. I say anything you say really.
Did you take it from the Welsh poet?
No, no...It's a name in my family, but, uh, it's from my uncle's family. It's not my first father's name, it's the name of my mother's...my mother's side of the family and it's uh, spelled D-I-L-L-O-N, and I uh, changed it!

Martin Bronstein Interview, 1966

"New South Hibbing" is a busy place. All those houses moved in and many more being built from scratch. Work begins on a 100-unit federally-financed low-rent housing project in Greenhaven subdivision. Downtown—the grand opening of newly-remodeled Feldman's department store. The National Tea store advertises the first *supermarket* in Hibbing.

There have been no traffic fatalities this year; yet, to discourage bad driving, the *Tribune* prints photographs of crumpled automobiles in which six Iron Range residents previously perished. Graphic photos are also published of a naked 8-year-old boy with bruises and lacerations covering his body. After his parents cut him with a nut pick, burned his feet with matches and tied him to a ten-pound iron brick, the boy is found hiding in the rafters of the Memorial Building.

Making news is Merritt Dillon, a 35-year farmer on Dillon road who has been tenacious enough to develop a modern dairy farm in the harsh climate and metallic topsoil. Dillon deplores the disposal of trash along ditches in and around Hibbing. *This obnoxious practice should stop.*

THE GARMAKER SYNDROME

Vince Bugliosi, back from Beverly Hills, Calif., with a new tennis grip and a newer "butch" haircut, can be seen almost every day inside and outside the Memorial Building, practicing for the state tournament. His June victory marks only the second tennis championship won by a player from north of the Twin Cities.

In June, a baseball game at Bennett Park pits the Duluth all-Negro "Travelers" against the Hibbing Greyhounds semi-pro team.

A "beautiful" new clubhouse opens at the Mesaba Country Club. To pay for it, members have to dip into the till a little more than expected. Might have helped to invite some prosperous Jewish businessmen to join—but the charter won't allow it.

OVER THE RAINBOW

I can sing as good as Caruso.
   Interview, 1960s

I remember we had a phone in the house, but I also remember there was a party line of maybe six other people. And no matter when you got on the phone, you know, there might be somebody else on it...When television first came in, it came on at like four in the afternoon, and it was off the air by seven at night. So you had more time to...I guess to think.
   Rolling Stone, 1984

You stop smoking those cigarettes...and you'll be able to sing like Caruso.
   Rolling Stone, 1969

Music in the air. Small local bands—the *Aristocrats, Chet Crippa, Jim Bauldrica, Jimmy Dall, Mickey Bentnix, Joe Cippeloni.* Big national bands. The high school band and city of Hibbing band. The Schubert Chorus. Live shows between feature movies. At a school festival, American folk songs, sung by the fifth grade.

Incomparable Hildegarde. The world famous chanteuse from New Holstein, Wis., plays piano and sings to a record crowd of 1,945 at the high school auditorium. "There still is plenty of entertainment money around in Hibbing and on the Range, providing the public is given what it wants, or what it thinks it wants," remarks the *Tribune*, noting that Hildegarde's "vivacious personality" enables her "to get to everybody and make everybody feel at home and feel as though in love with her." Her piano playing is "remarkable" but Hildegarde has "no singing voice to speak of."

"I have visited many small communities," Hildegarde says, "but nowhere have I found a more spontaneous, neighborly welcome than I did in the ore capital."

After her show, she visits the Hull Rust pit. "I certainly did not want to leave Hibbing without seeing one of the wonders of the world."

Television is received in Hibbing, usually poorly. The handy-man Alfred Schmidt, a.k.a. "Schmidty," tells the *Tribune* he is "pulling in" programs from Minneapolis, Chicago, Milwaukee, Nashville and Dallas.

Free Saturday morning movies at the State and Lybba theaters begin with the Zane Grey western, "West of the Pecos." Hibbing merchants hope to attract out-of-town shoppers with big screen baby-sitting. Same at Christmas.

At the State, the *Tribune's* George Fisher views *The Great Caruso*. He calls it "one of the screen's greatest contributions to good and wholesome films."

Halloween parties are held for 4,500 youngsters. Fourth-grader Gerald Bloomquist wins a pea-guessing contest.

NORTH COUNTRY FAIR

If I had any advantage over anybody at all, it's the advantage that I was all alone and could think and do what I wanted to. Looking back on it, it probably has a lot to do with growing up in northern Minnesota. I don't know what I would have been if I was growing up in the Bronx or Ethiopia or South America or even California. I think everybody's environment affects him in that way.
   <u>**Spin,**</u> **1985**

Varmints. Adjacent Itasca county pays $7,965 in bounties in 1950—for 291 brush wolves and 12 timber wolves. *June 15*. If old man frost keeps away long enough, the prospects of blueberry, currant and strawberry crops are the brightest in years.

AGUDATH ACHIM

I'm comfortable wherever people don't remind me of who I am. Anytime somebody reminds me of who I am, that kills it for me.
   <u>**Bat Chain Puller,**</u> **1990**

Shavuot, the "Feast of Weeks," commemorates the revelation of the Ten Commandments. "In warmer climates, people express their gratitude for the first fruits; on the Range, it is, of necessity, thanks for the final arrival of spring," comments local Rabbi Joseph Wiesenberg, immediately resigning and moving to Chicago. He is credited by the *Tribune* with influencing not only those of his faith but all creeds, with his broad-mindedness, articulate sermons and efforts in behalf of the community.

World Jewish Child's Day, commemorating the rescue of 50,000 children from the Nazis and their rehabilitation in Israel, is observed with films and a social hour sponsored by Hadassah. Mrs. Abe Zimmerman, president of the Hibbing chapter, urges a full attendance at the meeting.

BOBBY

I never was a kid who could go home. I never had a home which I could just take a bus to. I made my way all by myself.
  No Direction Home, pub. 1986

When I was about eight or nine I wrote...poems, rhymes, you know...about the flowers and my mother and stuff like that.
  Martin Bronstein Interview, 1966

MAURICE ZIMMERMAN'S philosophy, as I heard it expressed the other day, made me believe that chivalry has not passed from this world, writes George Fisher for the *Tribune*.

"My wife and I go everywhere together," declares Uncle Morey. "We fish together, we visit together, we travel together, and if she doesn't go I don't go either." With that, he buys a block of tickets for an excursion for couples. Later that year, he is elected president of the Hibbing merchants association.

Like it or not, everywhere Bobby goes is family. At the clothing store, Grandma and Uncle Lewis Stone; Grandma now lives with Lewis. At his new Chisholm furniture store, Uncle Henry Goldfine; Uncle Henry and Aunt Irene buy a nice two-story house on the west side of Hibbing. Not far away are Uncle Paul Zimmerman and Grandma Zimmerman. At the theaters, at school and all around town are numerous Edelsteins representing several generations. Lots more relatives with entirely different names in Duluth and Superior.

Bobby spends a lot of time at home. His dad, a furniture salesman who can play a few chords, buys a Gulbranson spinet piano wholesale and places it in the living room. Brother David loves lessons and quickly learns the scales. After one session with "cousin" Harriet Rutstein, Bobby quits. *I'm going to play the piano the way I want to.* He proceeds to bang away.

When visitors are present, Bobby usually escapes to his room. Sometimes he returns down the stairs with some words he has written. For Father's Day, he composes a poem praising his dad as "the best" in all the world, saying he keeps his father's picture on his desk and his father's handball medal above it. When Dad gets real mad, Bobby writes, he thinks it best to keep quiet so Dad doesn't get *more* angry. I'm very lucky to have a dad this good. *I try each day to please him in every little way.*

For his mother, he writes twelve stanzas. He hopes she will never grow old and gray and that all the people in the world will say, *Hello, young lady, Happy Mother's Day.*

Above: Hibbing High School vocal group rehearsing "Gondoliers," 1951-52. *Aubin Studio* • Below: Corner Bar, Howard and 1st. *Aubin Studio*

Chapter Seven
5th Grade
1951-52

Over the Rainbow

I have a brother, David, who is 20 years old. He is studying music at college. I remember when I was 10 years old, that our father had bought a piano. I have only had one lesson, but he did not leave the piano the whole day. He even had a teacher coming each week for him.

(1966) <u>Look Back #18</u>, *pub. 1988*

I wrote my first song to my mother an' titled it 'To Mother'/I wrote that in 5th Grade an' the teacher gave me a B+/I started smoking at 11 years old an' only stopped once to catch my breath/I don't remember my parents singing too much/At least I don't remember swapping any songs with them.

"My Life in a Stolen Moment," 1962

I saw a Negro musician playing his guitar on the street, and I went up to him and began accompanying him on the spoons. I used to play the spoons when I was little. My folks didn't seem to mind because I don't remember them saying anything. Maybe I was happy when I was little or I was unhappy, a million other kids were the same way. What difference does it make?

<u>Seventeen</u>, *1962*

I've been writing since I was eight years old. I've been playing the guitar since I was ten. I was raised playing and writing whatever it was I had to play and write.

<u>Playboy</u>, *1966*

I used to play the guitar when I was ten, y'know, so I figured maybe my thing was playing the guitar, maybe that's my little gift.

Studs Terkel Interview, 1963

From now on, I want to write from inside me and to do that I'm going to have to get back to writing like I used to when I was ten—having everything come out naturally.

<u>Hard Rain: A Dylan Commentary</u>, *pub. 1992*

POLITICAL WORLD

Korea.—In early October, Sgt. First Class Donald Sanborn, 20, is killed in action, the first National Guard casualty from Hibbing since World War II. *Politics.*—Averell Harriman and Sen. Estes Kefauver aspire to the Democratic nomination for President. Among "Leap Year Bait" are eligible bachelors Joseph McCarthy, Republican senator from Wisconsin; John Kennedy, Democratic congressman from Massachusetts; Sam Rayburn, Speaker of the House; and J. Edgar Hoover, FBI chief. *Flying saucers.*—Reported seen on radar above Washington, D.C.

KING HEMATITE

the only job around here is mining—but jesus, who wants/to be a miner...i refuse to be part of such/a shallow death
  Tarantula, 1966

Eerie silence over the Mesabi as miners again walk off their jobs to support a nationwide steel strike. Shut down: giant shovels, silent in the rust-red pits; seemingly endless rows of ore cars; railroad workers; suppliers of explosives; distributors; shops; and 16,000 miners. Hibbing employment drops from 8,593 to 4,887. With no benefits to strikers, sales on Howard Street plummet. *Hibbing's lifeblood is iron ore and when the ore isn't moving, economic life slows to a point close to zero.* The strike lasts 55 days and results in an increase in wages.

POSITIVELY HOWARD STREET

You can stand at one end of Hibbing on the main drag an' see clear past the city limits on the other end.
Hibbing's a good ol' town.
I ran away from it when I was 10, 12, 13, 15, 15 1/2, 17 an' 18
  "My Life in a Stolen Minute," 1962

Minnesota Historical Society members call the Ore Capital a "vanishing city." Not so! George Fisher, editor of the *Tribune,* counters the naysaying nabobs with a "bird's-eye view." One of the finest communities in the state boasts new shops, warehouses and gigantic shovels engaged in the greatest mining activity since World War II, beautiful new residences, a high school building affording quality education from kindergarten through two years of college, a handsome city hall, a Memorial Building copied all over the nation, and the second-largest county fair in Minnesota.

Old North Hibbing is on its way out for good reason. "We must have the iron ore to prepare ourselves for all-out war, if it comes." Technically, the population of "New Hibbing" has declined but an increase in the surrounding township of Stuntz more than compensates, Fisher says. *No indeed, Hibbing is not vanishing. It has just started on its way to greater fame and glory.*

Showing faith in the future, Minnesota Northwestern Bell, in a $1 million program, converts Hibbing's 7,000 telephones to dial service.

Fisher later characterizes the history of what has been called the "Richest Village in the World," "Biggest Village," "Town that Moved," "Razzle-Dazzle Village" and "Iron Ore Capital of the World." "Hibbing, at the turn of the century, was a lusty, brawling infant with solid lines of saloons flanking its main street. Miners and lumberjacks from Upper Michigan were dominant among the early settlers, but crowded Europe began pouring immigrants directly into the new labor market... Hibbing's population has remained static around the 16,000 mark for almost two decades, but development in the low and intermediate ore processes have stimulated optimism in the last few years."

Kids nowadays! In a mid-winter demonstration, students hurl insults and attempt to tip over cars on Howard Street. The chief of police had suspended teen-age dances when a teen group failed to obtain a permit and arrange for chaperones at an event following the Hibbing-Chisholm basketball game. High school Principal Kenneth Pederson lectures against demonstrations as a weapon of force. He says the situation shows the need for a youth center.

Many citizens are up in arms against hot rodders who "race their cars on Howard street, toot their horns and stage a pocket-edition of the speedway, annoying people who are trying to sleep, molesting patients in the hospitals and generally making fools of themselves."

The reprobates could profit by "the Horatio-Alger success story of Jeno F. Paulucci, former Hibbing High School student who dedicated a two-million dollars a year business—the Chun King food processing operations at Duluth." Paulucci's mother, Michelina, owns a small grocery store near Alice School. The Tribune also points with "home town pride" at another "local boy making good"—Russell Martin, who has introduced a safety program in numerous stone quarries.

Dillon. On Dillon road, the death of Mrs. Mary Dillon.

THE GARMAKER SYNDROME

For George Fisher, watching Chuck Edelstein, the "wonderful little field general" of the high school football team, brings back "blessed memories." Fischer recalls 1924, when Max Edelstein, Chuck's dad, played on the team that defeated Denfeld at Duluth for the district championship.

When the Minneapolis Lakers, featuring "Mr. Basketball," George Mikan, play the Indianapolis Olympians at the Memorial building, just under 6,000 turn out, short of the record 6,863 at the finals of the 1948 regional basketball tournament.

"The strange sight of a six-foot four-inch, well-built lad wearing galoshes and shooting a basketball at a home-made outdoor basket about 1 a.m." would be Dick Garmaker, who is averaging over 33 points a game for the undefeated Hibbing Junior College team. With Garmaker, the highest scorer the conference has ever known, the junior college finishes second in the national tournament.

The "fighting mad" Hibbing High School Bluejackets bring home the first state high school hockey championship.

OVER THE RAINBOW

I'm not Judy Garland, who's gonna die onstage in front of a thousand clowns.
<u>*Rolling Stone,*</u> *1986*

The "Iron Ore Capital," also serves as Northern Minnesota's Entertainment Capital, according to Fisher. In one week, Hibbing hosts the St. Paul Bible Institute Choral Club, the London Opera Company's "Carmen," a Jeanne Mitchell concert and Wayne King's concert orchestra. Standing room only for a Nelson Eddy concert soon after. A smiling, friendly Margaret Truman, the only daughter of the U.S. president, arrives for a cocktail party at the Androy and a concert at the high school auditorium. "The weather is invigorating, the air is bracing, your community is metropolitan and your mines are something to behold."

"Don't be too surprised if Judy Garland, Grand Rapids, Minn., musical and screen star who staged a sensational comeback in New York last week, comes back to the haunts of her early childhood, the Mesaba range, next year," writes the *Tribune*. "The little performer from Grand Rapids whom many Hibbing people remember as the child soloist who made appearances in a number of local theaters ... a human being, has become to Broadway within the past few weeks, a kind of goddess."

A few miles to the west, Mary Louise LaFreniere, Calumet, amasses a collection of 1,500 phonograph records while her brother-in-law runs a jazz radio program; some items are so rare they're worth $50. LaFreniere's own radio program over a Duluth station is rebroadcast in London.

Some of the more expressive songs of 1952 likely to affect impressionable youngsters are: "Cry" by Johnnie Ray; "3 O'Clock Blues" by B.B. King, "Goin' Home" by Fats Domino; "Lawdy Miss Clawdy" by Lloyd Price; "My Song" by Johnny Ace; "Juke" by Little Walter; "Jambalaya" and "I'll Never Get out of This World Alive" by Hank Williams.

NORTH COUNTRY FAIR

Where I grew up...I forgot about it once I went east. I couldn't remember very much about it even then. I remember even less about it now. I don't have any long great story to tell about when I was a kid that would let anybody know how it is that I am what I am.
<u>*Spin,*</u> *1985*

Spring: a house-to-house canvass seeks donations to help thwart the impending invasion by forest tent caterpillars, commonly called army worms. "No community on the Range has ever been more responsive to measures which retain community pride than Hibbing," writes Fisher of the response. "Hibbing never fails when a job has to be done. We will not and must not fail tonight."

Hibbing Area Tent Caterpillar Control, Inc. applies DDT, considered harmless. However, as sprayers move along the streets, residents are advised to keep clothes off the lines.

The worms make a mess anyway—along Highway 169; near Maple Hill Cemetery; on the Town line road; on the Swandale road; and on the Dupont highway. Trees are stripped of foliage and roadways turn black with squashed pests. At one farm home, they drop off the hen house like rain and you can actually hear *the squirming of the worms, worms, worms, worms.*

The caterpillars have metamorphosed into airy wraiths by the time throngs trek to the woods for the annual berry picking "and accompanying it, the usual number of lost articles, from false teeth to eye glasses." The more ethereal side of nature is shown when a lovely local girl, "a soloist," is preparing for her marriage and a beautiful double rainbow arches across the skies behind her house.

On the borderline. In Duluth, a movie opens, "just as rugged as the background it embraces and just as vibrant as the men and women, who helped to make the iron ore history of the Mesaba."

The movie is named *Woman of the North Country.*

AGUDATH ACHIM

When I was young, my life was built around the family. We got together all the time. There weren't that many Jews around.

Bob Dylan: Behind the Shades, pub. 1978

Rosh Hashanah. Agudath Achim synagogue prepares for the Jewish New Year in September—"a time when people of the Jewish faith try to make peace with their neighbors, themselves and their Maker," explains Mike Siegel, president of the synagogue. Services are conducted by Rabbi Milton Kopstein of Minneapolis.

The December 31 *Tribune* includes a photograph, "OBSERVE JEWISH HOLIDAY." Shown lighting Menorah candles for the Chanukah *feast of lights* are Dennis Chez, Norman Hallock, Benjamin Stone and David Zimmerman.

The beginning of September brings a self-proclaimed, widely-advertised, city-wide Bible-healing campaign at the Memorial Building arena. Appearing in person, Abraham Tanenbaum, "The Jewish Preacher," who offers to FORGIVETH THINE INIQUITIES HEALETH ALL THY DISEASES.

BOBBY

These people were my friends. I went to school with them, I lived with them, I played with them, y'know, I ate with them, y'know, y'know, we did good things, bad things, we went through all kinds of things together...they still seem to be the old way.

Studs Terkel Interview, 1963

Neighborhood boys play high above Fairview addition on an abandoned iron ore dump or below, in the Willows, where weeds are thick and high like a forest and little streams trickle by a club house fort. At night, they skulk through the back gardens, snitching carrots, onions and crab apples. Sometimes they mildly tease Bobby about his name or simply fail to pronounce it accurately. *Zennerman.* But his feelings are hurt a little more easily than most—and he goes home pouting. *Don't call me Zimbo.*

Bobby, the lone Ranger, does not take to fishing, hunting or golf, though he seems to enjoy swimming, which, in Hibbing's climate, is conducted mostly indoors at the high school. He tours the drug stores on Howard Street and 1st Avenue, looking for comic books.

In school, he mischievously pushes a girl, who chips her tooth on a water fountain. As Bobby walks home, a younger boy, just to be mean, calls out, "Jew!" though he doesn't know precisely what a Jew is. Bobby chases the big mouth and knocks him down. In winter, he shoves neighbor girl Nancy Aanes down and washes her face with snow. Mrs. Aanes says, *Sometimes boys do that.*

The first time John Bucklen sees Bobby, he thinks he's kind of a pansy, a puffy-cheeked brain always wearing new clothes, shirts buttoned to the top, hair nice and combed. One of *those* kids.

Bucklen doesn't know Bob is Jewish. The fact wouldn't bother him. When Bucklen's dad is hurt in a mine accident, there is no welfare, so Mrs. Bucklen tries to make ends meet as a seamstress. A neighbor, Mrs. Maurice Banen, a Jew, goes to the synagogue and tells her friends about the Bucklen's plight. All the Jewish ladies, including Mrs. Zimmerman, came over with sewing so John's mother can make a little money.

I really like these people, Bucklen thinks.

Aubin Studio

President Truman and wife, Bess, arriving in Hibbing, 1952.

Above: "Ore Gave Life to Hibbing; Ore Killed It." 8th-grade display at soon-to-be-demolished Lincoln School, 1953. *Aubin Studio* • Below: The St. Louis County Courthouse was one of the last buildings standing in North Hibbing. *Aubin Studio*

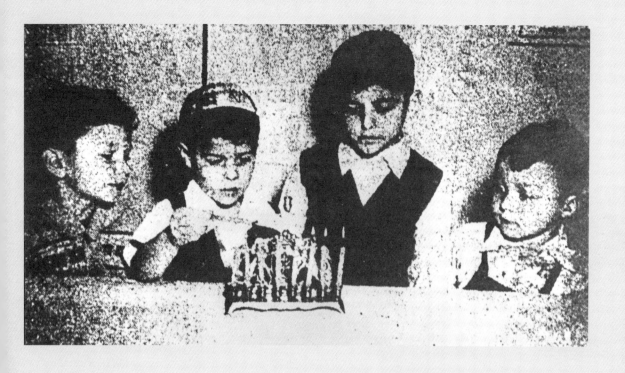

Above: Dennis Chez lights a Menorah candle for Chanukah, 1951. Also shown, from left: David Zimmerman, Norman Hallock, Benjamin Stone. *Hibbing Tribune*
• Below: Iron lung at Hibbing Hospital, 1950s. *Aubin Studio*

Looking east, 1949
Minnesota Historical Society

Above: Florence Stone Naturalization Papers, 1949. *IRRC* • Below: Music class, Bobby front, right (original photo not available). *William Pagel Archives*

Chapter Eight
6th Grade
1952-53

North Country Fair

My/youth was spent wildly among the snowy hills an/sky blue lakes, willow fields an abandoned open/pit mines
   To Emergency Civil Liberties Committee, 1963

POLITICAL WORLD

A Russian has three an' a half red eyes/five flamin' antennas/drags a beet-colored ball an' chain/an/ wants t' slip germs/into my Coke machine
   "11 Outlined Epitaphs," 1964

Republican Governor of California Earl Warren speaks to 600 at the Sons of Italy Hall in support of Presidential candidate Gen. Dwight Eisenhower. Outgoing Democratic President Harry Truman plugs the St. Lawrence Seaway and candidate Adlai Stevenson before 8,500 at the Memorial Building, while 22,000 wait outside for the motorcade. "Hibbing? Oh yes," says Truman. "That's the place where you have the high school with the gold door knobs." On an ore dump to the east, there burns, ten feet high, made of pipe covered with oil-soaked rags—a fiery cross. Police chief Chester Naeseth believes it is the result of a youthful prank; the Ku Klux Klan has not been active here since the Twenties. In November, Minnesota voters join the majority for Eisenhower. Hibbing continues to vote 2-1 Democratic.

Communism. Joseph Stalin, Soviet Prime Minister, ruler over a sixth of the earth's surface and a third of its people, dies. In June, Master Sergeant James B. Motherway, 27, of Hibbing, is reported killed in action in Korea. In July, generals of the UN Command and the Red armies sign a compromise armistice in the bitter, three-year war. Julius and Ethel Rosenberg are electrocuted at Sing Sing prison, New York, for delivering secrets of the atom bomb to the Soviets—the first non-military convicts executed for espionage by the U.S.

KING HEMATITE

Yeah, <u>everybody</u> was workin' there at one time. In fact, ninety percent of the iron ore for the Second World War came out of those mines, up where I'm from. And eventually, they said, 'Listen, this is costing too much money to get this out. We must be able to get it someplace else.'
   <u>Rolling Stone</u>, 1984

Mainly because of the strike the previous year, iron ore tax receipts are down 20 percent. Two state firms are shipping taconite, the low-grade iron ore that promises to reinvigorate Minnesota's mining industry. At the same time, Oliver engineers from Hibbing are developing iron ore mining in Venezuela. Oliver, a subsidiary of U.S. Steel, hopes to ship South American ore in 1954.

As the Hull-Rust mine continues to consume North Hibbing, three schools are sold to the mining companies: Jefferson, abandoned for many years; Washington Elementary School and the old high school, now Lincoln Junior High School.

POSITIVELY HOWARD STREET

But there are some people who don't get changed by the times. They can be living in any kind of time period, and I'm one of those people because everything gets filtered through me, and it gets filtered into the music I play. I was the same twenty, thirty years ago that I am now.

<u>*Icons-Intimate Portraits*</u>, *1989*

"What would you do if 20 Negroes moved into Hibbing tomorrow?" challenges Carl Rowan, a Negro from a white Minneapolis neighborhood, in a lecture at the Hibbing Presbyterian church.

What would you do with the pop from Pengilly who loiters four hours in a Nashwauk bar, leaving two progeny in the car with the engine running? The muffler is defective; there's a hole in the floor; and a son and daughter dead. What would you do if another daughter of that father had died the same way a year ago?

What would you do about the reprobates? Two large mirrors broken in the ladies rest room of the State Theatre and a paper cabinet set on fire. A dozen youngsters breaking into the Gopher Theatre after the box office closes. The good name of Hibbing is threatened, worries manager R.H. Hughes.

What would you do about the "boy gang" from Hibbing, decked out in cowboy outfits from a store robbed in Nevada, crashing their stolen car at 90 miles an hour on a New Mexico highway? Or the seven teen-age Hibbing boys in court for carnal knowledge of a 15-year-old girl?

How about a curfew? It's 9:30 p.m. for children under 16. How about a youth center? The Minors Club in the Memorial Building always has a chaperone. How about a Soap Box Derby? How about some fluoride in the water? *You owe it to your children.* Hibbing physicians and dentists recommend a "yes" vote. How about some pizza? The Italian tomato-cheese-topped bread is a novel new snack, having "won popular favor with the young moderns."

What would you do about the veil of prosperity that hides an unfriendly face? The celebration of Hibbing's 60-year history is highlighted by the grand opening of a new $275,000 public library. Record employment, new subdivisions (Greenhaven, Graysher, Merryview), new schools, churches and a planned county courthouse defy the observation "that the iron ore would soon be gone and Hibbing would quickly fade," according to the *Tribune.* "Now the thought is to the future, to the mountains of taconite and lean ores that can be processed and to the need of more men to work the processes to extract that tougher ore." Survey crews begin re-routing Highway 169 around overtaxed Howard Street.

What would you do if the multitudes complained about the new devices installed on Howard Street? Every day, the *Tribune* runs the following admonition:

*Hibbing's Parking Meters
are for YOUR convenience!*

THE GARMAKER SYNDROME

Are you crazy? I don't want to inspire any songwriters. If I made the basketball team in high school, do ya think I'd be here now?
Death of a Rebel: A Biography of Phil Ochs, pub. 1989

America is a divided nation right now. It doesn't know whether to follow the President or the Green Bay Packers.
Los Angeles Times, 1983

Bobby Dillon. A big year for Hibbing High School hoopsters as the Bluejackets win the Region Seven title but lose to Hopkins in the finals at Williams Arena, Minneapolis. Big year for football as the Green Bay Packers play an exhibition game in the "Iron Bowl." After an intense hailstorm, Packer quarterbacks Tobin Rote and Babe Parilli face off at Hibbing's Cheever Stadium. A rising star in the Packer defense is second-year, one-eyed defensive halfback and interception specialist, 23-year-old *Bobby Dillon*.

OVER THE RAINBOW

Was Hibbing an oppressive place? Did it just make you want to get out?

Not really. I didn't really know about anything else except, uh, Hank Williams. I remember hearing Hank Williams one or two years before he died. And that sort of introduced me to the guitar. And once I had the guitar, it was never a problem. Nothing else was ever a problem.
Rolling Stone, 1984

It was just like an adolescent...you find somebody to latch onto. I did it with so many people, that's why I went through so many changes. I wrote a lot of stuff like Hank Williams, but I never grasped why his songs were so catchy or so classic.
No Direction Home, pub. 1986

I started singing after I started writing. I started that when I was ten or eleven, and started out just country & western—Hank Williams and Lefty Frizzell kinda things. Hank Williams had just

died and I started playing some time around there...Hank Williams was the first influence I would think.
   Billy James Interview, 1961

An' my first idol was Hank Williams/For he sang about the railroad lines/An' the iron bars an' rattlin' wheels..."
   "Joan Baez in Concert," Part 2, 1963

He begins playing guitar at age seven. Before 20, he's the finest singer-songwriter in the history of his genre. But New Years Day, 1953, at age 29, he lies dead in the back seat of his Cadillac. Say good-bye to the composer of "Your Cheatin' Heart," "Hey, Good Lookin'," "I'm So Lonesome I Could Cry," and 100 more good songs—country-western legend in his own time, Hank Williams.

He tours the U.S., weaving magic with musical musings about mutability, while his extravagant tippling gets as much attention. Say gently, "Good-night." Dead of pneumonia and alcoholism is Welsh poet Dylan Marlais Thomas.

Among the latest entertainers to come to Hibbing is Vaughn Monroe, the country's "most popular" bandleader, who had won a trumpet contest in Wisconsin at age 14. Among musical association volunteers is Mrs. Abe Zimmerman.

She dies of a heart attack near the Santa Monica, Calif., aircraft factory at which she is employed: Ethel Milne Gilmore. She had not been on speaking terms for some time with her daughter, "Judy Garland." Garland was born in 1922 to Mrs. Gilmore and her first husband Frank Gumm, in Grand Rapids, where Frank ran the Grand Theater. The former Frances Gumm, at age three, performed with her parents and, later, in vaudeville with Virginia and Suzanne, "The Gumm Sisters."

NORTH COUNTRY FAIR

I had some amazing projections when I was a kid, but not since then...They were a feeling of wonder...I was born in, grew up in a place so foreign that you had to be there to picture it.
   <u>*In His Own Words*</u>, *1978*

Last year, "army worms" stripped most broadleaf trees in an 11-million acre area. This year, the total devastation is expected to hit 26-million acres. A "ballot" appears in the *Tribune*. "Are you in favor of spraying Hibbing to Control Tent Caterpillars and will you contribute to help do so—YES or NO." The outcome is 1,370 for and 188 against. A house-to-house campaign to fund the program follows. In June come torrents of rain. Battalions of worms crawling over roads at the crests of hills are crushed by traffic into greasy heaps two inches deep. To counter the slippery mess, crews are called out to sand sections of the highway.

AGUDATH ACHIM

There is nothing anybody can expose about me. Everybody thinks that there is such an exposé, on millions of little tiny things, like

name change. It doesn't really matter to me. Obviously there are people who like to read that shit.
   <u>*No Direction Home,*</u> *1986*

Once again, Agudath Achim sounds the "shofar" or ram's horn for Rosh Hashanah, the Jewish New Year. With no local clergyman in place, Rabbi Herman Himons of Chicago conducts the services.

In time for Chanukah, Mrs. Max Edelstein, Beatty Zimmerman's aunt, contributes Jewish "meat recipes" to be prepared ahead of time and served buffet style: corned or pickled meat; liver paste with rye bread, crackers, pickles and olives; and shrimp with cocktail sauce.

When Hadassah and the Council of Jewish Women hold their annual Donors Party at the synagogue, Mrs. Sher thanks Mrs. Abe Zimmerman for her work during the year. The theme of the evening is "crazy hats" festooned with cabbages, carrots, radishes, bananas and animal crackers. A photo appears in the Tribune of a capless Mrs. Zimmerman.

In November, a rabbi arrives—Reuben Maier, a German native who came to the U.S. 25 years earlier and had served in New York and Minneapolis. His son, Dr. Joseph Maier, speaks at Agudath Achim, to analyze the "age of anxiety." The younger Maier says he likes Hibbingites. *They are all so friendly and attentive. They seem interested in everything that is going on about them.*

BOBBY

Take Shane for example. That moved me. So when I go to see a film...I want to be moved, because that is what art is supposed to do, according to all the great theologians.
   <u>*Playboy,*</u> *1978*

Zimmerman brothers have expanded the now-named "Micka Furniture and Electric Co." from an electrical contracting shop to a furniture-and-appliance store. Abe is "furniture man" and bookkeeper; Paul, "boss" and salesman; and Maurice, the eldest—master electrician or "refrigerator man." The store now has three sections; one for used appliances; another for new appliances and the third "add on" section for furniture. They handle both "good" quality and cheaper items, allowing for the tough times that roll around pretty regularly. "Zimmerman's" is the largest electrical supplies outlet in Hibbing, although Kelly's in the Moose building remains a bigger furniture store.

"Sharp Clear Pictures Proved in TV's Toughest Reception Areas," claims Micka, advertising a General Electric 17-inch TV for $199.50—probably the same model Bobby's dad, Abe, brings home for the boys' room.

In school, "everyone who counts" plays in the junior high band. Accordingly, Bobby visits Crippa's music store and tries out a trumpet, trombone, saxophone, clarinet, whatever other instruments come to hand. Finally, he gives up on group harmonizing, rents an inexpensive acoustic guitar and goes home with Manoloff's Basic Spanish Guitar Manual.

From the radio, the faint cadences of rhythm-and-blues are beginning to come in from the distant south: "(Mama) He Treats Your Daughter Mean" by Ruth Brown; "Hound Dog" by Willie Mae Thornton; "I'm Mad" by Willie Mabon; "Crying in the Chapel" by the Orioles; "Money Honey" by Clyde McPhatter and the Drifters.

At the theater, when he views *Shane,* Bobby can identify with young Brandon de Wilde's Joey or with Joey's hero, the short, effeminate, long-haired, tough-but-sensitive one-named hero played by Alan Ladd. A drifter and retired gunfighter, Shane defends a homesteading family terrorized by hired guns.

"You can call me Shane."

"*Mister* Shane, Joey," the boy's mother insists.

Joey: *You wouldn't say nothin' no matter how much it hurt would you?*

Mr. Shane: *Fraid I would Joey if it hurt bad enough.*

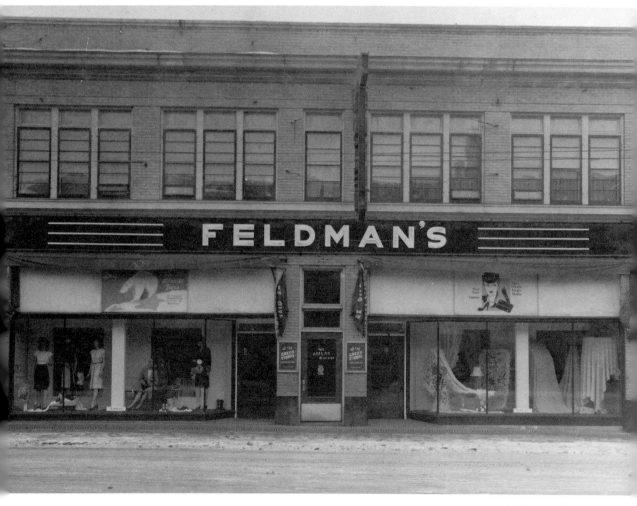

Aubin Studio

Beatrice Zimmerman worked at Feldman's on Howard Street.

Above: Moose Lodge, Howard Street, early 1950s. *Aubin Studio* • Below: The Zimmerman brothers owned Micka Electric. *Aubin Studio*

Chapter Nine
7th Grade
1953-54

The Garmaker Syndrome

I didn't go hunting. I didn't go fishing. I didn't play on the basketball team...I just played the guitar and sang my songs. That was enough for me. My friends have been the same as me, people who couldn't make it as the high-school football halfback, Junior Chamber of Commerce leader, fraternity leader, truck driver working their way through college. I just had to be with them. I just don't care what anyone looks like, just as long as they didn't think I was strange...All I did was write and sing, paint little pictures on paper, dissolve myself into situations where I was invisible.

<u>Saturday Evening Post</u>, 1966

POLITICAL WORLD

Communism. Keewatin welcomes home Cpl. Michael Milkovich, after three years as a North Korean prisoner of war.—Dien Bien Phu, epitomizing the Indochina war for 57 days, falls to Communist-led rebels.—In "Brown Vs Board of Education," the U.S. Supreme Court rules segregation in schools unconstitutional, stealing "the thunder that Communists have often used," writes the Hibbing *Tribune*, "mainly that people of different color and creeds have no equality in the United States and will also refute one of the accusations the Reds have been making to the people of their enslaved areas." It is considered newsworthy that, north of Virginia, Minn., lives the "colored" family of J. Gaskins, a farmer and active member of the Cook American Legion. His daughter, Alice, is a top student at the Northwestern hospital in Minneapolis.—With 5 percent of the world's population, Americans own 50 percent of its automobiles, 58 percent of telephones, 45 percent of radios; 29 million homes have television. With so much evidence that the Supreme Being is on our side, the phrase "under God" is added to the Pledge of Allegiance.

Congressman John Blatnick and Senator Hubert Humphrey, both of the Democratic Farmer Labor party, deliver an attack on the Republican administration of Dwight Eisenhower. The 1,500 persons served in the Memorial Building is believed the largest number ever at a banquet in northern Minnesota.

KING HEMATITE

*Come ye masters of war
you that build the big guns*

"Masters of War," 1963

Hull-Rust-Mahoning. The *Hibbing City Directory* for 1953-54 celebrates the largest and most productive iron ore mine in the world, which has given up more material than was removed from the Panama Canal. The U.S. produces 96 million tons of iron ore in 1953; 82 million from Minnesota, 76 million from the Mesabi Range, 25 percent from within the village of Hibbing. A 1954 publicity film calls Hibbing the "undisputed capital of the iron ore industry," describing a "Main Street" that is barricaded at the mine precipice, where Main drops into the "Grand Canyon of Minnesota." As Calvin Coolidge said in 1928, "That's a pretty big hole."

One of North Hibbing's most impressive structures, the Carnegie library closes. Books and equipment are moved south to the new library. The only public buildings still in use in North Hibbing are the courthouse and two schools.

POSITIVELY HOWARD STREET

I come from Minnesota; there was nothing there. I'm not going to fake it and say I went out to see the world or I went out to conquer the world...I had to get out...and not come back. Just from my senses I knew there was something more than Walt Disney movies.

<u>Los Angeles Free Press</u>, 1965

Hibbing, the metropolis. According to the 1953-54 city directory: Population: 17,572 • Assessed valuation, $21,190,935 • 1,510 feet above sea level • Average annual rainfall, 23 inches • 6 city parks totaling 55 acres • McCarthy Beach Memorial State Park • 2 golf courses • 8,264 telephones in service • 5,249 dwelling units, 12 hotels, 5 motels • 19 churches • 2 railroads • 150-bed hospital • Village hall • Highways: U.S. 169, state 65, 73 and 216 • 1 municipal airport served by North Central Air Lines • High school civic theater seating 1,800 persons • Memorial building arena • 5 moving-picture theaters, 1 drive-in theater • 10 public schools: 5,216 students, 230 teachers • High school building from kindergarten through second-year college • Cheever Memorial Stadium—concrete stands and night football • 1 parochial school • 2 public libraries, 85,000 volumes • St. Louis County Fair, Minnesota's second largest.

According to George Fisher of the *Tribune,* Hibbing is also home to the "meanest person in the world." On Halloween night, she wraps up potato peelings and garbage for treats.

Hibbing, the Metropolis. According to the *Tribune*, "multitudes" from "the outside" are arriving. More than 275 homes built, with as many expected the next year. Bennett Park revived with a public golf course, playground, pavilion, band shell, lighted ball diamonds, horseshoe courts and volleyball courts. Established in Hibbing's lush days of two million-dollar tax revenues, it had contained a zoo and greenhouse. Sam Perella opens the city's first "pizza palace," on Howard Street. Native son Jeno Paulucci's Chun King food processing company's payroll exceeds $1.5 million, more than 90 percent said to be brought into northeastern Minnesota. For Chun King's Chinese vegetable medleys, 10,000 acres of the "finest celery anywhere" are grown in the Zim-Sax-Meadowlands district, south of Hibbing.

"Hibbing will never be anything but a second-rate community as long as our main traffic arteries and the streets feeding into them are reminiscent of the horse-and-buggy days," maintains a planning commission's report. Needed are wider streets, one-way streets and off-street parking, it says. On Friday nights, Howard Street is bedlam. "Add to this a constant din of tooting horns, sudden bursts of speed and noise, and the tenants who live upstairs in apartments over business places must be suffering with badly upset nerves." A few blocks away, an auto driven by a drunken driver roars over the North Hibbing bridge and strikes a group of 11 children on the sidewalk with fatal results.

Flying saucers. A local mortician describes sitting in a car outside a Hibbing home and viewing an unidentified moving object in the South Hibbing skies; three bright lights almost blind him.

Bobby Dillon. In Windom, Miss Marcelaine Schreiber marries a young man from Hibbing. That makes her Mrs. Robert Dillon.

THE GARMAKER SYNDROME

I used to play hockey when I was growing up. Everyone sort of learns how to skate and play hockey at an early age. I usually played forward, sometimes center...I couldn't play too much baseball, because my eyes were kind of bad and the ball would hit me when I wasn't looking. I never played much basketball, unless I played with my kids. Football I never played at all, not even touch football. I really don't like to hurt myself.

<u>Spin</u>, 1985

Dick Garmaker, a Hibbing native, becomes the first University of Minnesota basketball player to score 400 points in one season with a "fabulous display of out-court shooting."

William Marinac, 13, is one of two *Minneapolis Star and Tribune* carriers selected as official mascots to the world champion *Minneapolis Lakers*. At the Memorial Arena, the Lakers paddle past the College All-Stars, 68-63.

With 1954's entry, the Hibbing High School Bluejackets count four teams in the modern state basketball tournament, all coached by Mario Retica—in 1948, with leading player Milan Knezovich, third place; in 1949, with Knezovich and Dick Garmaker, consolation; in 1953, with Bill Radovich, second place.

OVER THE RAINBOW

Now that was a lie, that was a downright lie. Rudy Vallee being popular. What kind of people could have dug him? You know, your grandmothers and mothers.

(1965) "Bob Dylan Interview," pub. 1990

"The opening of deer hunting season Saturday will send many hundreds of men into the woods from early morning until sunset and another 'dear' will bring them back to town in time to get into clean clothes and over to the Hibbing Memorial Building by 8 p.m. This particular 'dear' is pert, red-haired Barbara Becker, one of the lovely female stars of the Wayne King Show." The "fatherly" King performs before nearly 3,000 with a two-hour dance following the show. Sponsors lose money anyway; King charges a $3,000 fee and expenses run to $5,000.

Arthur Fiedler, conductor of the Boston Pops Orchestra, talks to Elmer Courteau from the *Tribune* over scrambled eggs at the Androy Hotel. Fiedler, "as common as an old pair of Prince of Wales' shoes," exhibits a keen interest. Hibbing, he says, is the smallest city and the farthest north on his tour.

Rudy Vallee, "star of stage, screen, radio and TV" fails to fill the high school auditorium in a show termed a "night club presentation without the environment." At a Monday concert by Harry James and his Music Makers is an 8th grader named LeRoy Hoikkala. He admires the orchestra's Buddy Rich, "the world's greatest drummer." Maybe LeRoy, a miner's son, can play like Buddy Rich some day.

A "forest of television aerials" sprouts in the Ore Capital as WDSM and KDAL in Duluth go on full power. Some $200,000 is spent almost immediately on television sets, many from Zimmerman's furniture and appliance store. The Hibbing *Daily Tribune* begins a daily listing of programs. To compete with the new medium, manager Julius Edelstein says the Lybba Theater will install stereophonic sound and a screen for viewing 3-D films without glasses.

Rhythm-and-blues music continues to be popular on exotic late-night radio: "The Things That I Used to Do" by Guitar Slim; "You'll Never Walk Alone" by Roy Hamilton; "Work With Me Annie" by the Midnighters; "Hearts of Stone" by the Charms.

In Hibbing, tastes tend to the ethnic. *Just Arrived ... RECORDS FROM FINLAND ... Chet Crippa Music Store— "Everything in Music."*

NORTH COUNTRY FAIR

That's where I feel rooted, you know. I feel more familiar with the landscape, the people and the...earth, I think...I feel more at home there.

I feel Minnesota more than I feel New York or L.A...My work reflects the thoughts I had as a little kid that have become superdeveloped.

<u>Minneapolis Star,</u> 1978

During a magical week in November, northern lights provide a spectacular show night after night.

AGUDATH ACHIM

The town didn't have a rabbi, and it was time for me to be bar mitzvahed. Suddenly a rabbi showed up under strange circumstances for only a year. He and his wife got off the bus in the middle of winter...He was an old man from Brooklyn who had a white beard and wore a black hat and black clothes. They put him upstairs above the cafe, which was the local hangout. It was a rock 'n' roll cafe where I used to hang out, too. I used to go up there every day to learn this stuff, either after school or after dinner. After studying with him an hour or so, I'd come down and boogie. The rabbi taught me what I had to learn, and after he conducted this bar mitzvah, he just disappeared. The people didn't want him. He didn't look like anybody's idea of a rabbi. He was an embarrassment. All the Jews up there shaved their beards and, I think, worked on Saturday. And I never saw him again. It's like he came and went like a ghost.

<u>Spin</u>, 1985

Newly-arrived rabbi Dr. Reuben Maier explains that during Rosh Hashanah, Jews contemplate the past year while God sits in judgment. Ten days of penitence close with the fast of Yom Kippur, the "Day of Atonement," the one evening in the year when even unobservant Jews make the motions of prayer and repentance. About a half hour before sundown, candles are lit and parents bless their children. For 24 hours, the devout abstain from eating, drinking, bathing and wearing leather shoes. *Today we are celebrating the commencement of the new year, the day on which we give specific emphasis to the fact that the Eternal, our God, is the King of the whole universe, the sole ruler and guide of all men, their judge and avenger.* Later, Rabbi Maier tells the Women's Auxiliary of St. James Church that if children will remember the commandment, *Honor thy father and thy mother*, the juvenile problem will be much lessened.

BOBBY

I happened to go to Detroit once when I was about twelve or so, with a friend of mine. We had relatives there...I found myself in a pool-hall parlor, where people were comin' to eat all day and play bingo all night, and there was a dance band in the back...Anyway, this was my first time face to face with rhythm and blues.

(1980) <u>Behind the Shades</u>, pub. 1990

When did you leave home?
When I was 12 years old and had had enough of helping my father transport refrigerators. I became manager for a very popular blues singer. Big Joe Williams. That was the first time I ran away.

(1966) <u>Look Back #18</u>, pub. 1988

First guitar I ever had was a very old guitar and the strings were about an inch from the keyboard. That's why I use a flat pick when I play now...because I could never <u>get</u> those strings—they were heavy strings—and my fingers hurt.
How old were you?
About ten.
Who gave it to you?
Down at uh, uh, I got it in Chicago on the South Side. I think from a street singer. I didn't get it from him, I got it from a friend of his—Arvella Grey. He was a singer and let's see, there's Sioux Falls, South Dakota. I learned a lot of songs there. I learned not a lot, but I learned—I don't learn songs—I just learned <u>ways</u> of singing I do...There was this fella there on a farm right in Sioux Falls, South Dakota, a little bit out—played autoharp. And he was just a farmhand there. He was from Kansas—I learned just ways of singing from people like that.

Billy James Interview, 1961

This here song's a good example ["The Girl I Left Behind"]. I learned it from a farmer in South Dakota and he played the autoharp. His name is Wilbur. Met him outside of Sioux Falls when I was there visiting people.

Oscar Brand Interview, 1961

First, I bought a Nick Manoloff book. I don't think I could get past the first one. And I had a Silvertone guitar from Sears. In those days, they cost thirty or forty dollars, and you had to pay five dollars down to get it.

<u>Rolling Stone</u>, 1984

I learnt a couple of chords out of some books and then just going out to watch people...how they're playing those chords...just to see what their fingers are doing.

<u>Westwood One</u>, 1984

I saved the money I had made working on my daddy's truck and bought a Silvertone guitar from Sears Roebuck. I was 12. I just bought a book of chords and began to play.
The first song I wrote was a song to Brigitte Bardot.
I don't recall too much of it. It had only one chord.

<u>In His Own Words</u>, 1978

My first song was dedicated to Brigitte Bardot. I saw her in a movie when I was fifteen, six years ago.

<u>Seventeen</u>, 1962

I always wanted to be a guitar player and a singer. Since I was ten, eleven or twelve, it was all that interested me...Henrietta was the first rock 'n' roll record I heard. Before that I'd listen to Hank Williams a lot. Before that, Johnny Ray. He was the first singer whose voice and style, I guess, I totally fell in love with. There was just something about the way he sang When Your Sweetheart Sends A Letter...that just knocked me out. I loved his style, wanted to dress like him too.

    Biograph, 1985

I was never gonna be anything else, never. I was playing when I was twelve years old, and that was all I wanted to do—play my guitar.

    (1984) in Behind the Shades, pub. 1990

My mother has hundreds of poems I wrote when I was twelve years old.

    Saturday Evening Post, 1966

Even beyond Hibbing, wherever you look, are Bobby's relatives: Duluth, Minneapolis, St. Paul, Superior, Wis., and Fargo, N.D. Two great aunts live in Sioux City, Iowa: Sylvia Edelstein Goldberg and Jeanette Edelstein Agranoff, whose husband, Abe, runs the Young-Town Clothing Store. Within walking distance of Bobby's house at 7th Avenue East and 25th Street is Uncle Maurice, at 2620 3rd Avenue West. *Tribune* Editor Fisher says of Maurice, that his heart is *as big as himself.* He notes the elder Zimmerman brother is looking for contributions to provide a television set for a needy Hibbing veteran. Grandma Anna Zimmerman lives with Maurice. Uncle Paul Zimmerman lives at 3505 3rd Avenue West. Grandma Florence Stone can be found in an apartment at 2144 1/2 2nd Avenue West, Apt. 3, with her son, Lewis Stone.

A lot of people know Bobby's dad, Abe, through Micka Furniture and Electric. He is quiet-spoken, friendly enough, polite. An athlete in his younger days, Abe's a social golfer at the public course. That he walks with a slight limp, caused by polio, is not always noticed. Abe likes to take his sons Bobby and David, all dressed up and shoes shined, for Sunday dinner at the Androy Hotel.

Almost everyone knows Bob's mother, Beatty, from Feldman's clothing store, where she is an affable and loquacious clerk. Always well-dressed, she loans items to neighbor girls and sells her fashionable clothes when she tires of them—not a "Range" thing to do. Bobby composes writings and drawings for her. *Look at the beautiful poem he wrote,* she says to friends. *You should hear the songs he makes up.*

Beatty has something of a reputation for her fudge bars. *Melt together 4 squares unsweetened chocolate and half a cup of butter or margarine. Add to: 4 beaten egg yolks and 2 cups sugar. Mix together and add 1 cup flour, half cup milk, 1 teaspoon vanilla. Fold in 4 egg whites beaten. Put into greased 13X9 inch pan. Bake at 325 degrees for 30 minutes. Frost with chocolate frosting.* Although Jewish moms cook "American" like anyone else, they also share recipes for rendered chicken fat, gefilte fish, chopped herring, knishes, chopped liver, pickled herring, chicken soup *(Jewish Penicillin)*, matzo balls, kreplach, borscht, cabbage soup, bagels, rye bread and date bars.

Not as many Hibbingites know Bobby, at least not very well. He's always been quiet. Ordinary in appearance, he's a bit short and chubby in the cheeks. When he smiles that shy, dimpled smile, an endearing twinkle appears in his eye. His wavy, light-brown hair is clipped and combed to his mother's specifications. He's smartly dressed in new clothes, the shirts buttoned to the top. Bobby and his brother, David, enjoy an abundance of toys and athletic equipment. His home has a piano and a chandelier over the dining room table. His parents make sure he studies. He makes the Honor Roll for Grade Seven: Dennis Wichman, Laura Wilcox, *Robert Zimmerman.*

On occasion, Bobby steps out with some of the other kids, hanging around the swings at Bennett Park or robbing wine grapes from the guy behind Sunrise Bakery, then sitting on the 4th Avenue West bridge, where the kids eat until faces turn purple. On the Dupont Lake lovers lane, Bobby ties on a monster mask and startles couples in steamed-up sedans. At the ice skating rink, he calls Echo Helstrom over to peek through a knothole at his fingers. He's walking them up and down a bench as if they are little legs.

To his neighbor, Bill Marinac, Bobby seems to be a normal sports fan. Marinac even says he considers Bob a good runner.

Bobby takes instruction in Hebrew from Rabbi Reuben Maier, in Maier's rooms above the L&B Cafe on Howard Street. About the time of his 13th birthday, May 24, he dons a white suit and fringed shawl, chants the required Hebrew scripture and speaks in English about the moral duty of the Jew. Some say he conducts himself beautifully. To others, the shtick isn't too different from any other. In the evening, Bobby's guests meet at the ballroom of the Androy Hotel. Beatty is proud to say that of 500 guests invited, 400 show up. Many are relatives from Duluth or the Cities, descended from mutual forebears with old country names like Zigman Zimmerman, Chana Greenstein, Shabsie Solemovitz, Lybba Edelstein.

That Bobby is Jewish is not as defining as it might be elsewhere. On the Range, everybody is *something*: Catholic, Lutheran, Orthodox, Serbian, Finnish, Italian. Sixth-grader John Bucklen, a miner's son of German-Swedish background, lives next door to Maury Banen, a Jew who manages the Mesaba Finance Co. Bernice Banen and Bucklen's father enjoy sitting together and arguing.

With Marsha, the Banen daughter, John thumbs through an encyclopedia. They find a picture of Jesus.

"Oh, we don't believe in him," the girl says.

Wow! Why not? Doesn't everybody?

Whether you're *Catholic* or not is probably the biggest divider. A Catholic is taught everyone else is going to Hell. According to the Pope, if you so much as set foot in somebody else's church, you're struck dead by lightning. As for Protestants, they're defiled former Catholics—and Jews, they killed Christ. So when Bobby has to go into the 4th Avenue West synagogue for his lessons, his Italian Catholic playmates wait outside.

Being Protestant, chances are, you hate all things Roman. Jews, you're not too sure about. The Bible involves them pretty heavily on various sides of Christmas and Easter. Other than having more toys than average, Jewish kids don't seem too different. They join in school activities like everyone else. They go out with their friends on Friday night, their Sabbath, like everyone else. And they have Sunday School on Sunday like everyone else.

Anyway, there are more important things than religion. One fine afternoon, John Bucklen walks up First Avenue with Bobby.

Sure, I'm interested in music, John says.

Bob laughs. *Sing something.*

John sings a little and Bob says to him, *Damn that kid's good. That kid's really good!*

You really think so? Well, thanks. Thanks a lot!

Bucklen believes him at first. When he realizes Bob is joking, that Bob has made a fool of him, he doesn't associate with him for a while.

Bobby has always been clever. Perhaps inspired by stories the previous year about an abused youngster found in the Memorial building, a composition surfaces that he may have written or copied, called "The Drunkard's Son," a poem-song about a boy hiding from a father who threatens to kill him if he fails again. Found dead of natural causes, the boy leaves a note, "I'm hiding with Jesus...and my mother who I love." The paper is signed, *Bobby Zimmerman*.

Looking east, 1953.
Hibbing Historical Society

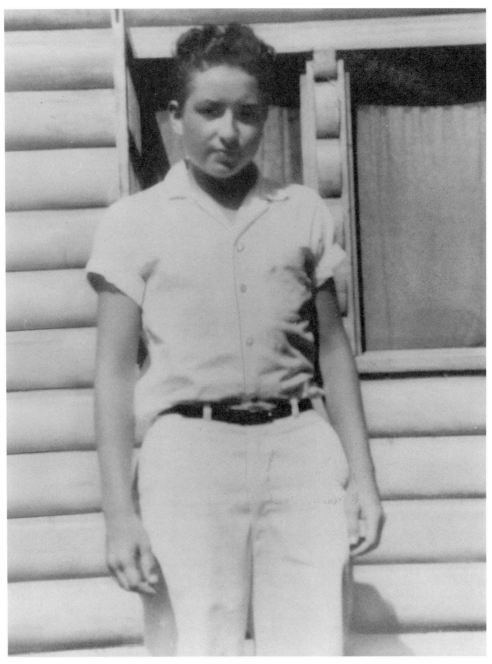

William Pagel Archives

Robert Zimmmerman at Camp Herzl

Chapter Ten
8th Grade
1954-55

Blackboard Jungle

You go to school, man, and what kind of poetry do you read? You read Robert Frost's "The Two Roads," you read T.S. Eliot—you read all that bullshit...And then, on top of it, they throw Shakespeare at some kid who can't read Shakespeare in high school, right? Who digs reading HAMLET, man? All they give you is IVANHOE, SILAS MARNER, TALE OF TWO CITIES—and they keep you away from things you should do. You shouldn't even be there in school. You should find out from people. Dig! That's where it all starts.
    <u>Los Angeles Free Press</u>, 1965

What did the school teach me?...I haven't used any of that stuff which I've learned in twelve years, except, you know, adding, maybe and reading and writing and how to, you know...
    Nat Hentoff Interview, 1965

THE POLITICAL WORLD

I am sick of people/praising Einstein...bourgeois ghosts—
    <u>Tarantula</u>, 1972

Even Einstein wasn't a genius. He was a foreign mathematician who would have stolen cars.
    <u>Saturday Evening Post</u>, 1966

Einstein, disguised as Robin Hood
With his memories in a trunk
Passed this way an hour ago
    "Desolation Row," 1965

It is a known fact that I was born and that is all that is necessary. Albert Einstein said that—dead at 76. Known also for his sense of social responsibility, Einstein's theory of relativity and work in nuclear fusion made the atom bomb possible. Yet, the small, bushy-haired, sockless, violin-playing, pipe-smoking, German-born Jew tried to work without the distractions of fame, his privacy protected by colleagues. "The door was slammed on the inquirer wanting simply to know about Einstein." In order that posterity might enjoy better access, Einstein bequeaths his brain to Dr. Harry Zimmerman of Columbia University.

In Washington, Wisconsin Senator Joseph McCarthy is censured by the Senate for his irresponsible harassment of "reds." In San Francisco, City Lights book shop becomes the mailing address for the "Beat Generation." In Montgomery, Ala., 23 Negro children are denied admission to elementary school. Saigon, Viet Nam: American-supported Premier Ngo Dinh Diem declares war against the rebel Benh Xuyen society.

KING HEMATITE

I was born with death around me. I was raised in a town that was dying. There weren't no need for that town to die. It was a perfectly valid town.

Life, 1964

Not so many years ago, radicalism ran rampant on the Range. Old-timers recall the red badges the I.W.W. wore at the 1917 May Day picnic; meetings in the old North Hibbing hall; notables—Haywood, Gurley, Flynn, Panter—visiting in *those stirring days;* the riot at the Security bank in North Hibbing when deputies attempted to prevent a Wobbly parade; "the North Street riot when an Indian agent, E. Ellis, trained his gun on a desperado Red who was aiming to hit some of the deputies below but dared not shoot because the deputy's gun was trained on him every minute of the battle."

The "enemy" is somewhere else now: Canada, Labrador, Africa and Chile. Venezuelan ore goes to Pittsburgh steel mills, traditionally a Minnesota market. Oliver closes the Godfrey underground mine near Chisholm, as the Fraser mine had been closed six months earlier. About 445 jobs will be affected in both mines.

POSITIVELY HOWARD STREET

J: Is it a physical Highway 61?

B: Oh yes, it goes from where I used to live...It ran right through my home town in Minnesota. I traveled it for a long period of time actually. It goes down the middle of the country, sort of southwest.

J: I think there is an old blues about Highway 61.

B. Same highway, lot of famous people came off that highway.

Sing Out, 1968

"Here is the city that was actually moved to make way for the rich iron ore deposits which lay beneath its streets," say American Automobile Association travel notes. "You can still see the abandoned section of town which now hangs precariously on the brink of the ever growing iron ore pits and to the south you can view the new model community which replaced the old section of the city back in 1918-1922. In recent years, the mining companies have become fully aware of the tourist attraction which man and machine have made in the search for iron ore ... In the red, orange, grey, purple pits you'll see huge electric shovels biting into tons of earth at a time and then dropping their mouthfuls into monster trucks with man-high wheels or into chains of ore cars pulled by diesels along the steel tracks which wind around the pits." The one-millionth guest in the four-year-old Mesaba Range tourist program visits the Oliver Iron Mining Division's mine observation platform.

Mines attract the biggest crowds, but the high school and new grade schools, Cobb-Cook, Greenhaven and Tourist Court, also draw tourists, claims the *Tribune*.

Range charm reaches the new Mesabe Coffee Shop in Minneapolis' Curtis Hotel, which displays photographs of mining equipment and specializes in "The pasty, toothsome and traditional dish of the Iron Range."

After successive annual epidemics, hope arises for polio prevention. In the summer of 1952, 58,000 cases in the U.S. and more than 3,000 deaths. In 1953-54, the disease "cripples" the Nashwauk and Gilbert football teams. Now, the vaccine developed by Jonas Salk "can virtually end the icy fear that long has gripped the hearts of parents." Joining a nationwide effort of mass inoculation, kids line up at Hibbing clinics on their way to a Friday night movie. *Don't faint or everyone else will.*

Dillon, Mrs. Gerald, Kerr Location, clips a lucky column and wins $50.

THE GARMAKER SYNDROME

My real name was Knezelvitz and I changed it to avoid obvious relatives that come up to you in different parts of the country and want tickets to concerts and stuff like that...uh?

It was Knevevitch?

Knevovitch yes.

That was the first or last name?

That was the first name. I don't really want to tell you what the last name was.

   (1965) <u>*Bob Dylan In His Own Words,*</u> *1978*

Wouldn't you change yours if you had a name like William W. Kasonavarich? I couldn't get any girlfiends.

   Craig McGregor Interview, 1966

Basketball. All-time scoring records smashed at the Memorial Building as the Minneapolis Lakers defeat Bob Cousy and the Boston Celtics, 129-118.

Hibbing's Dick Garmaker ends his career at the University of Minnesota, the only Gopher to score more than 500 points in a season and the only unanimous choice for the All Big 10 team. The Junior College standout, most valuable Big Ten player and the village's first All-America "cager" is presented with a new Plymouth sedan, purchased with funds contributed by 850 local fans. A basketball court at Bennett Park is named for him.

Bobby Knezovich's cousin? Garmaker's predecessor, former Hibbing High School standout Milan Knezovich, announces he will marry a Mankato girl.

OVER THE RAINBOW

Where I lived was really hillbilly country. The radio stations I used to listen to weren't local, but came up from Louisiana, right up the Mississippi river.

   <u>No Direction Home</u>, 1986

You know how, when you're a kid, you stay up late in bed, listening to the radio, and you sort of dream off the radio into sleep. That's how you used to fall asleep. That's when disc jockeys played whatever they felt like.

   "BOB" in <u>Esquire</u>, 1987

Folk music aficionado Alan Lomax, "a big, 40-year-old New Yorker," travels with his father for thousands of miles, recording mountaineers, Indians and Negroes. He edits 14 albums of songs including those of Huddie Ledbetter, or "Leadbelly," discovered in a Louisiana prison and recorded in 1933. At the Hibbing library, Mrs. C.A. Nickoloff illustrates "folk" music with recordings from the Library of Congress. Included are songs of the Mesabi area.

Now showing: Judy Garland and James Mason, in *A Star is Born*. Ethel Merman and Marilyn Monroe in *There's No Business Like Show Business*. Marlon Brando in *On the Waterfront*. Julie Harris, Raymond Massey and James Dean in *East of Eden*, based on John Steinbeck's novel. Fess Parker in *Davy Crockett*. How about a coonskin cap?

The audience wanes for radio shows like "Dragnet" and "The Great Guildersleeve" as television continues its absorption of American life forms. From Duluth stations come "Howdy Doody," "Life of Riley," "This is Your Life," "Bob Crosby," "Captain Video," "Arthur Godfrey and Friends" and "I've Got a Secret." The Hibbing Junior College talent show presents its "TV Edition."

A new kind of music insinuates itself further into late-night radio waves: rhythm-and-blues, formerly called "race" music, recorded by Negroes. "Earth Angel" by the Penguins; "Pledging My Love" by Johnny Ace; "My Babe" by Little Walter; "Bo Diddley" by Bo Diddley; "At My Front Door" by The El Dorados; "Lovey Dovey" by The Clovers; "Goodnite, Sweetheart, Goodnite" by the Spaniels; "Sh-Boom" by the Chords; "I Hear You Knocking" by Smiley Lewis; "Ain't That A Shame" by Fats Domino and "Maybellene" by Chuck Berry.

Closer to home, juke boxes "Shake Rattle & Roll" as Hibbing teen-agers "Rock Around the Clock" to Brylcreemed whites redoing Negro music: Bill Haley & His Comets, Carl Perkins, Jerry Lee Lewis, Johnny Cash, Roy Orbison. Elvis Presley cuts "That's All Right" for Sun Records. They are beginning to call it rock 'n' roll.

Live entertainment of national prominence continues in Hibbing, including Gene Autry, Fred Waring and Little Jimmy Dickens (4 feet 11 inches).

"Oh, what a voice!" exclaims *Incomparable Hildegarde* of "some sounds" she had just made on the Hibbing high school stage. "Hildegarde jokes about her voice and we won't disagree with her there," writes the Tribune. "She ended a lot of her songs in a loud blare that was particularly discomforting." After the performance, Hildegarde retires to one of Hibbing's newest eateries, *La Pizzeria,* for salad, spaghetti, chicken, dessert and plenty of coffee. She dines at the counter because the place is filled and tells proprietor Sam Perella, "What an elegant dinner."

NORTH COUNTRY FAIR

I can see God in a daisy. I can see God at night in the wind and rain. I see creation just about everywhere. The highest form of song is prayer. King David's, Solomon's, the wailing of a coyote, the rumble of the Earth. It must be wonderful to be God. There's so much going on out there that you can't get to it all.

TV Guide, 1976

Local poet Jean Wright, 14, contributes two poems about *the autumn queen*.

> Her scepter is the golden rod
> And scarlet is her cloak
> And she makes all nature a jester
> And the autumn world a joke.

AGUDATH ACHIM

During National Brotherhood Week, five windows in a Lutheran Church are donated by a Catholic and dedicated to the memory of his Jewish friend, I.R. "Izzy" Sher. When Our Savior's Lutheran Church had been built a few years previous, Sher collected money from fellow Rotarians to help defray the cost. "People of Hibbing, regardless of creed or nationality, mourn the passing of I.R. Sher," remarks the Lutheran pastor, Rev. Stolee. "He was a leader among his own Jewish people, but no less a sincere friend to countless of the Protestant and Catholic faith." The gesture is celebrated in the *Minneapolis Morning Tribune*, *The Rotarian* magazine and by Samuel Schriner, executive director of the Minnesota Jewish Council, who pens, "Hibbing has really become, through this incident, the 1955 brotherhood capital of the United States."

In the same spirit, Barbara Greenberg of Eveleth organizes Gentile girls to perform Hebrew songs and dances throughout the range.

Honoring the 300th year of Jewish settlement in America, four volumes depicting that history are donated to Hibbing Public Library by Hadassah, the Hibbing council of Jewish Women and the Hibbing B'nai B'rith Lodge.

BLACKBOARD JUNGLE

The teachers in school taught me everything was fine. That was the accepted thing to think. It was in all the books. But it ain't fine, man. There are so many lies that have been told, so many things that are kept back. Kids have a feeling like me, but they ain't hearing it no place. They're scared to step out. But I ain't scared to do it.

<u>Life,</u> *1964*

Hey man, ya oughta see some pictures of me. I'm not kiddin'. At Whitaker's. I look like Marlon Brando, James Dean, or somebody. You oughta see me. I had this blue turtleneck sweater on.

<u>Great White Wonder,</u> *1969*

Now showing, *The Wild One.* As the Black Rebels Motorcycle "Club" bugs a small town of squares, Xtra-cool actor Marlon Brando and his sidekicks promote the juvenile delinquent look to teen-agers everywhere: black boots, black leather jacket, motorcycle cap, ducktail haircut, tee shirt with a sleeve rolled around a pack of smokes, dark glasses, surly facial expressions, hepcat slang. "Do you pick up on this jive? Dig the rebop, daddy-O." *If you're gonna stay cool you got to wail.*

"Hey Johnny, what are you rebelling against?"
What'ya got?

Blackboard Jungle! "A Drama of Teen-Age Terror!" Glenn Ford—the school teacher; Sidney Poitier—the wiseacre student; Vic Morrow—the Marlon Brando imitation. Switchblade knives, sneaky Pete wine, hot rods, cigarettes, cool cats, jitterbugging juveniles who take over the school. *These kids can't be all bad,* says a teacher just before the degenerates destroy his collection of Bix Beiderbeck records.

D'ya like swing, daddy-O?

"Rock Around the Clock" by Bill Haley and his Comets introduces the movie and, in so doing, brings the new music to young ears from Hibbing to Helsinki.

One o'clock, two o'clock, three o'clock rock.

Accompanying *Blackboard Jungle* is the Tom & Jerry cartoon, "Dr. Jeckyll & Mr. Mouse."

Dig the rebop, daddy-O.

Teachers complain that high school students no longer read, being so distracted by football games, television, after-school jobs taken to pay for cars, guitars and record players and by extra-curricular activities in which they bang the piano, stand up on the stage, shimmy and shake and sing <u>Ricochet Romance</u>. "Some 12-year-old girls who can't add or tell you where the capitol of the United States is are permitted to smoke, drink, wear high-heels and lipstick and steady date, something well-bred bobby-soxers in our era didn't do," complains a syndicated columnist.

With its own selection of rock 'n' roll, the Hibbing Youth Center at the Memorial Building is "bursting at the seams" for Friday and Saturday dance nights. The "Minors Club" is self-operated by teen-agers and is open to grades 9-12. Critics call it a "rendezvous" where young persons pick up a "date" and move somewhere "less desirable." A defender counters that, "The social problems which arise from the fact that the automobile makes it easy for young persons to go and come were not created by the Youth Center, and will not be solved by it."

BOBBY

There are a lot of people afraid of the bomb, right. But there are a lot of other people who're afraid to be seen carrying a MODERN SCREEN magazine down the street, you know. Lot of people afraid to admit that they like Marlon Brando movies.
    Los Angeles Free Press, 1965

D*' ya like rock 'n' roll Daddy-O?* Walking home past the Alice School where he had attended first grade, Bobby exults to LeRoy Hoikkala, *This is really great. This is exactly what we've been trying to tell people about ourselves.*

Since second grade, when the Zimmermans moved to 7th Avenue, Bobby's personal blackboard jungle has been located a couple blocks from his house. The massive Hibbing High School was built in the early 1920s as a monument to the "World's Richest Village," then being relocated further south of the Hull-Rust mine. Six oil paintings by David Erickson decorate the main entrance. Murals, statuary and spacious corridors contribute a museum-like quality to the interior. In the library, pupils whose attentions drift from the 20,000 books muse over a 1913 mural by Minnesota-native David Tice Workman, depicting the journey iron ore makes from the mine to the mill. It is accompanied by a slogan as massive as its meaning: THEY • FORCE • THE • BLUNT • AND • YET • UNBLOODIED • STEEL • TO • DO • THEIR • WILL.

The 1,828-seat auditorium, designed after the old Capital Theater in New York City, is adorned with priceless wall decorations, draperies, and chandeliers of European manufacture. With a ceiling 90 feet high, the stage accommodates 45 backdrops. At the rear are single dressing rooms such as found in Broadway theaters. The Barton vaudeville pipe organ is a complete orchestra in itself.

Encompassing kindergarten through grade 14, the building's population is about 1,750, with 34 nationalities recognized. The majority are on the college-bound track; about 70 percent of those actually continue their education. With a junior college on site, they don't have to leave the building to do it.

Joining the school board is former junior college sophomore president turned dentist Rudy Perpich. The principal is 50-year-old Kenneth "K.L." Pederson, a disciplinarian who actively recruits good staff. "This is about the only place I could have taught," says Charlie Miller, who had been working on a doctorate when he applied for a job. "If they didn't have freedom of speech, I wouldn't have come."

Benefits for students are the envy of the state. A doctor visits routinely; a dentist provides fluoride treatments; school supplies, such as compasses and protractors, are free. As they are pampered, the students normally return the favor. Violence is rare; graffiti, almost unknown. If you light a fag in the can, a square might squeal. "We do not smoke in Hibbing High School!"

In the early grades, the infectious spirit of Miss Katherine Hessler instilled in many youngsters a love of music. In junior high, Bobby and his classmates "take" vocal music from Val Peterson, who introduces a variety of styles, including classical and folk. The pupils create percussion instruments from inner tubes. A photograph from 6th-grade or so shows Bobby smiling in the front row of the nine-member "band," holding what appears to be a hand-made drum and drumstick. Ms. Peterson notices that, unless something really excites him, Bobby doesn't excel. He has lost interest in classical music in favor of the new craze they're calling rock 'n' roll. He misses the early 8th Grade honor rolls but finishes strong, taking his place among his usual alphabetical companions: Dennis Wichman, Laura Wilcox, Robert Zimmerman.

Cousin Barbara Edelstein is selected to represent Hibbing at Minnesota Girls State, St. Paul. She's an active, award-winning honor student, unlike Bobby, who avoids organized activities.

During noon hour and after school, Bobby often stops by Crippa music. *How do you like Hank Williams?* he asks Crippa clerk Jim Nehiba, while hoping to charge sheet music and records to Abe's account. "Go ahead, as long as your father's got money," Nehiba says. Bobby also likes the lachrymose lyricism of Johnnie Ray's "Cry," "Just Walking in the Rain," and "You Don't Owe Me a Thing."

After some years living with Uncle Maurice, Bobby's grandmother Zimmerman is moved to Sholom nursing home in St. Paul. She dies of arteriosclerosis April 20 in a St. Paul hospital and is survived by five sons, a daughter, and 14 grandchildren. A member of the ladies auxiliary and Hadassah, Anna Zimmerman is buried at Duluth's Tifereth Israel cemetery in the vicinity of her husband, Zigman. An encapsulated photograph shows a dark-haired, middle-aged woman frowning into the afternoon sun. *May her soul be bound up in the bond of ever lasting life.*

1955
Iron Range Research Center

Looking east, c.1955. Howard Street at angle to top left. 1st Avenue, bottom, left to right. High school, top center. Hospital, center. Blessed Sacrament church, 7th Avenue East and 24th Street, top right. Zimmerman house at 7th Avenue and 25th Street (one block to right of church). Memorial Building, right. *IRRC*

Above: Howard Street, Budweiser Clydesdales on display, 1950s. *Aubin Studio*
• Below: Collier's Bar-B-Q and Rex Hotel, 4th Avenue East, 1950s. *Aubin Studio*

Leather jackets are the order of the day for these high schoolers, probably at Colliers Bar-B-Q. *1956 Hematite* • Below: Looking toward the front entrance, Hibbing High School. *1956 Hematite*

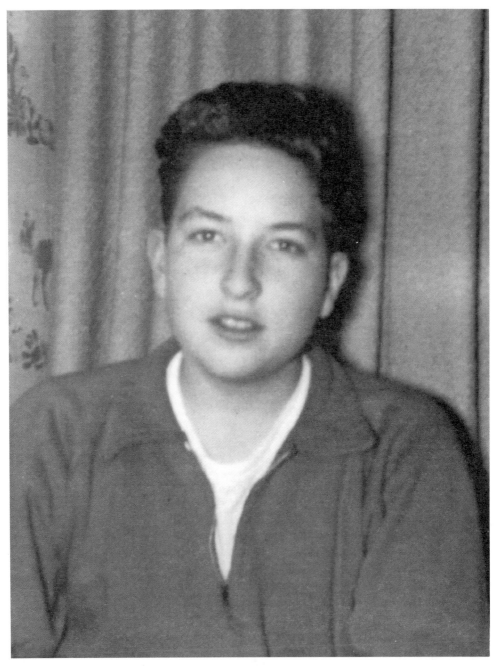

William Pagel Archives

Robert Zimmerman, 1955-56

Chapter 11
Freshman
1955-56

Rebel Without A Cause

An' I'll sing my song like a rebel wild/For it's that I am an' can't deny
   "Joan Baez in Concert, Part 2," 1963

When I was fifteen, I said to myself: 'They treat me pretty low-down here now, but I'll be back one day and then they'll all run up and shake my hand.'
   No Direction Home, 1986

THE POLITICAL WORLD

Bowel movement a good one, reports Dr. White, physician for hospitalized President Dwight D. Eisenhower. "The country will be pleased about that *because it is a bowel-minded country.*" As a result of Eisenhower's heart attack, Vice President Richard Nixon is accompanied by the Secret Service.—Six-time Socialist candidate for President Norman Thomas speaks to 250 at the Iron Range Executives Club. *War should be just as objectionable to us as cannibalism.*—Democratic candidate Adlai Stevenson, seeking support in the presidential primary, brags up the new taconite industry. The next day, Estes Kefauver, Tennessee's Democratic senator and also candidate for President, spends the night in Hibbing. In the primary, Stevenson hands Kefauver a stunning defeat.—A simulated nuclear attack requires the temporary relocation of government units in 34 states and Canada.

KING HEMATITE

...which tells you something about the people out there, who can ravage the earth, create pits and slag heaps and towns where the houses are all red from the ore dust and you could choke to death—and they brag about it.
   Bob Dylan, 1971

Most of original Hibbing, "the North Forty," has been transported: the buildings to new South Hibbing; the earth to steel mills on the Great Lakes. Oliver Mining Co. pays $750,000 for what remains: the old library, the streets and alleys.

The high-grade hematite ore that created the Ore Capital is being depleted at a precipitous rate. Tax revenues are the lowest in more than three decades; in 1953, there were 101 million gross tons of taxable ore; in 1954, 98 million; in 1955, 92 million. Consequently, taxes for individuals rise steeply.

In July, joining a nationwide steel strike, more than 1,200 Oliver employees sign up for unemployment compensation. The 28-day strike results in wage increases, holiday pay and supplementary unemployment benefits. It's a Pyrrhic victory. The *Tribune* reaches the "sad conclusion" that *Hibbing is no longer one of the richest villages in the world.* It has in fact fallen well down on the list.

POSITIVELY HOWARD STREET

where i live now, the only thing that keeps the area going is tradition—as you can figure out—it doesn't count very much—everything around me rots
   Tarantula, 1972

Prospects degenerate but Hibbingites have never acted so prosperous as shopping on credit replaces scrimping as a way of life. First, Piggly Wiggly jiggles in. Then Graysher Shopping Center, placed by Max Gray and the late I.R. Sher at the edge of the planned Highway 169 beltline. Gray expects a large variety store, complementary small stores, a drive-in restaurant and a playground where parents can leave children while doing their business. The parking lot holds 400 cars. The shifting population, the increase in the use of autos and the change in retail merchandising have made the shopping center a must, says the *Tribune*.

The new courthouse formally opens at the east end of Howard Street. Downtown, a powerful spotlight from the roof of Micka Electric Shop and Furniture Store "throws its beams on the spire of the Catholic Church of the Blessed Sacrament and illuminates this beautiful house of worship, adding much to its attractiveness." "Tourist Court School" and the junior high are renamed Washington School and Lincoln Junior High School after the North Hibbing schools they replaced.

Political Dillon. "To Pledge A Sound Township Program Elect George Dewey Dillon for Township Supervisor."

THE GARMAKER SYNDROME

Pastimes? I would love to say, y'know, bowling or sailing or roller-skating...but really, I can't tell you anything...
   Martin Bronstein Interview, 1966

Former Hibbing High School and University of Minnesota gunner Dick Garmaker makes his first pro appearance at the Memorial Building, as the Harlem Globetrotters and Minneapolis Lakers play separate games. Also with the Lakers is Bob Williams, their first Negro player, signed by general manager George Mikan, "Mr. Basketball."—Vince Bugliosi, former Minnesota state high school tennis champion and now University of Miami senior, is called by the Hibbing *Tribune,* "unquestionably the best net player ever produced on the

Range."—Perennial pro-bowler Bobby Dillon leads the Green Bay Packers with seven interceptions.

OVER THE RAINBOW

When I was a youngster the music they were playing...was Frankie Laine, Rosemary Clooney...Your Hit Parade. Dennis Day? Or Dorothy Collins and...the Mills Brothers...Mule Train...Johnny Ray was the first person to actually really knock me out.
<u>Westwood One</u>, 1984

I used to sing these songs way back, a long time ago, even before I played rock 'n' roll as a teenager...Sinatra, Peggy Lee, yeah, I love all these people...
<u>Los Angeles Herald Examiner</u>, 1985

When I first heard Elvis's voice I just knew that I wasn't going to work for anybody and nobody was gonna be my boss. Hearing him for the first time was like busting out of jail.
<u>US</u>, 1987

PLAYBOY: What quality did Dean represent?
DYLAN: He let his heart do the talking...
PLAYBOY: Did you read <u>Catcher in the Rye</u> as a kid?
DYLAN: I must have, you know. Yeah, I think so.
PLAYBOY: Did you identify with Holden Caulfield?
DYLAN: Uh, what was his story?
PLAYBOY: He was a lonely kid in prep school who ran away and decided that everyone else was phony and that he was sensitive.
DYLAN: I must have identified with him.
<u>Playboy</u>, 1978

Guy Lombardo opens the Winter Theatre series, sticking to tried-and-proven favorites with "no unpleasant surprises." Lombardo says he is thrilled by the audience at the high school auditorium. "Your city is reflected in your enthusiasm. It is one of the finest small communities I have been in." Lombardo band members scour local beaches for driftwood to decorate their homes.

Sponsored by the Hibbing Police Relief Association, Duke Ellington and his orchestra appear at the Memorial building. The Mesaba Civic Music Association presents the U.S. debut of Israeli violinist Ivry Gitlis at the high school, which also hosts the "comic genius" of Spike Jones.

Locally, the College Capers talent show begins to admit contestants from outside the junior college. A high school student council talent show includes instrumentals, vocal numbers, marimba, pantomimes and dramatic readings. At least three freshmen are involved. Dave Karakash plays western tunes on his guitar. Barbara Bianchini and Roberta Johnson sing, "The Man In the Little White Coat."

Now showing: *The Wizard of Oz* —starring Judy Garland, formerly of Grand Rapids.

On the radio: "The Lone Ranger," "Chet Huntley," "Dragnet," "People Are Funny," "Widder Brown." No rock 'n' roll on Hibbing's WMFG—as long as Bobby's cousin, Les Rutstein, is manager.

On TV. From Duluth's KDAL: "Patti Page," "Robin Hood," "Burns & Allen," "Dateline Europe," "I Love Lucy," "December Bride," "Studio One," "Mickey Mouse Club," "Uncle Harry and the Western Playboys," "Frankie Laine," "Phil Silvers," "$64,000 Question," "My Little Margie." From Duluth's WDSM: "Superman," "Sid Caesar," "Rocky Teller Show," "Milton Berle Show," "Fireside Theater," "I Led Three Lives," "Bishop Sheen." A guest on Art Linkletter's "House Party," Mrs. Bruce Cook, Hibbing, wins $10,000. On the Tommy Dorsey show, Elvis makes his first television appearance. "Gunsmoke" introduces a slow talkin', slow walkin,' fast drawin' hero, Marshal Matt Dillon.

Wild Bill Boone and His Rock and Roll Boys, *the most famous colored Rock & Roll Trio in America,* wail at the Tibroc in downtown Chisholm.

NORTH COUNTRY FAIR

She could not be found./So I watched that sun come rising/From that little Minnesota town.

"Went to See the Gypsy," 1970

Local pickers hit the barrens in August. "Nothing better than the jam you make from these wild Minnesota strawberries." In winter, 4,500 attend the second Dupont Lake fishing contest; another 1,000 are turned away. A 13-ounce crappie takes first-place prize, a car-top boat.

International headquarters of the 2,400 member Friends of the Wilderness are located in Hibbing. From Ely, Sigurd F. Olson publishes *The Singing Wilderness,* an appreciation of the Quetico-Superior wilderness area. "You realize that he expresses your very own feelings," writes the Tribune, "only you do not have the gift, as he has, of putting them into words."

AGUDATH ACHIM

Passion Play. To great publicity, the Black Hills drama depicting the death of Jesus, is performed in the high school auditorium.

Prior to an appearance at the synagogue, the regional president of Hadassah, Mrs. Martin Lebedoff, visits at the home of Mrs. Abe Zimmerman. A *Tribune* photo shows Mrs. Lebedoff, Mrs. Roth, Mrs. Edward Spector, Mrs. H.J. Feldman and Mrs. Zimmerman. Beatty is also among those giving bridal luncheons prior to the wedding of Shirley Feldman to Ronald Goldman.

Agudath Achim. A fire during remodeling is quickly extinguished but the front of the synagogue is damaged.

BLACKBOARD JUNGLE

Ah, well, I was playin' music in high school too and I was workin' in high school...My mind was always outside the classroom...There were some good...teachers at Hibbing High. But I had teachers that my mother had so—

<u>Minnesota Daily</u>, 1978

Cars cars cars. Drag races on Howard Street. A "drag strip" on the outskirts of Hibbing. Triple Digits car club: you gotta hit 100. *Har dee har har.* Kids cruise the circuit. West on Howard Street, south on 1st Avenue, around a block and back to Howard toward the Androy. Round and round, hoping for action. *Har dee har har.*

Clean-cut guys wearing white bucks and gals with poodle skirts—at the Deluxe Sweet Shop on west Howard, where a jerk in a white suit dispenses cherry Coke and ice cream. The *Blackboard Jungle* crowd frequents the L&B Cafe on east Howard. Anyone hungry can take a booth at Sammy Perella's "La Pizzeria"; the people call it "The Pizza."

Juke boxes feature popular 45 rpm rock 'n' roll records: "See Ya Later, Alligator" and "Rock Around the Clock" by Bill Haley & His Comets; "Dungaree Doll," by Eddie Fisher; "The Rock and Roll Waltz," by Kay Starr; "Sixteen Tons," by Tennessee Ernie Ford; "The Great Pretender," by the Platters; "Teen-Age Prayer," by Gale Storm; "Tutti Frutti," by Little Richard ("She almost drives me crazy/Whooo"); "Maybellene," by Chuck Berry.

Now showing. *Rock 'n' roll Midnite Show*—"70 Minutes of Crazy, Real-Gone Fun!" with Nat 'King' Cole, Duke Ellington, Lionel Hampton and the Delta Rhythm Boys—*Rock around the Clock* with Bill Haley & His Comets, the Platters and Alan Freed—*The Girl Can't Help It* with Jayne Mansfield. "If she's a girl then I don't know what my sister is." And a line-up of rock 'n' roll idols: Eugene Vincent Craddock, better known as Gene Vincent; Eddie Cochran *(That guy ain't got a trained voice either and he's one of the top record stars in the country—why? Because he has a new sound)*. Fats Domino and the mop-headed, effeminate, wild-eyed Little Richard, standing at the grand piano, struttin' out "Ready Teddy."

"Flash! Dave Karakash was rushed to the hospital following the student council talent show," joshes the Hibbing High School newspaper, *Hi-Times*. "Somebody stepped on his 'Blue Suede Shoes.' Apparently he hadn't recovered by the time of the JC orientation program, much to the regret of the girls who swoon at his singing."

Teen-agers can find their music on the juke box in the Memorial building's Minors Club, operated by teen-agers and supervised by adult directors such as Beatty Zimmerman. Besides rock 'n' roll, there's television, radio, ping pong, a putting green, shuffle boards, games, soft drinks and candy machines. Dances on Friday or Saturday are attended by hundreds. Officials refute charges of drinking and lovemaking in the parking lot as "insidious" and "exaggerated yarns."

"Did your thoughts turn to the party at the Memorial building, tricks or treats, or an evening of destruction?" challenges *Hi-Times*. For some, Halloween means waxing windows, false alarms and dumping garbage cans. For three friends, an eve of destruction on another date includes stealing cars, gin, beer, clothes, money, guns, hunting knives, gloves and socks. For big city addicts, destruction includes drug addiction, said to be at an all-time high—but the sheriff of adjacent Itasca County assures the Hibbing Lions a dope ring would be impossible here in the predominantly rural area. Perhaps, as many believe, "Comic books are the evils of the times." *Har dee har har.*

"Young people are not crazy mixed-up kids—but the world they live in is," asserts child psychiatrist Dr. Ralph D. Rabinovitch. "In some families, it is thought parents no longer dare direct a child after he has reached the magic age of 16."

"The kids of 1956 are no worse than those of 1906 or 1856," agrees a judge, echoing Minnesota native F. Scott Fitzgerald. "They just have more machinery for getting into trouble." To keep teen-agers and their parents on the straight-and-narrow, free re-play for high scores on pinball games is ruled illegal gambling.

BOBBY

My daddy, he didn't leave me too much. You know, he was a very simple man. But what he told me was this...he did say, 'Son...' [long pause] He said so many things, you know? [Laughter] He said, 'Son, it's possible to become so defiled in this world that your own mother and father will abandon you. And if this happens, God will always believe in your own ability to mend your ways.'

Accepting Grammy Lifetime Achievement Award, 1991

It's like my daddy once said, when he was twelve years old he asked his dad something and he didn't think his dad knew too much about what he was talking about. When he got to twenty five, he asked him the same question and he got the same answer and he was amazed how his father got to be so smart.

Australia, 1986

"You know, my father worked real hard all one winter on this room."

<u>*Duluth News Tribune-Herald*</u>*, 1986*

Why turn over a good basement to the mice? "Your wife, if she runs true to type has probably mentioned a hundred or more times that it is just the place for a family room—where television set, record player and radio may be kept for the amusement of the young set or where Junior's rocking horse, toy trains and games may find a home." With prompting like this, Abe Zimmerman goes to work on a paneled "rec" room in the basement. Adults can gather at the bar; nine-year-old David can set up his toys; and Bobby can play that loud music.

Like most houses in Hibbing, Bobby's is a good, family home. In an upstairs bedroom he shares with his brother can be found horses-and-saddles wall paper and comics, including some high-toned Illustrated Classics: *Cyrano, Hunchback of*

Notre Dame, Corsican Brothers, Pathfinder. On a shelf, medicine for asthma. Bobby's drawings for *Les Miserables.* Stashed in cracks—cigarettes.

From the room, you can hear the marching band and the cheers of fans from Cheever Stadium or the Memorial Building. You can feel the roar of races at the fairgrounds and the hubbub of Howard Street. But it quiets quickly and the last squalling infant sleeps, the last boyfriend says good-night at the door across the street, the last of the Triple Digits rumbles by on the way to nowhere. After midnight, you hear nothing, nothing moves but cats and a stray cop. There *is* nothing, except the mercury of the thermometer silently sinking, in summer down to the 40s, in winter, to minus 20, 30, 40.

No matter how cold outside, Bobby's room is extra-heated, like rooms in Hibbing tend to be; some owners are spoiled by nearly free steam from the "Water & Light." When the little GE television and local radio station WMFG sign off, you pull your head under the covers, and, in the privacy of the pillow, can hear the magic of a faraway place where *something is happening.* Oh baby, gimme some jive talk, juke moves, rhythm-and-blues, all night long. *Dig the rebop!*

Downstairs, a silver-plated lamp casts warm light on the family album. Someone has been looking at pictures that show Abe before Bobby, a slight but serious athlete; Beatty, a perky socialite. Abe and Beatty together, looking like tourists. Then Bobby as a curly-locked infant. Bobby and David. Bobby as a Boy Scout; a bullfighter caped in a bathrobe; Bobby banging on bongo drums. School pictures. Bobby posing between curtains. Vacation pix: *Paul Bunyan, the headwaters of the Mississippi.* Honor roll: three times as a freshman.

Waiting to be pasted in, something new, a clipping from the *Tribune.* And they say Bobby's a loner?

TEEN-AGE BOWLING CHAMPS.

And they say he's not athletic?

According to the caption, the winners of the 1955-56 Teen-Age Bowling League competition are *The Gutter Boys.* Wearing a plaid flannel shirt rolled up to the elbows, Bobby, the bowler, appears lean, confident and at ease. *Gutter Boys.* His dark hair is the longest, combed fashionably high on the top.

Another clipping shows Bobby's little brother, "Dave," at the Memorial Building, receiving an autograph from the famous band leader, Guy Lombardo. David is the pianist of the family, diligent with practice and lessons.

Bobby refuses piano lessons, preferring to ad-lib without critique. Though he does not join the school chorus, junior high music teacher Val Peterson thinks Bobby has potential—for something or other. If the school puts on a music show, Bobby's there, whether he's invited or not.

In English class, he passes a note to a friend, "I'm going to make it big. I know it for sure, and when I do, you bring this piece of paper and for two months, you can stay with me, no matter where I'm at."

Neighborhood pal and classmate Bill Marinac plays bass violin in the school orchestra. Like Bob, he has an affinity for rhythm-and-blues and rock 'n' roll. Another high school acquaintance, LeRoy Hoikkala, is getting good on his drum set. He too likes rock 'n' roll. *Hey, maybe we can jam some time.*

When summer comes, Bobby is sent off, as usual, for a couple weeks at Camp Herzl, near Webster, Wis. With other Jewish boys and girls, mostly from Duluth and the Twin Cities, he enjoys swimming, rowing, playing tennis, listening to ghost stories, playing jokes on counselors and cooking over an open fire. He also must speak Hebrew in the dining hall, call buildings by Hebrew names and dress in white for the Sabbath. The campers play at Zionism. It's Arab versus Jew, just like cowboys and Indians, pelting the neighborhood bullies with flour. At sundown, religious services are held at an open-air amphitheater next to the lake.

Some see Bobby with a harmonica jammed in his back pocket, hanging around with maybe one friend all summer. Some see a shy boy who scribbles thoughts on scraps of paper and tucks them in a back pocket, preferring to express himself in writing. Yet, sitting around a campfire, Bobby recites a poem about a helpless dog that brings some to tears. Some see Bobby sitting on the bathroom roof with *those guys*, Louis Kemp, Steve Friedman, Stevie Goldberg, Larry Keegan. They're up there a lot, Bobby strumming on the guitar and singing. He yells and taunts counselors until a rabbi appears with an appropriate sermon.

This kid has a chip on both shoulders!

A teen-ager who thinks he has to be *bad* to make good! A kid from a 'good' family caught in the undertow of today's juvenile violence: He's Jim Stark, the boy sensation of *East of Eden,* James Dean in REBEL WITHOUT A CAUSE—at the Lybba, December 1955.

Down in Memphis, Tenn., Elvis Presley says he wants to be "the James Dean of rock 'n' roll." In Hibbing, Bobby Zimmerman, Bill Marinac, John Bucklen and LeRoy Hoikkala want to be moody, hurt and soulful. *Just like Jimmy Dean.* To them, Dean isn't just *acting* the role of Stark. He *is* Stark or Stark is Dean. Bobby gets a red jacket, *like Jim Stark* and affects angst. Too bad that, whatever he shares with Jimmy Dean, Bobby resembles more the Sal Mineo character, the hapless, effeminate, tormented Plato. Maybe it's the hair.

Just like Jimmy Dean. When the actor's Porsche Spyder, *Little Bastard,* is demolished by a head-on collision, September 30, Dean's truest fans in Hibbing search the news stands of Howard Street and 1st Avenue, studying the photographs.

Just like Jim Stark, Bob is not getting along with his parents. He doesn't like history or physics. So what if he wants to be an artist or a writer? Abe and Beatty don't understand—just like Jim Stark's parents. They want to know, "What's so terrible about going into your dad's business? What's so terrible about going to school and learning something about making a living?"

They argue about his *attitude*. One night he is late; the next, skips homework; soon, drag racing, motorcycles, bad girls, vandalism, juvenile delinquency. What next?

Above: TEEN-AGE BOWLING CHAMPS. Winning the 1955-56 Teen-Age Bowling League competition are the Gutter Boys—second from left, Bob Zimmerman. *Hibbing Tribune* • Below: Latin Club—Bob Zimmerman, bottom, third from left. *1957 Hematite*

1st Avenue, Hibbing, looking north.
Aubin Studio

Above: Mike Retica of the state consolation champ baseball team completes a home run. *1957 Hematite* • Below: Hibbing's "B" football squad, apparently in dark uniforms. Larry Fabbro wears #38, Chuck Nara, #26. *1957 Hematite*

Scenes from the 1957 *Hematite:* Above left: Probably Crippa's music store.
• Above right: L&B Cafe. • Below left: "Hey! Someone's getting too much ..."
• Below right: "Simmer down, Sharon; it's just a cut-out." Elvis at the State Theatre.

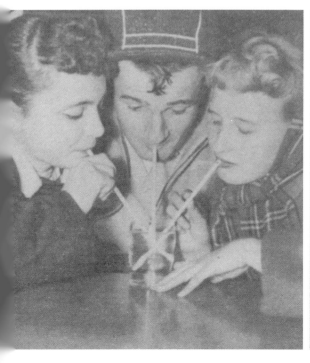 

1957 Hematite

Robert Zimmerman

Chapter 12
Sophomore
1956-57

Daddy Cool

Don't know which is worse—doing your own thing or being cool.
  "Gonna Change My Way Of Thinking," 1979

It's funny. In high school, I just couldn't get rid of my baby fat.
  Look Back #15, 1987

THE POLITICAL WORLD

When did Abraham break his father's idols? I think it was last Tuesday. God is still the judge and the devil still rules the world so what's different? No matter how big you think you are history is gonna roll over you.
  Biograph, 1985

"Whether you like it or not, history is on our side. We will bury you," declares Soviet premier Khrushchev to "the West," about the time he crushes a revolution in Hungary. In Nevada, blue light blinds watchers as the U.S. explodes its 15th atom bomb, hoping to bury Khrushchev before he buries Bovey.

The race problem continues to trouble America. They're rioting in Tennessee over the attempted admission of Negroes to schools. At Knoxville, dynamite explodes outside a concert by Louis "Satchmo" Armstrong's Negro-white band.

"Man, the horn don't know anything about it," Satchmo says. "I'll play anywhere they'll listen."

Democratic Hibbing votes 2-1 for Adlai Stevenson but the national electorate gives Dwight "Ike" Eisenhower a big victory for President. With the federal surplus at $1.6 billion, Ike is able to recommend a third balanced budget.

Henry Ford II announces the "sophisticated" Edsel, with a new vertical-front styling theme and Teletouch push-button transmission controls.

In Brooklyn, N.Y., crew-cut 13-year-old Bobby Fischer emerges as a dominating force in chess. "If he continues to proceed the way he has the past year or two, he's likely to become one of the greatest players of all time."

Dillon, George Dewey. The member of CIO Local 1663 and the First Settlers of Hibbing, runs for Township Supervisor: *Let's have roads of tomorrow and not roads of yesterday.*

KING HEMATITE

...old north Hibbing...already dead...old stone courthouse decayin' in the wind...windows crashed out...the old school...where my mother went to...standin' cold an' lonesome...

"11 Outlined Epitaphs," 1964

With the "world-famous" Mesabi Range running out of "direct shipping ores," each scoop from the Hull-Rust mine is a bite out of the future. Yet, even in its twilight, the Mesabi accounts for two-thirds of U.S. iron ore mined. "One of the busiest industrial periods in Hibbing's history" is predicted in the near future, through the mining of recently-vacated North Hibbing.

"Hibbing residents were treated to an extremely unusual sight recently," writes the high school newspaper, *Hi-Times,* "when a 1,200-ton dragline 'walked' three miles from the Morton mine to North Hibbing where homes, schools, a court house, streets, and sidewalks are being abandoned to clear the way for new mining operations ... that ... will turn the former site of Hibbing into an addition of the Hull-Rust-Mahoning pit, better known as the largest man-made hole."

What's left are a half-dozen weather-worn homes and a few forlorn public buildings—the former Lincoln High School, the library and the courthouse—surrounded on three sides by open pit mines.

POSITIVELY HOWARD STREET

beer halls & pin balls, polka bands...snowstorms, family outings with strangers...ducktails all wired up & waiting for Eisenhower, waving flags & jumping off fire engines, getting killed on motorcycles whatever...

Planet Waves cover, 1974

Dick Kangas speeds toward the Chisholm Sweet Shop in the 1950 Olds he bought the night before. He passes seven cars, slides on glare ice and slams into the Mitchell bridge going 85 mph. The car is totaled and Kangas, with a major bruise on his forehead, catches a ride back to Hibbing with the highway patrol. Then he hitchhikes to Chisholm to visit his buddies—waiting to see his new hot rod.

Leonard R. Venditto, 18, sells his motorcycle and takes it for one last ride on Memorial Day. When he crashes into a Sturgeon Lake bridge abutment, a passenger is thrown into the river and not critically injured. Venditto dies of a skull fracture. Among the honorary pallbearers is LeRoy Hoikkala. LeRoy and Bob Zimmerman later sit in a convertible and talk about Lenny's death.

A strange little man in a long black coat. Paul Huttonen, who had traveled the town, picking up junk only he valued—toys, hoses, lawn mowers—and storing it in basements, rented rooms, sheds and warehouses. Huttonen also possessed an uncanny ability to open old safes, according to the *Tribune.* "Pioneers will

THE GARMAKER SYNDROME

All I do is write songs and sing them. I can't dig a ditch. I can't splice an electric wire. I'm no carpenter.
   Cavalier, 1965

"If a man can't curl on this ice he just isn't a curler!" chirps a visitor to the first "Last Chance" International Bonspiel in the Memorial Arena.—Cleveland Indian rookie outfielder Roger Maris' first major league home run is also the season's first grand slammer. The 23-year-old Maris (or "Maras") is a former Fargo, N.D. football star and Hibbing native.—Bobby Dillon leads the Green Bay Packers with nine interceptions.—"Only" 750 show up for the Chisholm-Hibbing game, half of those from Chisholm, a great insult. "Well, maybe you think the old six-pack you waste your money on instead of going to the game," chides *Hi-Times*, "will make you popular with the 'crowd.'"

OVER THE RAINBOW

has anybody/ever told you, you look like/james arness?
   Tarantula, 1972

Now showing. *Face in the Crowd*: The director who gave you Marlon Brando and James Dean presents *Andy Griffith,* in "one of the most powerful performances the screen has known," playing a young nobody who becomes the idol of millions!— *Bus Stop* with Marilyn Monroe. Co-star Don Murray visits Hibbing in November for the Democratic presidential ticket of Adlai Stevenson and Estes Kefauver.—*Teenage Rebel* with Ginger Rogers. "Recommended for everybody except parents with a guilty conscience."—*The Bad Seed*, not suitable for younger people "without worldly experience."—*April Love* with Pat Boone. As he begins his second film, "America's new boyfriend," faces a moral dilemma. Should he, a married man, kiss actress Shirley Jones? "I still don't know whether I can reconcile myself to doing something on the screen that I wouldn't do in my personal life."— The top-rated television program is *Gunsmoke*: James Arness plays the John Wayne-style marshal, Matt Dillon.

Jay Lurye's Winter Theatre offers music, plays and "artists" of stage, screen and television bearing "the metropolitan brand." Mesaba Civic Music lists four concerts: an "evening with Johann Strauss" features Beverly Sills, lyric soprano. Local composer, soldier and dance band pianist Donald Peterson, 24, says he once turned out nine songs in seven days. His first musical composition was a 1950 "boogie woogie."

How to Play the Harmonica. With Dr. Sigmund Spaeth's advertised pamphlet, a novice can master practically any tune—or make up his own.

Judy Garland. The Grand Rapids native, who, as a young girl, performed at Hibbing's State Theater, is quoted in the Minneapolis *Star*, "The train stops in Grand Rapids, Minn., just for laughs."

"Grand Rapids has always felt kindly toward the Gumm (Judy's real name) girl. It's too bad she ever left town, really," editorializes Ken Hickman, Rapids columnist. "Here she'd be soloist in some church choir, she'd have had one husband, a normal life and real friends. Instead, she has fame, money, a crazy mixedup life without any of the important and worthwhile things. She could have stayed here and laughed right back at the train every time it stopped."

NORTH COUNTRY FAIR

I hate bears.
    "Talking Bear Mountain Picnic Massacre Blues," 1962

Celebration of September. "The coloration of the woods bordering area highways, lakes, fields and rivers now is something that would rival the gaudiest billboard ... blueberry bushes, scattered cherry and plum trees, dogwoods and spireas at an old homestead ... ferns, milkweeds ... asters, brilliant yellows of paper birch, basswood and popple leaves."

Celebration of March: More than a foot of snow, whipped by 60-mile-per-hour winds, drifts up to ten feet high, stuck cars abandoned and schools closed.

Celebration of summer: Early-rising Kitzville residents are startled by a black bear wandering the streets. A poor blueberry crop is blamed. The previous great invasion had come in 1949 with hundreds of bears shot.

AGUDATH ACHIM

Now showing: War and Peace at the State. Tolstoy, who wrote the book the movie is based on, was an acquaintance of his, says the local rabbi, Reuben Maier. He had met the Russian author at the University of Heidelburg. The newly-arrived Maier announces he is retiring and joining his family in New York City. If he were younger, he might stay in Hibbing, he says. Maybe not. Many believe his Orthodox ways are out of touch with Hibbing's modern congregation.

Aluminum siding completes the renovation of Agudath Achim, "one of the finest synagogues in northeastern Minnesota." Among the children of the Religious School presenting the annual Chanukah program is Bobby Zimmerman's little brother, David.

In Winnipeg, Dr. Bertram Sachs competes in the Jewish curling bonspiel.

BLACKBOARD JUNGLE

Were you kind of an outcast?
I really couldn't say...To me, I was perfectly right. (Laughing)
    <u>*Duluth News-Tribune and Herald,*</u> *1986*

Joe Teen—doesn't think it's proper without his parents' permission *but* has had a drink; has smoked a cigarette; *must* have the family car once a week; plans to attend college; quarrels a lot but is reasonably satisfied with home life; thinks his father lives in the past (only 11 percent say they would follow their parents' way of life); hates report cards and curfews; does chores around the house and gripes about them heartily; may earn over $4 a week; feels bored from time to time; and faces the future with optimism.

Jane Teen has also had a drink. She thinks dope peddlers should get the death penalty; averages an hour-and-a-half on the telephone per day; believes a woman's place is in the home while Dad brings home the bacon; used to have a crush on Elvis but now considers Pat Boone *the most.*

Joe and Jane Teen like: pizza as an after-date snack, new cars with enormous tail fins, drag racing, going steady and I.D. tags with the other's name inscribed to make it official. They pore over *The Hematite,* Hibbing high school's yearbook, and the sometimes humorous "destinations" of the class of '57.

"To Side Lake," "to Vecchi's Market," "to the old malt house," "to Crippa's," "to look for a job at Micka's," "to Indianapolis Speedway," "to an 'urban' community," "to make a recording of 'Tenderly,'" "to compete with Gene Krupa," "to hear 'Wild' Bill Boone," "to the Chisholm Sweet Shop."

"To become a nuclear physicist," "to become another Al Capp," "to publish his stories," "to run film strips," "to manage 'Hurricane' Jackson,'" "to be another Elvis."

"To get a pair of elevated hockey skates," "to get another pink slip," "to change her name."

"As a 'Kool' character," "Elvisly," "to a sauna," "in his hot 'Merc,'" "at 'Coke Time,'" "as one of the few true blondes," "Blue JEAN BOP," "with her Pepsodent smile," "in her 5 inch heels," "in his alligator shoes," "in his pink pants," "with a knife in his back," "with his guitar," "with bongo drums," "on the pool table," "with a tube of Gleem," "with her chicken—'Wanna neck?'"

To be another Elvis. "The teen-agers' rock 'n' roll idol took his Hollywood lady fair out for a fast whirl on a motorcycle last night. Elvis (The Pelvis) Presley, dapper in tight jeans, leather jacket and peaked cap, roared out of his driveway, past a small cluster of fans, and sped away with screen star Natalie Wood clinging behind him on the seat." As Elvis appears on the Ed Sullivan television program, his songs "Heartbreak Hotel," "Don't Be Cruel" and "Hound Dog" top the charts. To promote his film debut in *Love Me Tender*, a life-size cutout figure is bartered at the State theater for the best letter, "I Like Elvis Presley Because."

Besides Elvis. The tops in pops encompass rhythm-and-blues, rock 'n' roll and novelty: "My Prayer" and "The Great Pretender" by The Platters; "Be-Bop-A-Lula" by Gene Vincent; "Blueberry Hill" by Fats Domino; "Long Tall Sally" by Little Richard; "Corrina Corrina" by Joe Turner; "See You Later Alligator" by Bill Haley & His Comets; "Roll Over Beethoven" by Chuck Berry; "I Walk the Line" by Johnny Cash; "Transfusion" by Nervous Norvus; and "The Flying Saucer" by Buchanan & Goodman. "Jamaica Farewell" by Harry Belafonte, 29, ignites a "calypso explosion."

Now showing. Shake, Rattle and Rock bashes the "squares" in "The rockin', rollin', boppingest jam session you've ever seen ... Even Santa's rock'n and roll'n to bring you this grand Christmas entertainment of Jumpin Jive!" During *Rock Around the Clock,* London's Teddy Boys riot to "See You Later Alligator." *Don't Knock The Rock.* Little Richard bebops at a piano in front of his band. "Saw Aunt Mary comin' and he duck back in the alley." "Hey, Teen-Agers! Dig This!" A special midnight show, *Rock, Pretty Baby,* with Sal Mineo, John Saxon and Luana Patten. *Rock Rock Rock* presented by Alan Freed, the "King of Rock 'n' roll" with Frankie Lymon and the Teen Agers, Chuck Berry and LaVern Baker.

Facing intense moral fervor to ban the new music, an executive retorts that rock 'n' roll directs the tensions of growing up into harmless channels while providing a means of expressing inner urges. Better to jitterbug in youth centers than to boogie woogie in a '51 Ford. Meanwhile, a law by the Minnesota state legislature prohibits persons under 17 from driving between the hours of midnight and 5 a.m.

Other than soda fountain juke boxes, the most pervasive source of the new music is radio. While cruising Howard Street, Joe and Jane try to pull in WDGY, Minneapolis. Out of Duluth come WEBC and WDSM—710 on the dial, at 5,000 watts, with Pat Cadigan. *Pat the Cat* has been spinning vinyl for teen-agers since 1955. For a "brutal" effect, he rubs records on the cork floor and backs them with an echo chamber. He and Lew Latto host dances in armories and VFW halls where the old hardwood floors bounce so much you have to hold the record player or the needle will jump.

More powerful 50,000 watt stations, such as WLAC Nashville, beam up from southern states with rhythm-and-blues and rock 'n' roll. By the time Chuck Berry's "Maybellene" hits the charts in 1955, black and white songs blend into the exploding teen market, promoted by black-sounding white disc jockeys like "the Big Bopper," who sets a 122-hour world record for continuous broadcasting.

At the grand opening of Forest Lake Lodge, Grand Rapids, Ginny, 318 pounds of dynamite, performs "Rock Around the Clock." Returned by popular demand, "LIVE AT" the Tibroc bar and lounge in Chisholm, the Wild Bill Boone Trio, "the hottest rock 'n' roll in the Midwest."

To keep up with the times, Arrowhead furniture, competitor to Zimmerman-owned Micka Furniture & Electric, runs a continuous 32-hour "Rock Around the Clock Sale."

BOBBY

I carry that other time around with me...the late Fifties and early Sixties...The singers and musicians I grew up with transcend nostalgia—Buddy Holly and Johnny Ace are just as valid to me today as then.

<u>The Rolling Stone Illustrated History of Rock and Roll</u>, pub. 1976

The only music I heard up until I left Minnesota was...country and western, rock 'n' roll and polka music...Lefty Frizzell, Faron Young...all the people that were around. Elvis Presley, Carl Perkins, Gene Vincent, Buddy Holly, Jerry Lee Lewis.

<u>Nat Hentoff Interview</u>, 1965

I can tell by the way people hold their cigarettes if they like Ricky Nelson. I think it's fine to like Ricky Nelson; I couldn't care <u>less</u> if somebody likes Ricky Nelson...There <u>isn't</u> any Ricky Nelson.

<u>Playboy</u>, *1966*

I'd remembered a Gene Vincent song. It had always been one of my favorites. Baby Blue...'when I first met my baby, she said how do you do, she looked into my eyes and said...my name is Baby Blue.' It was one of the songs I used to sing back in High School.

<u>Biograph</u>, *1985*

Late at night, I used to listen to Muddy Waters, John Lee Hooker, Jimmy Reed and Howlin' Wolf blastin' in from Shreveport. It was a radio show that lasted all night. I used to stay up till two, three o'clock in the morning. Listened to all those songs, then tried to figure them out. I started playing myself.

<u>Playboy</u>, *1984*

The songs I wrote at that age were just four chords rhythm and blues songs. Based on things that the Diamonds would sing, or the Crewcuts, or groups like this, the uh, the, you know, 'In the Still Of The Night' kinda songs, you know...I used to play great piano, very great. I used to play piano like Little Richard stuff only an octave higher...I played everything high and amplified it.

Billy James Interview, 1961

When the class of '32 holds its 25-year reunion at the Androy Hotel, Bobby's mother finds herself on the decorations, contact, registration and identification committees. She's always been popular. Having grown up in Stevenson, a nearby mining location, Beatrice Stone moved with her parents to Hibbing and, later, back again from Duluth with her husband and two sons. Her grandfather, Benjamin H. Edelstein, had owned several of the city's movie theaters. Now, on his 87th birthday, B.H. is feted by the Jewish Center of Superior, Wis.

A native of Duluth, Beatty's husband, Abe Zimmerman, has been, since 1947, bookkeeper and salesman with his brothers at Micka Electric. When the Zimmermans are short on help, he asks Bobby to work around the shop and go on deliveries in the hope his son might become interested in the business. According to Abe, the boy's as strong as football players twice his size. *Bobby can hold up his end of a refrigerator.* But it's not easy to get him near the "Frigidaires." When the subject comes up, Bobby always seems to be somewhere else. When you do get him there, he's not much interested in something as boring as pushing a broom. He's more likely in back, pounding on a piano. *Don't make so much noise!*

Often during strikes and mine shutdowns, Ben Orlando takes Bobby to pick up repossessed appliances, allowing him, Abe says, "to see the other side of life."

Dad, those people haven't got any money.

"Some of *those people* make as much money as I do, Bobby. They just don't know how to manage it. You don't buy something and not expect to pay for it."

Sometimes there's a scene. As a television set is hauled to the truck, the drunk and dispossessed former owner curses. *Jew!* Embarrassed, Orlando puts the truck in gear and drives off. *Dirty Jew!*

Bobby gets real quiet.

Orlando kids him, "Don't let your dad catch you with those cigarettes."

What cigarettes?

When Orlando comes back, the truck is full of smoke.

In the well-waxed hallways of Hibbing High School, wearing the newest of slacks and sweaters, Bobby looks to many a miner's kid like a mama's boy, maybe an egghead. He has a 9:30 curfew on week nights and doesn't seem to have a lot of friends. If you had to put a word on him, you might say *loner,* without meaning "lone wolf" or anything really cool.

Teachers view a fairly good student when you get his attention. Quiet and reserved, he is capable of a polite greeting and usually has his work done. Mother probably sees to that. She offers to help him with math. *I just don't like it.* History, too, is a problem. All you have to do is remember what you read, Mother says. *I don't like it,* he says. Why is it so hard for you? *There's nothing to figure out in history.* He's on again off again the honor roll: Dennis Wichman, Laura Wilcox, Robert Zimmerman.

Though he's likely to appear at football or basketball games, Bobby is notably *not* active in school activities. He belongs, technically, to Latin Club. If your parents want you to be a doctor or lawyer, you take Latin. If you take Latin, you're in Latin Club. In business-typing, he's an adequate tapper of keys.

The state basketball tournament highlights the school year. After losing to Fergus Falls, the Hibbing Bluejackets beat Bemidji and Rochester to win the "Consolation" title. To attend the games, he says, Bob borrows the family car. He meets Chuck Nara and the two scout shops for rhythm-and-blues records. Nara is amazed Bob knows so much about music yet cannot read a note. He's even acquainted with some young, black musicians.

For anyone who cares to notice, a change seems to be coming over Bobby. He's becoming more and more ... nervous, maybe. *Stop shaking your leg. It's driving me nuts.* You know, like he's looking for something to do but can't find what he wants. The sound of his cleats sends a message to the lockers lining the long hall. He poses privately, wearing a cowboy hat, a cigarette dangling from his mouth.

Jimmy Dean.

Actor James Dean's biggest legacy is *Giant.* A January review for *Hi-Times* by Jean Edelstein, Bobby's cousin, terms the Warner Brothers epic a "spectacular." "James Dean, in his last and greatest role, plays the part of Jett Rink, a poor ranch hand who becomes rich when he discovers oil on a piece of land given to him by Luz Benedict, portrayed by Mercedes McCambridge." *Giant* also stars Elizabeth Taylor and Rock Hudson.

Most critics agree the flick is excellent; but there's a problem at the Lybba Theatre. "We Apologize! Yes, we are sorry that we were unable to accommodate the many hundreds of people who wanted to see GIANT."

You like things your own way, don't you Jett? From the cinematic was-punk-now-magnate, Bobby learns how to mumble, wear sunglasses, twitch his right leg, carry a chip on his shoulder and live outside the law. He learns how to do things his way. *Boy howdy,* declares Jett. *Nobody's firin' me. I quit!*

Jett Rink doesn't go over so good at home. *Bobby, is that you?* He stays out too late. *What are people going to think?* He neglects school work, hangs around with juvenile delinquents, has an attitude problem. *We've given you everything.* He doesn't show up for work at the store. *Robert, for cryin' out loud, why don't you get a hair cut? Robert, come back here!* But he's escaped down the stairs to the basement rec room.

It's that hoodlum movie star.
No!
Abe rips a portrait of Dean from the wall.
Don't raise your voice around here.

Bob has known Bill Marinac, "always good for a laugh," since fifth grade. In Marinac's basement looms a big Zenith radio hooked up to the TV antenna, bringing in programs like *No Name Jive* from places like Rochester, N.Y., Cleveland and Little Rock, Ark. At Bob's house is a similar setup. There, the two also load up Bob's 45-rpm RCA record player with the Clovers ("Lovey Dovey," "Devil or Angel," "Little Mama"), Spaniels ("Baby It's You," "Goodnite, Sweetheart, Goodnite") Mickey and Sylvia, Johnny Ace, Pat Boone, Webb Pierce, Hank Williams, *Hank Snow Sings Jimmie Rodgers*, Nat "King" Cole, Gene Vincent ("Baby Blue"), Elvis Presley. They turn it up for all it's worth—which, with the small speaker, is not a whole lot.

Marinac, who has learned string bass in a tamburitza band, gets Bob together with Larry Fabbro, a trumpeter who is picking up guitar, and Chuck Nara, a clarinetist giving drums a try. The others are into jazz; Bob has a lot of rhythm-and-blues records. He demonstrates Little Richard on the piano in the corner of his living room. *Tutti frutti. Oh rutti.* The others don't know much about Little Richard. *Hey how about working up an act?*

From the school, Marinac borrows the big bass violin, Nara a snare drum and a cymbal. Fabbro brings his Silvertone guitar and Gibson amp. The four practice after school at Bob's house, because that's where the piano is.

If Bobby appears withdrawn at Hibbing High, he's out front when it comes to making music. From his favorite records, he teaches songs the others have never heard. They find themselves becoming a backup band, like Gene Vincent's Blue Caps. Dance steps are copied from rock 'n' roll movies Bob has seen. By his inspiration, they prepare to perform.

The student council variety show April 5 announces that a local jazz "quintet," including Larry Fabbro, will perform. "Surprise numbers are also on the program, and there are rumors concerning a sensational novelty number which at the moment is top secret," announces *Hi-Times*.

Everything Bob does is on the q.t. until he does it. The boys slick their hair back and strap on sunglasses, sport coats and whatever pink shirt is available. On a

Broadway-styled stage that has held major entertainers from Harry James to Hildegarde, the four take their place before an audience of almost 2,000. From the audience's left, the band consists of Zimmerman on piano, Marinac on bass, Fabbro on guitar and Nara on drum and cymbal.

When the act jolts into being, tittering follows like a reverberation. Little Bobby Zimmerman jumping around. Shouting, banging on the piano keys. At the grand piano, belting out two Little Richard tunes: "Jenny Jenny" *Whoo! Jenny Jenny Whoo! Jenny Jenny* and "True Fine Mama" *Whoo! Honey honey honey honey honey honey.* The only amplified instrument is Fabbro's guitar. It's all so loud and disorganized, he cannot follow the piano playing. The band forges ahead anyway. Most of the volume is provided by Bob's piano pounding.

Among the audience are those who don't know whether to applaud or boo, whether to cover their eyes or their ears. Well, the boy has *chutzpah,* Marinac's bass teacher tells him. *Whatever that means.* Certainly, performing stirs Bobby's soul. To Fabbro, an involved student used to the stage, the event is little more than a lot of fun, something no one else is doing, *something to make you feel hep.*

An encore follows. When an audition doesn't turn up sufficient talent, the Junior College "College Capers" again needs outside acts. Some of the panel have seen the high school show and ask the boys to perform—along with pantomimes, folk dances, a cafe scene, dances and skits. Bob's repertoire is about the same. *Jenny Jenny whooo!*

He thrives on the action and doesn't pay much attention to the reaction. He begins to talk about going into the entertainment business. He's gonna put together a band and make rock 'n' roll records. *I'll call myself Little Bobby.* Why not a movie? *(The boy with chutzpah can't help it.)*

The others consider the prospects. They had agreed to put on a show, not begin a career. There are plenty of other things to do, including being high school students and playing in the high school band. *Thanks, Bob, but no thanks.*

Nara writes in Fabbro's yearbook: "You and I will never forget the talent show and our band. We did turn out good for the amount of practice. I would like to keep monkeying around and work up a combo." From a pretty blonde classmate: "It's funny. I've been sitting here by you for about half a year and I really haven't got to know you. Only in these past few days have we ever said a few words. I want to tell you that I really liked the way you played the guitar in the talent show. I was surprised to see you up there with that git box. An English Pal, Echo Helstrom."

High school freshman John Bucklen is struck by the vision of *this little kid, Zimmerman,* this snide guy who had once made fun of him, now standing with rare courage, hammering at the piano and damn near screaming. Bucklen does not realize Bob is emulating Little Richard. Sure, half the kids are laughing. *But Zimmerman's up there. He's really doing it.*

At the L&B Cafe on Howard Street, John and Bob strike up a conversation with some girls—and find themselves talking with each other. They quickly settle on a common interest: late-night radio. Bucklen thinks, *this guy has a handle on things. This guy is really interesting.*

After school, Bob and John also visit Mal-Rad's on 1st Avenue to eat cherry pie, drink Cokes or coffee, smoke cigarettes, plunder the magazine rack, talk smart and play the jukebox. Bob likes "Donna," "La Bamba" and "Angel Baby." In the opinion of Bob and John, everybody else is backwards. Like a motorcyclist friend says—*they're bongs.*

At Crippa's Howard Street music store, Bob grabs a Gene Vincent album. At Feldman's clothing store, they buy blue caps with little visors, like Vincent's boys wear in the movies. Back in Bob's room, they spin the record while John pretends to bang a guitar and Bob takes the part of the rockabilly rebel: *Be bop a lula she's ma bay-ba...be bop a lula don't mean may-ba.*

Abruptly, there's an audience. *Whooo!*

My God, it's Abe. Standing in the doorway staring.

Like Jett Rink sez, *Boy howdy!*

At Mal-Rad's with LeRoy Hoikkala, Bob can be amusing, like when he takes a napkin and folds it into strange shapes or tells his story about a mouse named Hermie, moving his tongue in a funny way. Bob does not talk politics, parents, gossip or personal matters. He speaks of motorcycles, James Dean, music, maybe girls—topics the other guy is interested in.

Like Zimmerman and Marinac, John Bucklen hooks up with Frank "Gatemouth" Page's *No Name Jive,* broadcast from KTHS, Little Rock, Ark. The sponsor is Stan Lewis, from Shreveport, La., one of the first distributors of rock 'n' roll records. Because of Stan's ads, some listeners think the name of the show is "Stan's Rockin' Record Shop Review." Brother Gatemouth lays down a lot of rhythm and a lot of blues: Muddy Waters, Howlin' Wolf, Etta James, Bo Diddley, Chuck Willis, Chuck Berry, Ray Charles, the Dominoes, Orioles, Crows, Drifters, Moonglows. Electric guitar, bass, saxophone, background choruses along with a lot of Gatemouth's big mouth jive. *Nothin's shakin' but the leaves on the trees. Wouldn't be shakin' were it not for the breeze.*

Packages of six records retail at $3.49 or 98¢ for a single, but Stan can get it for you wholesale. John and Bob order the Blind Lemon Jefferson special, the Chuck Berry special, Big Bill Broonzy, John Lee Hooker. Bob is one of the few who phones in orders rather than mailing them. For a special deal, Gatemouth says, "I'll send you my picture." Bob and John figure Gatemouth *has to be* colored but when they get the photo, he's a white guy, half-bald. *What a drag.* Like with "Splish Splash," when they find out Bobby Darin is a white guy.

With John's Sears Silvertone tape recorder on Bob's piano, they attempt songs; Bob pounds chords and John kind of tinkles along on the higher keys. They mimic Stan Freberg, a popular comic who has parodied Elvis, Belafonte and "Sh-Boom." When they ad lib, the sessions can get raunchy.

You ain't nothin' but a horehound.

A couple of kids smoking, coughing, joking, laughing, screaming. "The Diarrhea Blues."

You stink. That's Bob. His and John's voices are nearly indistinguishable. Next, it's John, singing Buddy Holly's "Peggy Sue."

Briefly, lyrics fall into place, backed by Bob's four chord progression, now sounding vaguely like "Earth Angel" or something by the Turbins or Crests. Bob's voice is clear and almost sweet:

I wanna rock—I wanna cry—
I wanna rock—I wanna cry—

Lotta times, you can't tell where the official lyrics pause and Bob's imagination takes off. Like he says: *I make up a song. I know it's gonna sell a million copies but the writer of the song might sue me 'cuz it's so much alike.*

He narrates, like Gatemouth. Jive talk. Blues. Dig the rebop, daddy-O.
I'm walkin' down the street one sunny afternoon
A cop pulls me over asks me what I'm doin' ...
Here's the good part:
Cop asked me if my name was Henry ...
With Bucklen:
Daddy Cool, Daddy Cool ... cool Daddy ... Daddy who? Daddy Cool!
I got a girl, she lives on a hill, she's my baby and I love her still.
Barbara won't you come back to me?
I need your lovin'.

They place the tape recorder on the piano in the living room, facing west, where they can see the driveway.

A car pulls up:
Oh God you know who they brought.

With hushed tones, Bob speaks into the microphone like a newscaster: *John Hultstrand pulls up with some girls in the car—if you call them <u>girls</u>. If you call them girls you never saw a girl in your life!*

Talking to Bucklen while ostentatiously chewing gum.
Hey Josh.
Yeah, Oiving.
Hey Josh, what d'ya think of these girls?"
Don't bother me I'm reading a comic book.
I thought Checco'd have more sense that that.

I'm Bobby Zimmerman how she go ... I would write you a letter but they won't let us have sharp things in here.

When he hammers into Little Richard, his voice becomes harsh and strained.
Don't I sound just like Jerry Lee Lewis?

In Bucklen's bedroom, they record with acoustic guitar backing instead of piano.
Long Tall Sally. Tutti Frutti.
Jenny Jenny. Whooo. Jenny Jenny.
John: Don't you think it should be faster?
Checco! Hey Checco, you think that's too fast?
John and Bob: *Hey Little Richard! Ho Little Richard!*
Bob: *This is Little Richard. Little Richard's got a lotta expression. You think singing is just jumpin' and screamin'? You gotta have some kinda expression.*
John: What's the *best* kind of music?
Bob: *Rhythm-and-blues. Rhythm-and-blues is somethin' that you really can't explain, see. Why, you hear a good rhythm-and-blues song, chills go up your spine. You wanna <u>cry</u> when you hear one of those songs.*
Bob: *Ricky Nelson's another one of those guys.*
John: Ricky Nelson's out of the question.

Bob: *Well he copies Elvis Presley.*

John: He can't sing at all. Ricky Nelson, so we might as well forget him.

Bob: *Now, when you hear music like the Diamonds for instance. They're popular big stars. Where did they get all their songs? They got all their songs from little groups. They copy all the little groups. Same thing that Elvis—he copies Clyde McPhatter, he copies Little Richard: "Rip It Up," "Long Tall Sally," "Ready Teddy." "Money Honey," he copied from Clyde McPhatter. He copied "I Got a Woman" from Ray Charles.*

Bob sings about his friend, LeRoy Hoikkala: *Lee Roy—LEE Roy!*

LeRoy. Like John and Bob, the miner's son emulates James Dean. *Always in trouble* for drinking, smoking or staying out late. Feeling rebellious in school, he wears the DA, the leather jackets; wants a motorcycle. Likes rock 'n' roll and has a set of drums.

After school, LeRoy works at Feldman's department store. His good friend, Monte Edwardson has a part-time job at Sapero's clothing store. Walking down Howard Street, LeRoy and Monte run into Bob.

Hey, we should do somethin', Bob says. *We should try jammin'.*

They convene at Bob's house to hear Monte play his electrified acoustic guitar. Oh yeah, Monte is a naturally talented cat. Schooled in country-western and dance bands, he models his finger-picking style after Les Paul and Merle Travis and also can play rock 'n' roll style—with his teeth, behind his back and bending over backward touching his head to the ground.

Bob shows them music from *No Name Jive. I heard some neat stuff. This is how it goes.* He hums the parts. *This is what I want.* He's got the whole thing in his head. On the drums, he shows LeRoy the beat. He sings the guitar parts for Monte. On Bob's reel-to-reel tape player, the three lay down licks imitating Bob's rhythm-and-blues records, most memorably the Jive Tones' "Flirty Gerty." When Bob allows it, Monte and LeRoy contribute the more popular rock 'n' roll they prefer. There are also a few tunes that Bob has seems to have started writing.

To free himself from the piano, Bob comes up with an old box guitar and asks Monte to teach him chords, so he can play rhythm and still front the band. Monte shows Bob where to put his fingers on the guitar neck. Bob does not read music so he memorizes what he needs to and improvises the rest.

Bob also works on guitar-playing with his cousin, Stevie Goldberg, of Duluth. Sometimes, the two visit another Jewish kid, Dan Kossoff, in Superior, Wis. All three have guitars and strum back and forth, showing off chord progressions. Gimme a G. *Which one is that?*

With Bucklen, Bob goes to the Moose Lodge to see a piano player. After the performance, they go in and talk for a long time. Bob asks him a lot of questions about show business. *How do ya get bookings?*

Another early performer of rock 'n' roll in Hibbing is Dick Kangas, who borrows a guitar and amp from his guitar instructor and appears on the high school stage, performing Elvis Presley's "All Shook Up."

"You really ruined that song," he is told, "but you had more guts than I have getting up on stage."

Two years older than Bob, his 1957 graduation photo in the yearbook, *The Hematite,* is inscribed, *To Be Another Elvis.*

Dick's brother, Jeff, introduces Dick to John Bucklen. One day on Howard Street, Bucklen introduces Dick to Bob.

When Bob learns to chord along with Monte, the ruckus really starts in the garages around 7th Avenue and 25th Street. The neighbors shut their windows but pretty much keep their opinions to themselves. *Boys will be boys.* The Aanes family lives across 7th from Bob. When Nancy's mother is gone, Bob asks if he and his friends can practice there. Okay. Nancy's car salesman dad doesn't care how much noise they make. The band also plays in the basement of Monte's house out toward Keewatin.

Adding Bill Marinac on standup string bass for the night, they get a gig playing for the Moose Lodge above the L&B on Howard Street. The way it's going, they might even get paid some day.

I love Barb.
"Ya, you love Barb."
Boy, I really love Barb.
"Oh shut up."

When Bob's "girlfriend," Barb, moves down along the Iron Range to the smaller town of Buhl, Bob and John see her a few times. She moves to New Brighton and they visit her there too but she recedes from their attention.

Bob also courts an Italian girl in Brooklyn neighborhood—but her parents don't approve. Neither would his parents if they thought it might go anywhere. Bob is *not Catholic*; she is *not Jewish.*

Bob and his family are by heritage and practice *very Jewish*. Each summer, with boys and girls from Duluth and the Twin Cities, he attends a Hebrew summer camp where he dazzles the dilettantes by playing piano and singing like Jerry Lee Lewis. *You shake my nerves and you rattle my brain!*

In Duluth, he appears with "his gang" at the Jewish center and at parties in basement rec rooms. This dampens the ardor for some young couples who had planned an evening of Platters but now have to put up with the great pretender himself, Little Bobby pounding on the piano.

William Marinac   Larry Fabbro   Charles Nara

Above: Bob Zimmerman's first ensemble was made up of three high school band musicians. *1957 Hematite* • Below: 1959 ad. *Hibbing Tribune*

MICKA FURNITURE and ELECTRIC

Abe Zimmerman

WHEN IT COMES TO FURNITURE COMPARE BEFORE YOU BUY!

Above: Memorial Building, probably the Hibbing High School band, 1957-58. *Aubin Studio* • Below: Looking south from the mines at Hibbing, 1950s. 1st Avenue extends top to bottom, Howard Street left to right. Bennett Park, foreground. The Zimmerman house is two blocks east and a block south of the Memorial Building (curved roof at center). *IRRC*

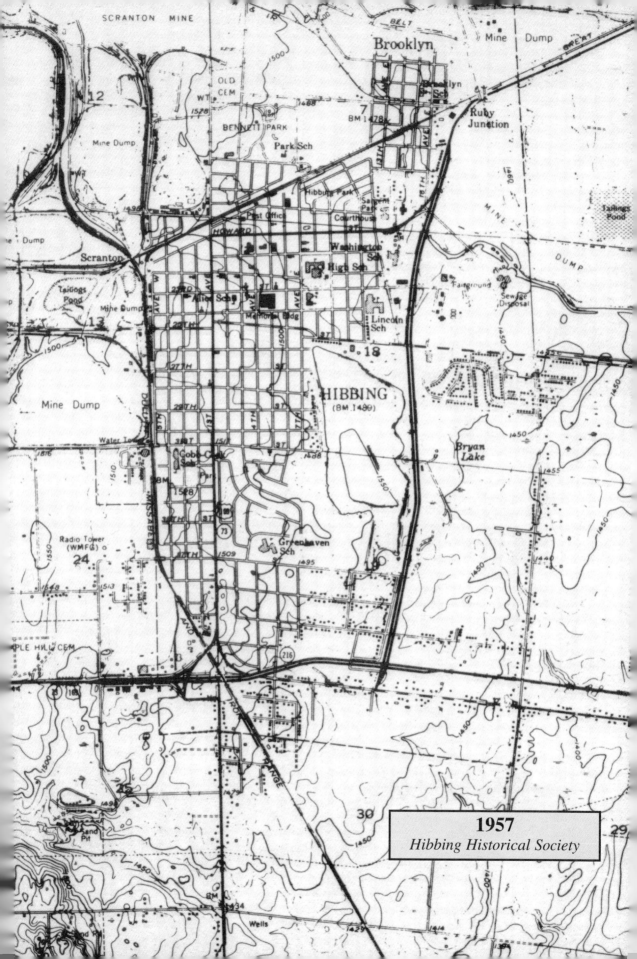
1957
Hibbing Historical Society

Howard Street, looking east, c. 1960.

1958 Hematite

Robert Zimmerman

Chapter 13
Junior
1957-58

Golden Chords/Glissendorf

I always needed a song to get by. There's a lot of singers who don't need songs to get by. A lot of 'em are tall, good-lookin', you know? They don't <u>need</u> to say anything to grab people. Me, I had to make it on something other than my looks or my voice...Well, now, Chuck <u>Berry</u> was a rock & roll songwriter. So I never tried to write rock & roll songs, 'cause I figured he had just done it. When I started writing songs, they had to be in a different mold. Because who wants to be a second-rate anybody?

<u>Rolling Stone</u>, 1987

THE POLITICAL WORLD

I grew up in the same area as Charlie Starkweather and I remember that happening...everybody pretty much kept their mouth shut about it. Because he did have a sort of a James Dean quality to him.

<u>Los Angeles Times</u>, 1984

& these people consider themselves gourmets for not attending charlie starkweather's funeral ye gads the champagne

<u>Tarantula</u>, 1972

Nigger, go back where you belong. A crowd of whites taunt as national guardsmen stop a teen-age Negro girl at the door of Little Rock Central High School. To enforce the federal court order for integration, President Eisenhower sends 1,000 paratroopers. Klan types dynamite synagogues in the deep South.

I always wanted to be an outlaw. Charles Starkweather, 19, admits 11 slayings in two western states.—Ed Gein, Plainfield, Wis., is arrested for murder, mutilation and necrophilia.—The treason indictment against poet Ezra Pound, 72, is dismissed, opening the way for his early release from a mental institution.—Cancer, heart disease or innocent pleasure? According to the *American Cancer Society,* smoking is directly linked to lung cancer.—Russia launches Sputnik, the first man-made earth satellite. The U.S. counters with the Explorer series.—Whether WACs should enhance their figures with falsies becomes a minor issue.—Fidel Castro's rebels seize Cuban radio and television stations.—A military coup ousts King Faisal, the pro-Western 23-year-old ruler of "one of the Middle East's richest oil countries," namely Iraq.

KING HEMATITE

This was not a rich or a poor town, everybody had pretty much the same thing and the very wealthy people didn't live there, they were the ones that owned the mines and they lived thousands of miles away.

Biograph, 1985

"We don't have the rich ores anymore, but we are not out of business," the Oliver Mining Co. public relations director tells Hibbing Rotary. With little ore to assess, property tax rates for 1957 increase by 42 percent, the largest jump in history. The greatest of iron ranges has become "middle-aged" and inadequate for the future, faced with "young and lusty competitors in Canada and South America."

POSITIVELY HOWARD STREET

Like picking up a high school yearbook, and just...
Oh, I love to do that...every once in a while.

Bob Dylan: A Retrospective, pub. 1972

Defying the terminal illness of King Hematite, the building boom continues. Everywhere you look is something new: library, courthouse, schools and "additions": Lebanon, Greenhaven, Graysher, Merryview and Court House.

The high school is crowded, despite its large size: 71 classrooms, two gyms, swimming pool, auditorium, and Hibbing Junior College, which meets wherever space is available. The high school band travels to New York, Washington, D.C., and the dedication of the Mackinac bridge. For boys, "letters" are awarded for football, cross-country, swimming, basketball, hockey, wrestling, track, golf, tennis and baseball. For girls—cheerleading and the Girls Athletic Association. In October, Asian Flu causes an all-time-high 551 student absentees.

What's so great about Hibbing? According to young writers, nice people and stores. New buildings. Peaceful streets. A long winter with lots of snow. Plenty of ore dumps on which to hike and hunt—and lakes to fish and swim in. "But most of all I like it," writes one proud junior Hibbingite to the *Tribune*, "because I have always lived here."

"Parents are honored in many ways by their children, but there's probably only one mother in the world whose son has paid tribute to her on the label of a tin can." Jeno Paulucci, Hibbing native and Duluth's leading employer, markets spaghetti sauces based on recipes of his mother, Italian-born Michelina Buratti Paulucci.

THE GARMAKER SYNDROME

Impressed by the success of the Milwaukee Braves, formerly of Boston, in the World Series, the New York Dodgers and New York Giants make plans to move to California. For the seventh year, defensive back Bobby Dillon leads the

Green Bay Packers in interceptions. December 19: The McHales have a baby and name him Kevin.

OVER THE RAINBOW

I don't have to go on other people's trips of who they think I am. A person doesn't like to feel self-conscious, you know? Now, Little Richard says if you don't want your picture taken, you got no business being a star. And he's right, he's absolutely right. But I don't like my picture being taken by people I don't know.
    <u>Bat Chain Puller</u>, pub. 1990

My uncle was a professional gambler. I'd see him once in a while.
    Nat Hentoff Interview, 1965

I've heard these songs before when I was young...the people sitting on their porches...They'd be singing folk songs, you know. But who would want to hear 'em? Like, they were a drag.
    Nat Hentoff Interview, 1965

I first heard Burl Ives when I was knee-high to a grasshopper. I guess everybody's heard those old Burl Ives records on Decca, with a picture of him in a striped T-shirt, holding up a guitar to his ear, just wailing.
    <u>Sing Out</u>, 1968

Now showing: "The real story of the most talked-about star of our time." James Dean, long dead, *plays himself* in The James Dean Story. At the other theater, the *awesome materialization* of "Jimmy Dean," the *ethereal form* of Elvis Presley and the *posing apparition* of Marilyn Monroe, along with living corpses, ghouls and slave maidens at the mercy of hideous beasts.—Michael Landon in *I Was a Teenage Werewolf.*—*Invasion of the Saucer-Men.*—*Hot Rod Rumble.*—*The Careless Years, Eighteen and Anxious.*—Elvis Presley in *King Creole* and *Jailhouse Rock.*—Tommy Steele's "wild pulse-pounding rock 'n' roll from overseas!" *Rock Around the World.*—Gregory Peck and Joan Collins in *The Bravadoes*. "Due to the unusual ending no one will be seated during the last ten minutes and please do not reveal surprise ending when recommending this picture to your friends."—Dirk Bogarde in *Man of the North Country.*

The Ore Capital is, as usual, alive with music. At the National Guard Armory, the *Grand Ole Opry,* with Jimmy Newman and Hank Locklin. Sponsored by the Civic Music Program: Richard Dyer-Bennet, presenting folk and art songs from Britain, Europe and America. *He sang with a concert-trained voice, possessed articulate diction, and was a skilled guitarist.* Climaxing the state Centennial year is a Broadway-style musical about Hibbing by native Donald Peterson. Songs included are "Union Party," "Give Me a Miner, Not a Cowboy," and "Our Range."

Television can be hazardous to your health. Tribune columnist George Fisher cautions that the new sets, if left plugged in, can spontaneously burst into fire.

NORTH COUNTRY FAIR

First robin, a time to put away bulky clothes and stuffy habits, the day the mercury hits 70, lilac-scented nights, and the "wonderful smell of grass fires on the outskirts of town." Signs of spring fever, according to the High School newspaper.—On a summer night at McCarthy Beach, campers huddle in tents as a tornado-like storm knocks down trees. A 9-year-old Minneapolis boy is killed.—Two lost children are found alive near Elephant Lake, having left a cabin to pick berries, wandering for 52 hours in "the worst type of Minnesota wilderness" and sleeping with their puppy for a pillow.—Sigurd Olson, the "Ely Woodsman," speaks at the library, to the "nature loving" minority, about his latest book, *The Singing Wilderness*.

AGUDATH ACHIM

"Sacred Days of The Jewish People." In September, the *Tribune* sends its "Jewish friends and neighbors" the traditional greeting: *May you be inscribed in the Book of Life, for a healthy, happy and prosperous New Year.* During Chanukah, there are decorations, games, gifts and food. Recipes from Mrs. Bert Chez and Mrs. Herman Feldman for potato pancakes and sesame cookies are published. Synagogue children, including David, Beth, Laura, Amy and Gary Zimmerman, present a program followed by a party.

A national survey shows that 86 percent of young Jews do not attend services regularly, compared to 68 percent of Protestants and 24 percent of Catholics. The proportion of faithful seems to be higher in Hibbing.—B.H. Edelstein, 88, great-grandfather of David and Bobby Zimmerman, recovers from an illness at St. Mary's Hospital, Duluth.—Joining the cast of the popular local musical, *Growin' Pains*, are synagogue members Bert Chez, Harriet Chez, Herman Feldman, Lester Hallock and Bobby Zimmerman's aunt, Irene Goldfine.

BLACKBOARD JUNGLE

There was always some kind of resistance. If it wasn't about religion, it was about the style of music. If it wasn't style, it was about the clothes you wore. If it wasn't clothes, it was about the people you knew. There was always something that people didn't like. I've been used to that since I was born.

<u>Los Angeles Times</u>, 1983 (<u>Absolutely Dylan,</u> pub. 1990)

Somehow, way back then, I already knew that parents do what they do because they're up tight. They're concerned with their kids in relation <u>to themselves</u>. I mean, they want their kids to please

them, not to embarrass them—so they can be proud of them. They want you to be what they want you to be.
The New Yorker, 1964

Me Tarzan, you Jane. *Funky. Raunchy. Square. Cube. Beat-nik. Bird-dog. What a blast! Shook up. Goof. Put down. Stow it. Scratch off. Shape up or shove off. Hit the deck.* Slumber parties and going steady—class ring on a gold chain around the neck, I.D. bracelets, matching clothes. Pearl studs in perforated ear lobes of girls. Bloody Mary jokes. Frisbees. Bobby soxers. Peroxide-streaked hair. Pale pink lipstick, pony tails, baggy sweaters (LSMFT), Bermuda shorts, sack dresses, straight skirts, wool socks, car coats. Sloppy Levi's and dungarees *or* the "hip" charcoal-grey slacks. Bola ties, V-neck sweaters over white T-shirts, flowered vests, crazy hats, loud argyle socks, loud and large cufflinks, raccoon coats and paratroop boots, "Libs"—patent leather shoes like Liberace's. "Only the duck-tailed haircut prevails in their return to sartorial splendor." *Me Jane, you Tarzan.*

There is trouble in International Falls over a dress code but not in Hibbing, according to Principal Kenneth Pederson. "Slacks and levis have not been school garb for more than 10 years. But we have no ban. We have used a positive plan of encouragement. If a girl wears slacks to school, the next time she wears a dress the teacher will comment 'how nice you look today.'" A committee of Hibbing teen-agers complies, calling for trimmed hair, clean jeans, "a belt which properly supports the trousers and an avoidance of unduly long hair," buttoned shirts, collars turned down. No tight, Elvis-type clothing. Girls must wear skirts or dresses to school.

What Young People Think. Gilbert, in the *Tribune:* "To the modern teen-ager the sweetest thing about being sweet sixteen is that most states allow you to get a driver's license at that tender age." In Minnesota, it's age 15. Nationally, by age 18, one boy in 20 has a car but less than one girl in 100. Two out of three vehicles are 1951 models or earlier, often converted into hot rods with special carburetors, superchargers and manifolds to see who can accelerate to the fastest clip in a few blocks. Drag races on Howard Street, the Kelly Lake road, the Dupont Lake road or Highway 5. Big crowds until the cops break it up. In town, vandals tear off auto aerials and smear lavatories with lipstick. *Bug the fuzz. What a blast!*

For some, the role models come from *The Beat Generation.* As portrayed in the *Tribune,* the "Beatniks" dig madcap parties, speedy sports cars, motorcycles, cool jazz, lots of loving and lots of drinking—all "without emotional response." *The object is to live life to the fullest but not to enjoy it.* The term *beat* was coined by Jack Kerouac in his novel, *On the Road,* "which now serves as a sort of manifesto for his beaten followers whom he claims are 'mad to live, mad to talk, mad to be saved.'"

The "depressive frenzy" is rejected, according to Gilbert; 84 percent of teens are not "beats" nor do they want to be. Fact is, 87 percent of teens want to live in suburbs. They want a home, garden, better schools, less traffic, congenial neighbors, fresh air, room to raise a family and freedom from the gangs of juvenile delinquents that are destroying the cities. Heroes of teen-age boys polled are

President Eisenhower, 31 percent; Elvis Presley, 14 percent; Vice President Nixon, 6 percent; Babe Ruth, 4 percent; Albert Schweitzer, 2 percent; and Arthur Miller, 3 percent—not as a playwright but as husband of Marilyn Monroe.

The more doleful, "beat," students are deplored by parents, athletes, achievers and squares in general. Reprinted in the *Tribune* from *Reader's Digest* which had reprinted it from magazines that reprinted it from the *Tribune,* is a "Letter to a Teen-ager" from a Hibbing housewife. "Always we hear the spoiled plaintive cry of the teen-ager: 'What can we do: where can we go?' I can make some suggestions. Go home! Paint the woodwork. Mow the lawn. Wash the car. Learn to cook. Scrub some floors. Repair the sink. Build a boat. Get a job!"

Hit the deck!

Music for teen-agers, according to the high school newspaper, *Hi-Times*, is dominated by "pop": "Peggy Sue," "That'll Be the Day" and "Every Day" by Buddy Holly & the Crickets; "Lucille" and "Keep A-Knockin" by Little Richard; "All Shook Up" and "Jailhouse Rock" by Elvis; "Bye Bye Love" by the Everly Brothers; "Party Doll," by Buddy Knox; "Whole Lotta Shakin' Goin' On" by Jerry Lee Lewis; "Rock and Roll Music" by Chuck Berry; "Lotta Lovin'" by Gene Vincent; "At the Hop" by Danny & the Juniors; "Summertime Blues" by Eddie Cochran and "The Stroll" by the Diamonds. Critics predict a sharp rise in the popularity of the Pat Boone style, and a practically extinct Presley. Calypso, now at its height, will soon make a quiet exit. "The sudden success of any extreme type of music depends on the fickle nature of the American public. Take heart, you calypso and Presley fans, there is always something new and exciting just ahead."

At "hops" and "sock hops" in high school gyms, squares gather in one clump and Elvis types in another. Chaperones are plentiful. Music is by local bands or 45 rpm records played by a clique of knowledgeable girls or by a local DJ. Dances, copied from "American Bandstand," include the Stroll, the Bop and the Chalypso.

"Say, Mom and Dad, maybe you'd better get those artillery-type ear plugs after all," advises the *Tribune*. "This rock 'n' roll racket is going to be around quite a while." With allowances averaging $8.50 per week, teen-agers account for 90 percent of all single 78 or 45 rpm record sales and 50 percent of the new 33 1/3 albums. "Instead of three minutes of sustained blues shouting, parents of hep teen-agers will now be exposed to 20 minutes or more. There have been continuing complaints that besides the basic savagery of its two beat rhythm, rock 'n' roll lyrics cater to the baser instincts by suggestion, double entendre and little concealed blue meanings." Never mind. *They never listen to the words*, claim 73 percent of teen-agers polled.

"In this nether world between childhood and manhood, Elvis Presley emerges as a symbol of destruction. Presley is unacceptable to the adult world and, to the unadjusted teen-ager, seems to mock its cultural taboos. Through an alliance of the spirit with Presley, the teen-ager is able to act out his infantile desires of striving for power through the destruction of adult standards and symbols. He can satisfy his need to belong by uniting with other youngsters of similar aim."

Yeah but Elvis is actually a shy, polite, religious, white, small-town boy who favors his mother and lives with his grandmother. Just like Bob Zimmerman. However, he does have an affinity for black performers and motorcycles. On stage, he seems to become another person, one already much imitated. In *Sing Boy Sing,*

Tommy Sands, a young Southern boy, rocks-and-rolls "to movie stardom" as the idol of the nation's teen-agers. Also showing: *High School Confidential* with Jerry Lee Lewis pounding the ivories. *Shakin' at the high school hop—Rollin' at the high school hop—Everybody's hoppin'—Everybody's boppin'.*

BOBBY

You put me on the stage without a guitar and I probably would hide. I feel uncomfortable in front of people without my guitar.
   <u>Icons-Intimate Portraits</u>, 1989

Back in the '50s, when I was 14 or 15 years old playing with four-piece rock 'n' roll bands back in Minnesota...there weren't any sound systems or anything you had to bother with. You'd set up your amplifiers and turn them up to where you wanted to turn them.
   Los Angeles <u>Herald Examiner</u>, 1985

I had a couple of bands in high school, maybe three or four of 'em. Lead singers would always come in and take my bands, because they would have connections, like maybe their fathers would know somebody, so they could get a job in the neighboring town at the pavilion for a Sunday picnic or something. And I'd lose my band. I'd see it all the time.
   <u>Rolling Stone</u>, 1984

Not everybody has the courage to sing like I do!
   WBAI radio, 1966

What voice I have, what little voice I have—I don't really have a good voice. I do most of my stuff with phrasing...I guess my voice sounds pretty close to a coyote or something.
   <u>Icons-Intimate Portraits</u>, 1989

They stone ya when yer playin' yer guitar.
   "Rainy Day Women #12 & 35," 1966

Local legend says that at the Hibbing High Jacket Jamboree someone cut the electricity on your band because you were so loud.
   Yeah, I wasn't very popular when I was there...I don't remember that, but it could've happened.
   Did people sometimes not understand what you were doing?
   Nah, we were just the loudest band around, it was mostly that. What we were doing, there wasn't anybody else around doing...there was one other band in town with trumpet, bass, guitar and drums. Mostly that type of stuff. And you had to play polkas.

Did you actually play polkas?
Yeah. Oh yeah.
<u>Duluth News-Tribune & Herald</u>, 1986

Back then it was mainly <u>polka bands</u>. If you went to a club it was more like a tavern scene, with a polka band. There was <u>country music</u>, too, that I remember. My girlfriend, Echo was her name— Echo Helstrom—her father played guitar.
<u>Duluth News-Tribune & Herald</u>, 1986

They say she was free-spirited.
Mm hm, she was just like me. We're both the same.
<u>Duluth News-Tribune & Herald</u>, 1986

Can you cook and sew, make flowers grow,
Do you understand my pain?

"Is Your Love in Vain?" 1978

You give me a woman that can cook and sew and I'll take that over passion any day.

<u>No Direction Home</u>, pub. 1986

Nearsighted, Bobby occupies a front seat in English class; for Business, he sits in the back, representing the letter, "Z." He is short, "baby-faced," a bit chubby, mild-mannered, well-dressed, slightly odd but not overtly obnoxious. In class, he doesn't say a word unless called on, though he is capable of answering well. He hates certain subjects. *I am not going to take physics. Let me drop it.*

Though you might take him for shy, he's not afraid to let you know he's going to *be something* some day soon. For his 1957-58 yearbook photo, he adopts an uncharacteristic sneer. *Hey, trying to look rebellious?* His right leg twitches when he's nervous or restless. His heritage, religious beliefs and intimate activities are all secret. He keeps his distance with a cutting sense of humor. That ability to *put on* and cut down an innocent auditor. His brown, curly hair is getting longer on top.

He smokes cigarettes regularly, sucking cough drops afterwards. He prefers the OP brand—Other People's. The way he bums, you'd swear he's broke all the time, even though he has a nice house, nice clothes, his dad drives an expensive Buick and he has a full pack of Luckies in his pocket.

Bob says his uncle is a professional gambler. *Maybe he is, maybe he isn't.* He shows a picture he says is his aunt with Elvis Presley's arm around her. *Maybe he is.* In February, the *Tribune* features a former Hibbing resident, written up in the *Wall Street Journal*, "A Las Vegas Veteran Trains Cubans in Arts of Wheeling and Dealing." *Maybe he <u>is</u> telling the truth.* The article says Professor Vernon Stone, 45, formerly of Hibbing, runs a card-playing and roulette school for fancy new gambling casinos opening in Havana, "this hustling city of riffle and roll." *See what my uncle sent me from Las Vegas?*

Then Bobby calls up his friend, John Bucklen, in early summer and plays a record he says he recorded, "Do You Want To Dance?" Remember, he's always making tapes. *You have gotten really good, Bob.* Then Bucklen finds out "Do You Want To Dance" was recorded in 1958 by 17-year-old Bobby, yeah—Bobby Freeman.

When Bob and John listen to "Bluebirds over the Mountain," they are intrigued by the singer's name, "Ersel Hickey." *How about the name, Elston Tornado?*

John Bucklen is Bob's best Hibbing friend, his best non-Jewish, non-relative friend. In December 1957, just before John's 16th birthday, LeRoy Hoikkala stops by. "I'm not going to school today," John says. He does not mention that he had found his crippled father dead that morning of heart failure. After that, John doesn't see Bob for a few months. Then one day, John's mother calls, "Oh, there's Bob" and he's at the back door like he used to be.

John adopts the juvenile delinquent look in imitation of LeRoy who is imitating James Dean. It begins with a haircut called *The Hollywood:* flat on top, long on the sides, slicked back into a ducktail. *A little dab'll do ya.* Shirt open three buttons with collar up. Leather jacket. Cigarette hanging on lip, a pack rolled in a T-shirt sleeve. A hard-case hood—on the surface only. Inside, John's more of a weasel. Bob's no tough guy either. But he *can* be a *wise* guy.

Glissendorf. An impromptu word game with no purpose other than to confuse an innocent third person.

I see it's raining.
"It isn't raining."
You say it isn't? Okay, if you wanna be difficult, it isn't. So let's move on. What's the next first thing to come to your mind?
The what?
The what? Just what I thought. I won! You won!
"I don't understand."
That's exactly right. You don't understand. <u>You don't understand.</u> (You're stupid.)

After a round of Glissendorf, one girl starts crying and John thinks, *maybe this is a little too—cruel.*

They listen to the radio whenever they can: while studying, talking, riding in a car. Local DJ Ron Marinelli hosts an hour-long local program. After running down the top ten, he says, "Now we go by remote to Jim Dandy in Virginia." Then another guy takes over with an *amazing* show. It's the real down and true, growling, nitty gritty blues: Lightnin' Hopkins ("Baby Please Don't Go"), Howlin' Wolf ("Sitting on Top of the World"), Big Bill Broonzy, Son House, Robert Johnson, Bukka White, Lester Young, Charlie Parker. *Raunchy!*

Bob and John show up at Marinelli's office.
Who is that guy, Jim Dandy in Virginia, Minnesota?
Here's the phone number; give him a call.
Bobby borrows his dad's car and off they go—30 miles east to Virginia and WHLB radio. *Are you Jim Dandy?*

To the rescue. It's Jim Dandy, like in the 1956 song by LaVern Baker. His real name is James Reese. All right so far, but coolest of cool, gonest of real gone, the cat is colored. Bobby, especially, loves to dig colored cats.

He and friends go many times to Jim Dandy at the radio station or up the long flight of stairs to the second floor Dandy apartment by the Virginia Library. There, you find the master, a slight, slender black man in his late twenties. He lives up there with his wife and a whole lot of records. *Jim Dandy to the rescue.*

"I like blues," Dandy says, "I like rock 'n' roll. But there's no depth to it like jazz." And it's jazz in which he tries to interest late-night audiences.

"People up here aren't tuned into that," station engineer Conrad Gabrielson warns Dandy. "Up here they like popular music, polka, standards."

"I'm going to *teach* them to like it."

He has his audience: Bobby Zimmerman and his high school friends, sitting with legs crossed on the living room floor, absorbing every word, every note.

Bob, not usually much interested in books, connects with John Steinbeck. When Bucklen gets the same English teacher as Bob had previously, he borrows Bob's paper on *The Grapes of Wrath.* John's mother types up Bob's hand-written script word for word. Yet Bob got an A and John gets a B.

Following his 1957 graduation from Hibbing High School, Dick Kangas drives a truck for Kelly furniture, which uses a warehouse in the alley behind the Zimmerman house.

Hey, how's it goin'?

Pretty cool, Bob.

At times when Kangas' car is out of commission, one of them walks the mile between Bob's Fairview Addition house and Dick's in Home Acres, where they listen to records, play guitars and sing. They exchange chords and lyrics with each other and with Bucklen. Kangas likes John's guitar playing, modeled after the much-admired Scotty Moore.

Hey when I make it.—

They all say the same thing. *When I make it big I'll give you a call, show you around Hollywood.*

Dick and Bob visit Ron Marinelli with the tape recordings they make in Dick's bedroom. The songs admittedly are not too much different from the other teen-age pop of the day. *I love you; you love me. Oh how happy we would be.* Marinelli agrees to play Bob's tapes and not Dick's.

When Kangas gets his '53 Ford, he picks Bob up after "shows" at the teen center—although Dick never actually views Bob on stage—same as he never sees him drive a vehicle. To Kangas, getting out on the highway is a lot more fun than hanging around the claustrophobic village. His classmates want to stay in Hibbing driving big trucks around the mines. Dick makes it clear he does not want that future. Bob doesn't say much about it. Why should he? His parents are sending him to college.

On a Saturday night when he has a car, Dick picks up Bob and John. With a supply of beer or gin-and-orange juice, they cruise 169, east to Virginia or west to Grand Rapids. Check out the dances and the bands. Crash a party. Pick up some girls. Or just ride around and get drunk and sing to the car radio: *Rave on it's a crazy feelin'!* On a summer night, white clouds roll by a dark blue sky and you feel like you're driving a ridge on top of the world. Lightning snaps along the Range, thunder rolls on by, and finally, to the chirping of crickets, the biggest yellow moon in the world balloons up from Chisholm. *Rave on!*

The boys get to know Johnny Dark. A 1954 graduate of Coleraine High School, William John Krznarich is a miner for the Hanna company and a role model of some proportions. His nickname, from a Tony Curtis movie, reflects a dark, Croation complexion and a costume inspired by *Dig!* Magazine. Johnny combs his hair back on the sides and down in the front. He wears clothes from "down south," favoring pink and black, the pants legs "pegged" wide at the top and narrow at the bottom. He displays a skull-and-crossbones on the back of his leather jacket. After seeing *The Wild One,* he adds "BRMC": Black Rebels Motorcycle Club—of which he is the only local member.

Johnny Dark takes a picture of himself on his fine aqua Harley motorcycle and sends it to *Dig*, entitling it, "The Highway Terror of 169." They respond, *This guy is a highway terror? Why is he in a field?* But they put it in anyway.

Johnny is a regular at the L&B Cafe. Sometimes, he talks to John, Dick or Bob. Johnny has been into rhythm-and-blues since he heard "Lonely Avenue" in 1954. When he gives Echo Helstrom a ride home from the L&B one stormy night, she notices a 45 rpm record player in the front seat of his car. If new records come in the mail, sometimes he calls Bobby Zimmerman.

Bring 'em over, says Bob. *We'll listen to 'em at my house.*

Bobby plays the piano a little. Johnny likes Bob's style of performance; he's like a wild man. Like Little Richard.

Johnny has a lot of records he orders from Shreveport, from Stan the Man. Some, he takes to Jenny Fontigrossi at the Chisholm Sweet Shop for the juke box: "Blueberry Hill," by Fats Domino; "Rain In My Heart" by Slim Harpo; "What'd I Say?" by Ray Charles; "Bo Diddley" by Bo Diddley; "Slow Down," "Short, Fat Annie," "Bony Moronie" and "Dizzy Miss Lizzy" by Larry Williams.

With his leather and sideburns, Johnny Dark looks tough. Unlike his young buddies, Bob and John, he *is* tough. The winner of numerous Golden Gloves bouts, they call him "Elvis" when he boxes.

One time at a dance at the Meadowlands, a visiting DJ of their acquaintance tells Dick to tap Johnny Dark and tell him Bob wants to fight him. A lot of guys *do* pick fights with him so Johnny turns and walks toward Bob.

It's just a joke.

Quite often, Abe lets Bob borrow the family Buick. But Bob wants his own car. More specifically, a pink-and-white '51 Ford convertible. It's a customized job, lowered in back, minus the nose piece, with added dual exhaust pipes, fender skirts, fancy hubcaps. *Gotta have that car,* he tells his dad, who does not approve. *Don't ask unless you're prepared to hear me say "No."* Bob keeps it up until they go to look at the car, where Bob dickers with some old guy in his twenties.

Can it get t' Minneapolis on a tank of gas?

"Yeah, I could get down there and halfway back."

Oh, that's good, real good.

A few weeks later the Ford is sitting out in front of the house. Bob has it painted blue. It's a neat car to drive around town in with the top down.

But Bob seems to be prone to fender benders. No matter what the particulars of the mishap, he calls and tells Abe, *I broke the fan belt.* Kind of a one-sided joke. After one accident, Abe apparently has to settle a claim out of court for several thousand dollars. There's nothin' to say about that! *I broke the fan belt.*

Soon enough, Bob finds a killer Harley-Davidson "45" motorcycle for sale in a garage on the west side. Abe again opposes the purchase. *Don't ask.* But Bob is excited. *Gotta have that cycle.* He tells Micka driver Benny Orlando, *Gotta have it.* He asks George Haidos at the L&B to help him convince Abe, who comes in every day for lunch. Abe says, *I told my boy to quit smoking and settle down and I'll get him a motorcycle.*

When the inevitable purchase approaches, Abe enlists Hoikkala's guidance. "You've got a bike, LeRoy. Make sure Bob gets a good one, and if you can, come over with us when we pick it out. And teach him how to drive it."

In the car, Abe follows the two wild ones home. What a picture they make!

Out on the West Side, LeRoy teaches Bob how to drive. They get a couple of Harley hats; Bob paints the cycle black. His brother's baby-sitter sees Bob fooling with the motorcycle in the garage. What a surprise! He *had been* such a nice Jewish boy. Unfortunately, Bob finds the cycle hard to handle. Lotta times he hits a corner a little wide: *Whoa!*

Bob goes over to a girl's house and asks her if she wants a ride. *Aw come on. It'll be cool.* She gets on and Bob blasts out of the driveway. When he turns up Howard Street, she begs, *Please let me off.* Nice girls don't ride on motorcycles, especially when they're afraid the driver will run into a parking meter.

After a teen dance somewhere out by Kelly Lake, Bob and LeRoy get off their bikes and take shelter in a vacant church. Concerned adults show up. *What do you think you're doing in here?*

Delivering appliances with Orlando, Bob talks more about his motorcycle than anything else. Likewise, the motorcycle is about the *only* personal thing Abe ever broaches to acquaintances. He desperately wants it gone.

"Leave him alone," Orlando argues. "He'll get out of it."

He'll get out of it. Bob, John, LeRoy and LeRoy's cousin, Dale Boutang, are driving Harleys to see a girl or at least make some impression on Brooklyn neighborhood. On the way, they must wait at the railroad tracks for a long, monotonous string of ore cars. Rattle and shake. Car after car going by in the red dust. Shake and rattle. It seems to take an awfully long time. Shake, rattle and roll. You know Bob. He's getting kind of antsy, twitchy. *Nervous Norvous.* When the train finally rumbles by, he guns the Harley and takes off.

But whoa!

The warning signal springs suddenly and he sees a second train's coming from the opposite direction, almost upon him.

Boy howdy!

Bob shoots forward and bam! throws 'er down, skids 'er sideways in the dust. He lies in the track bed and watches the train go by, the guy in the locomotive window looking out, shaking his head. *Juvenile delinquents.*

Bob picks up his cycle, pushes it across the track, puts his head down.

James Dean and Dean James. In October of 11th grade, Bob and John saunter into the L&B Cafe. If the Sweet Shop is the hangout for squares, football players, cheerleaders and student council members, the L&B is for rebels like them, with or without causes. *BRMC.*

In a booth, Echo Helstrom and Dee Dee Lockhart sit sipping cherry Cokes. Dee Dee happens to know Bob from years ago and Echo wants to meet him. Earlier, she had seen him on the sidewalk playing his guitar and singing in the falling snow like some weirdo. She can appreciate weirdos.

Echo Helstrom, this is Bob Zimmerman. Bob, this is Echo.

Echo knows she and Bob are classmates, but can they be any more than that? He normally looks like a little Sweet Shop goody-goody in an expensive sweater and she's an L&B regular in jeans and a black leather jacket. He's Howard Street business and she's poor folks from the wrong side of Highway 169. For kicks, he probably reads comic books; she and her girlfriends hitchhike the Range looking for adventure. But he's cute and seems nice and she likes to meet new people. She says she has seen him playing the guitar.

Hey, didja know I play the piano too? I'm startin' a band. We been rehearsin' up in the Moose Lodge.

"What do you play?"

R&B, mostly.

"You do? I listen almost every night. You have to put the radio right up to your ear to get it. Did you ever hear of *No Name Jive*?"

No Name Jive! You listen to Gatemouth Page? I love that show. Little Richard, he's my favorite. Some day, I'm going to be like Little Richard. I'm gonna be big!

"I hope to be in the movies."

I'll getcha <u>in</u> the movies. My uncle <u>owns</u> the <u>theaters</u>.

Both vow to succeed in show business and knock out the squares of Hibbing.

Let's go upstairs. I wancha t' hear my piano now.

They duck in a doorway next to the L&B and find their way up a long stairway to the Moose Lodge—but the door is closed. Echo stands and picks the lock with her jackknife, "one of my many talents." Just to make conversation, she says, "Gee, *Zimmerman*, that's a funny name. Are you Jewish?"

Without answering, Bob goes in. Bathed only by light beaming in from Howard Street, he plays the piano until they get scared and sneak downstairs.

Hey, come over to my house and I'll play you my records, okay? You c'n hear me perform.

At school later, John takes her aside. "Try not to ask Bob about being Jewish. He doesn't like to talk about it."

Bob and Echo begin meeting after school. They walk to the L&B for Bobby's favorite: cherry pie *a la mode*. They smoke cigarettes and play the juke box. They stroll up Howard Street, Bob in tight jeans, hands squeezed into pockets. Kind of a cocky smart-aleck from the beginning, but he can't help looking well-scrubbed, with rosy cheeks and a bit of a tummy. Sometimes they duck into the Sportsmen's Cafe for Cokes and hamburgers. Maybe popcorn or cotton candy at Kitchen's "Kitchenette." He gets her into one of the movie theaters his mother's family owns, the Lybba—but makes her enter alone and meets her inside.

Bob likes to joke around. In Crippa's music store, he demands records he knows they don't have. The clerk says, "Little Who?" or "Fats What?" and Bob says, "Well, how 'bout such and such—or so and so's new one?" He keeps it up until the clerk is really ticked off, then Bob puts on his hurt look. Grabs Echo by the hand and they amscray, almost ready to burst, then laughing like crazy.

In the short north-country summer, Echo and Bob ride the motorcycle. On the way to her house, they often stop at the A&W where Bob asks her to buy him a hot dog with mustard and relish. *Please Echo, please, I'm starving.*

He sets her on the Harley and explains the controls. She takes off but, realizing her feet don't reach the ground, tries to put on the brakes. The engine revs instead of stopping, the thing hits a stone and she flies head over heels. The motorcycle lies on the ground, rear wheel spinning, sparks flying, and Bob staring with big eyes.

When he has his Ford, they drive up Maple Hill to survey the great, plundered Mesabi Iron Range to the north, east and west—and the vast forest extending infinitely south. *It's pretty sometimes but there's nothin' happening!* They drive or hike along Fire Tower Road. Out to Big Sandy Lake.

They practice telephone mental telepathy.
I'm thinking of a color—

At Dee Dee's house on 5th Avenue West, Bob sits on the steps and plays guitar, singing folky songs and telling stories. To her, he's good-looking, well-dressed and well-mannered. When her little sister, Joey, follows Bob around, Bob tells her he'll pay her to go out and find some bottle caps for his collection. *If you take the corks out you can put them on your shirt like a button.* It's an excuse for him and Echo to disappear into the woods for a while.

After about a month, he kisses Echo, gives her his I.D. bracelet and they go steady—prompting a spell of possessiveness. At a party, he's banging on a guitar. Echo grabs a hula hoop and shows off her tight pants—very sexy. *Hey cut it out.*

Arnie Maki, custodian at the youth center, gets Bob and Kangas interested in Los Angeles, where the weather is great and, he says, every place you look, there's a beautiful girl. A semi-professional photographer, he shows them glamour shots he has taken of Echo, who is very blonde and blessed with beauty reminiscent of Marilyn Monroe and Brigitte Bardot.

For a session at the old cemetery, the photographer has Echo wear black leotards, then asks her to take off her top so he can shoot her unclothed back; she refuses. Bob scolds, *I don't want you hangin' around with that guy no more.*

Bob asks Echo to prove her qualifications as a housewife by preparing pizzas and sewing him a pair of royal-blue slacks. He calls her *Angel Baby.* They talk about *hopes and dreams,* how someday they'll show the ignorant, pick-you-apart bongs of Hibbing by making it big.

Bob and Echo spend a lot of time at the Helstrom place by Maple Hill, at the edge of the great forest. The house remains unfinished; a garage fire during construction destroyed most of the building materials. Studs separate the rooms but some walls have not been paneled over.

Bob sits on the front steps and plays guitar—music he's picked up from the radio: mostly quiet songs, country kind of songs. He talk-sings like Hank Snow does in "Prisoner of Love." He revises an old song about a little kid hit by a car. The way he does it, you have to laugh. Some situation will come into his head and he'll build on it. He and John play "Over the Rainbow" in hillbilly style.

Bob gets along pretty well with Echo's mother, Martha Helstrom. She has a collection of country music on 78 rpm records that he tries to duplicate—sad songs like "Ohio Prison Fire," cowboy songs and the *Grand Ole Opry*. He and Echo tell Mrs. Helstrom they plan to get married, live on Maple Hill and call their child "Bob" whether it's a boy or a girl. But Mrs. Helstrom can see it won't happen. Bobby is restless, impatient, a young man with some place to go.

About the only good part about Mr. Helstrom, as John and Bob see it, is that he owns several guitars, including a big-necked Hawaiian job. On the bad side is that the well digger, welder and repairman does not approve of boyfriends in general and this boyfriend in particular. A hide tacked on a shed from a bear he has killed seems suggestive.

Echo is baby-sitting for the son of her sister, who lives next door, when Bob and John arrive to keep her company. Unexpectedly, Helstrom arrives home. The boys jump out the front door and scramble down the road as Helstrom beams the flashlight at their retreating forms. *Hey you!*

Late one night, Kangas drives Bob out to Echo's and they park by the bedroom window. Bob, in the back seat, starts singing and begging Echo to come with them. She crawls out the window and they take off for a midnight ride across the range—Keewatin, Nashwauk, Pengilly, Calumet, Bovey, where the northern lights dance like the ghosts of ancient electricity.

At the Maple Hill homestead, there are the usual arguments, sometimes including Echo's parents. After that, maybe they don't see Bob for a couple days. Then the doorbell rings and there he stands, beating on his guitar. He pushes past Echo and sings, parading around the house until they're all laughing so hard they forget what the fight is about.

One day, he comes over to her house with the book *Cannery Row* in his hand. *Steinbeck is a great writer. Didja know he wrote <u>East of Eden</u>, that James Dean movie?*

Sometimes, Bob and John park a car at Echo's and go hitchhiking, feeling very adventurous. She has to laugh; that's how she usually gets around. They often find their way down 169 to John's sister's place in Pengilly. Ruth, seven years older than John, enjoys sitting on the couch with John and Bob and singing along to "Swing Low, Sweet Chariot" and "Satisfied Mind." It's fun to listen to Bob and John try to copy falsettos they have heard.

Ruth finds Bob charming. He would make a good salesman. Sitting and bumming her cigarettes. They're on the same frequency. About her singing, he tells her, *You're a natural second.*

She kids him. "When you're rich and famous you can buy me a pack of cigarettes."

That's okay, Ruth, I'll never forget you.

Ruth and her husband are members of a Croation tamburitza band. One night, when they return home, they find Pete's tamburitza guitar hanging from a light fixture. *Pete, you're losing your mind,* she says. Later, John calls. "Did you notice anything unusual?" He tells her that he and Bob had climbed in the bathroom window to get out of the rain. The hanging bugarija is their signature.

Bob doesn't talk much about his father. Obviously, he doesn't get along with him. The Harley runs out of gas and Bob sends Echo walking. Of all people, here comes Mr. Zimmerman! Abe drives Echo to get the gas and back. When Abe has gone, Bob starts yelling. *What'd you do that for? Why'd ya let him give you a ride?*

Another time, Bob sees Echo downtown and pulls her into an alley. He feels terrible about what has happened, he says. A three-year-old kid holding an orange ran into the street from between two parked cars and collided with his motorcycle. He says the boy needed to go from the Hibbing hospital to the Duluth hospital and Abe arranged for an ambulance. The boy recovers but Bob agrees to sell the motorcycle. *I can still see that orange rolling across the street.*

Held in the boys' gymnasium, May 2, 1958, from 9-12 p.m., the Junior Prom features conventional dance music by George Pogue's orchestra. The theme is "Bewitched, Bothered, and Bewildered."

Echo's sister comes over from her house next door to take pictures of Echo in a pale-blue, floor-length gown, accented by a corsage from Bob.

Bewitched.

Before the Prom, Bob insists he and Echo drive thirty miles to Virginia to see Jim Dandy.

Bothered.

Still, when they arrive (a little late), there is possibility in the glittering three-dimensional stars beneath a ceiling of blue, silver, and gold streamers. Outlining the dance floor are white trees draped with pink angel hair and surrounded by silver stars.

Bewildered.

But who could feel more out of place among so much Hibbing High School pride? Bob is as poor a leader as she is a follower. He takes "little teeny steps" and keeps saying, *What's the matter, can't you dance?*

Can't you dance?

Finally, he says, "Let's get out of here." A post-Prom supper dance is held at the Moose lodge club rooms for the righteous; but Bob and Echo fall asleep in the car. Later, they find out the pictures her sister took do not turn out.

At the end of the school year, Bob writes a long letter to Echo about *that time when it was 20 below zero and he was running down the road in the rain her ol' man's flashlight on his ass...about the time they sat and talked in the L&B until two o'clock in the morning and the time I was such a complete idiot, thinking back, that the car was in the driveway all night long.*

Well Echo, I better make it, huh—Love to the most beautiful girl in school, Bob—

By now, Bob has put together a real band, consisting of himself on piano, rhythm guitar and vocals; Monte Edwardson, lead guitar; and LeRoy Hoikkala, drums. From LeRoy's golden Ludwig drum set, they take the name *The Golden Chords.*

The band practices in living rooms, basements and garages. They play PTA and Moose Lodge meetings. On Sunday afternoons, when the place is closed, they play at Collier's Bar-B-Cue, a narrow, block-long restaurant just north of Howard Street, owned by the father of Jerry Van Feldt, an acquaintance of Bucklen's. The boys haul their gear past the kitchen where employees are peeling potatoes for the next week. They move the booths away from the window and face the back.

Inside, it's so loud you can't hear the words. Sometimes they're moaning instead of singing. Sometimes, they work on their own songs, such as the instrumental, "Big Black Train." With the door propped open, the racket reaches Howard Street and beyond. Collier's goes over pretty good. It's free and "by invitation" only.

Bob, John and LeRoy occasionally drop by local teenage parties, where they might be asked to entertain or might entertain without being asked. The popular choice is Buddy Holly. *Pretty pretty pretty Peggy Sue uh hoo oo oo oo oo hoo.* The boys' habit of singing on Bucklen's porch roof brings threats of calling the cops from the neighbors.

Bob's first guitar is an old acoustic job with strings painfully far off the neck. When he learns to chord along with his younger mentor, Monte Edwardson, he orders a turquoise Silvertone solid-body electric guitar from the Sears Roebuck catalog. Having saved $20 for the down payment, he hides the instrument from Abe until he has the remaining $19.

Though he does not join the Golden Chords, John Bucklen buys a $22 blue-and-white Stella guitar from a little music store on 1st Avenue. As his strumming improves, he becomes interested in performing with a group.

He and Bob are walking down 1st Avenue when they find some new guitars displayed in the window of a former bakery. Inside, they pore over a guitar catalog with Mr. Hautala, the elderly Finnish owner—*I'll give them to you for half price.* They each order a black solid-body sunburst-finish Ozark Supro electric guitar in the Stratocaster image. The price is $60 apiece, which Hautala tells them is *at cost.* Bob says, *Wow! Did we ever get a deal!*

Now, where to get the dough? Bucklen goes home and begs and cries to his mother. "I need this guitar. It's the most important thing in the world." He and Bob both manage to get $60 and pick up the guitars. However, when they unwrap them, they realize amplifiers are needed. Bob holds his new ax up to the window to hear the vibrations. Soon, John picks up a small Fender amp.

But it is the piano that Bob plies in his most memorable Hibbing performance: the Jacket Jamboree of his junior year.

The school newspaper, *Hi-Times*, of Jan. 28, 1958, provides the scenario. The coronation of homecoming queen Shelby Clevenstine, Thursday, Feb. 6, at 2 p.m., is to include entertainment assembled by the Pep Club: a magic show, a skit by Hibbing High School cheerleaders plus a "local rock 'n' roll instrumental group and several vocal selections." Bob keeps his exact plans pretty much secret.

For the afternoon program, the entire school audience of 1,800 assembles beneath the chandeliers in the ornate Hibbing High School auditorium. To cope with the august setting, Bobby has augmented the amplification system with a microphone in the piano, at the modest amplifiers, in front of the bass drum and three at his side for vocals.

There is some uncertainty as Bobby bounds on the stage, takes his place standing at the piano and peers at the audience, which, due to myopia, he can't see clearly. His long-for-the-times wavy hair is piled straight up on his head like Little Richard's. He's small but the sound is big. In fact, it's the biggest, loudest music anybody has heard. Painfully loud, as Bob bangs away. *Rock 'n' roll is here to stay!* He's halfway through the second number, jumping around and thumping the piano so hard the pedal breaks off.

The program has abruptly become rambunctious and reaches a condition school officials consider "out of character" as Principal Kenneth L. Pederson cuts the house mikes, leaving only the band's amps. The piano and drums don't need power so the hullabaloo continues, every painful second seeming way longer than it really is, until Pederson feels he has to pull the curtain.

Even Bob's most liberal teachers, such as social studies teacher Charlie Miller, are a little shaken. *Wasn't that awful?* says Val Peterson, the junior high music teacher who periodically befriends Bob. Student reactions vary. Here is one really strange, *different* kid performing as if he were Little Richard. Some think it's a big joke. Some think it's terrible.

It's most difficult for Echo, who gets upset days ahead when she knows Bob will perform. At the evening version of the Jacket Jamboree, she squirms down in her seat, shuts her eyes and puts her fingers in her ears. The band gets into a Ray Charles kind of song, really loud (*I got a woman way 'cross town*). The usual—the band is too loud *and* she doesn't want to hear the boos and laughter. But the girl next to her pulls Echo's hands away, "Listen!"

It's Bob, shouting over and over, *I gotta girl and her name is Echo.* He's seemingly making up verses as he goes along—the first time she hears him sing something that has not been written by somebody else, and it's her song.

Bob walks her around in the cool evening air, excited. *Didja like it?*

Shortly after the Jacket Jamboree is the Chamber of Commerce Winter Frolic, including a dance, a bowling tournament, ski jumping, cross country skiing and a skating show. A Thursday afternoon "Carnival Talent Contest" held at the 250-seat Little Theater of the Memorial Building, selects finalists to perform prior to the Winter Frolic Queen Coronation that night. Preliminary success means Bob's "piano and song," will compete with a mime, an acrobat and tap dancers.

Bob tells LeRoy, *We're gonna take 'em.* Though the setting is considerably more intimate, the show is about the same as that at the Jacket Jamboree.

"This is way too loud," says a spectator standing in the back, his niece a queen candidate.

"Hold 'er down!" others shout.

A number of teen-agers in the audience seem to think the Golden Chords have won. Older, more conventional thinking grants the first-place prize to Raymond Reed, pantomime artist. Second place: Bob, Monte and LeRoy.

At Sammy's pizza, after the relatively positive reaction from the Little Theater crowd, Bob's knee gets to bouncing. *Hey, we really reached 'em. We knocked 'em dead.*

In March, the high school student council talent show is held in the high school auditorium. The school administration informs the students they will be liable for any further damages to the equipment, namely the grand piano; Bob is not asked to perform.

Not to be denied, the Golden Chords, in partnership with a disc jockey, reserve the Hibbing Armory. They drive around town in a convertible, advertising through a rented loudspeaker. *Dance tonight!* A 50¢ ticket gains admission to a "Hop for Teenagers." *Rock 'n' roll!* Your favorite 100 top records "plus intermission entertainment by Hibbing's own GOLDEN CHORDS featuring Monte Edwardson, Leroy Hoikkala and Bobby Zimmerman."

Again, the sound is turned up so loud, Bob's voice can't be clearly heard. "Turn down the amplifiers!" Echo shouts from the side of the stage.

Bobby strikes some as rather bizarre-looking with his chubby cheeks and pompadour hair. Furthermore, he always seems to be one step off. Again, he plays on like they're applauding when some are really booing.

In an attempt to "get famous," the Golden Chords travel the 75 miles to Duluth for the Chmielewski brothers "Polka Hour" television show. They spend two hours waiting at the downtown studio, then wing the usual Little Richard bit and go home.

Less than a year after they convened to practice, Monte and LeRoy, who want more commercial success, begin to evaluate their prospects. Maybe some younger listeners enjoy the music of the Golden Chords as a show. But the older, paying audience, accustomed mainly to polkas, wants music to dance to. Providing a ballroom backdrop is not one of Bob's priorities.

Then there's the singing—the raspy voice and the way he bends the songs way out of shape; they don't come out the same twice. He also *acts* peculiar. Range bookers are not looking for Little Richard-style gyrating. His personality can be difficult. *Take me in my weird way or forget about it.*

After a talent contest, junior college students Jim Propotnick and Ron Taddei approach LeRoy and Monte. They recognize in Monte Hibbing's best young guitarist, a versatile musician able to accompany several acts in one show: a country singer from college, a trio with a steel guitar, the Chords. You can replace a singer easier than a good guitar player.

The prospective new band members set up a record player outdoors, get out the guitars and the *Rockets* are born. "We can't do anything with this band around here," they inform Bob and his Golden Chords enter the afterlife of history.

Propotnick's Fender electric bass is one of the first on the range. Taddei, who bears a resemblance to Buddy Holly, asks Jim and Monte to help him learn to play his Gretsch hollow-body electric guitar. With the support of their parents and the community, the Rockets quickly become popular, entertaining at PTA meetings, youth centers and armories on the Range and, with experience, traveling down to Minneapolis. The St. Louis County Centennial Talent Show holds auditions May 22. Performing are Dave Karakash, singer and guitar player, the Belle Tones from Keewatin, the Rockets and a "local instrumental ensemble."

Monte works on "The Big Black Train," the instrumental he had begun with the Golden Chords, and "Shari Ann," both recorded at Kay Bank studio in Minneapolis. The Rockets sign a contract with Aladdin Record Co., Hollywood, Cal., for "Let Me Know."

"They're The Coolest!" An August newspaper article uses a group photo by Jim's dad, Louis Propotnick. "The Sensational Young Rockets," "a genuine portrayal of the modern trend in music and the interpreters of the 'rock 'n' roll' and the Beat Generation" are preparing to participate in the pageant, "Mesabi—from Arrows To Atoms." With plenty of "the spice and variety that makes great shows greater" the reporter says the Rockets are "tops in modern music."

Bob calls Bill Morris, his drummer cousin in Duluth. *How about getting together?* Morris, originally named Cohen, has been playing jazz with another "cousin," Marsh Shamblott, on piano and Dennis Nylen on stand-up bass. Counting Bob, they comprise "three Hebes and a Swede." The four travel up to Hibbing on weekends. They practice in Bob's living room or bedroom and try to get jobs, such as playing at high school dances. No dice. Bobby is just too wild, such a screamer, they are told.

Now and then, they take a ride in Bobby's blue Ford convertible, usually down to Crippa's to replace guitar strings Bobby has broken.

During the summer of 1958, Bob and Echo continue to go steady. They double-date with Dee Dee Lockhart and Thomas Strick, a 25-year-old miner living on strike insurance. Strick has a 1951 primered Mercury with dual exhausts, fashionably lowered in back—and he's old enough to buy wine and beer. The four drive out to Dupont Lake, Side Lake, and the outdoor theater. There's a party at Dee Dee's, when her parents are gone. Bob is fascinated by a box of poetry Strick says he has written. For his part, Strick sees in Bob dry humor, subtle innuendo and sly comebacks. *But, to love Bob, ya gotta know him.*

Bob travels often to Minneapolis or St. Paul, to listen to music, he tells Echo, but she knows he's seeing other girls. He comes back and rambles on tactlessly about how great everything is in Minnesota's twin metropolises. Everyone so hep, so cool. So different from the bong town of Hibbing. With Bucklen, he visits a black St. Paul neighborhood at Selby Avenue and Dale Street, where Bob introduces John to some young musicians. In Highland Park, he tells Jewish friends he and John are in town to cut a record. Says John is the bass player.

In summer, Bob attends Camp Herzl for the last time. While others play ping pong, he appropriates the piano on the porch of the social hall. Most of the campers don't really dig the kind of music Bob plays any more than the people of Hibbing do. Hard to identify, they guess it might be big-city rhythm-and-blues or else something he wrote himself. One song to be remembered repeats the refrain, "Red lights, red lights."

Red lights. Red lights.
That's what sticks in your mind.
Red lights.

Louis Propotnick

The Rockets, 1958. From left: Ron Taddei, Jim Propotnick, LeRoy Hoikkala, Monte Edwardson.

Above: Junior Prom, 1958. *1959 Hematite* • Below: Band concert, Hibbing High School auditorium, 1959. *Aubin Studio*

Above: John Bucklen. *1958 Hematite* Echo Helstrom. *1958 Hematite* • Below: Johnny Dark aboard "The Wild One." *Johnny Dark*

Howard Street looking east, c. 1960.
Star Tribune/Minneapolis-St. Paul

Above: Looking east from 1st Avenue onto Howard Street. At left, Sammy's Pizza. Stone's clothing store is near the Delvic Hotel, right. *Aubin Studio* • Below: The Rockets join a Howard Street parade to promote an appearance. *LeRoy Hoikkala*

Above left: Post-crash lament for Dick Kangas' car. Above right: Dick Kangas in bedroom "studio" also used by Bob Zimmerman. • Below: A party in Virginia, Minn. Guitarists: John Bucklen, left; Dick Kangas, right. *Richard Kangas*

Above left: *1957 Hematite* • Above right: *1958 Hibbing Tribune?* • Below left and right: *Tribune*.

Above left: Duluth *Herald?* Above right: Bobby Vee, 1959. *Bobby Vee* • Below: Buddy Holly, center, Dion and Frankie Sardo at Green Bay, Wis. *Larry L. Matti*

1959 Hematite

Robert Zimmerman

Chapter 14
Senior
1958-59

Elston Gunn

I think back sometimes to all those people I once did know. It's an incredible story, putting together the pieces. It's like a puzzle, as far as stories go. I meditate on it sometimes, all that craziness.
   <u>Rolling Stone,</u> 1972

THE POLITICAL WORLD

Dillon, Joseph. The St. Paul mayor, defeated in a primary election for Congress.— *McCarthy, Eugene*: Democratic Congressman easily elected to U.S. Senate. McCarthy and Gov. Freeman push "Hubert Humphrey for President".—*Sandburg, Carl.* Democrats fete "rich proletarian poet," creator of "Lincoln Industry" and "minstrel of homespun school of doggerel and affectation."—*Guevara, Ernesto.* Castro lieutenant killed in fighting between the Cuban government and rebel forces.—*Pineapples, Dole.* 50-star U.S. flag unfurled as Hawaii becomes a state.

KING HEMATITE

They say that your ore ain't worth digging./That it's much cheaper down/In the South American towns/Where the miners work almost for nothing.
   "North Country Blues," 1963

"What Iron Ore Mining Means to Me and My Community." A Chisholm high school senior writes: "To those on the Iron Range, mining means everything. The business establishments of each community are patronized mainly by mine workers. If the mines suffer a setback, so do the people of the town."

Approaching the Christmas shopping season, the Hibbing *Tribune* castigates local Scrooges: "The only thing wrong with just a few Hibbing people is that they are a menace which contaminates everything about them by preaching the doctrine of hopelessness and pessimism." But all too soon, comes the chill of New Year Present. "No one need inform the Range that a recession exists here, and that men and women are out of employment, but we don't like the idea of it being publicized over the breadth of the land, due to a news feature that appeared in a recent Sunday issue of a Minneapolis paper... True, there are breadwinners out of jobs, a situation we know is acute, but to point to the entire area as suffering from lack of food, clothing, medical aid, etc. is exaggerated indeed. The Range country can take care of its own unemployed. It needs no pressure from the outside."

A national strike in July is joined by 13,606 workers on the Mesabi. Registration of the unemployed begins at the Memorial building but strikers are expected to manage without assistance as long as possible.

Fanning the flicker of hope, *National Geographic* puffs a putative "New Era on the Great Lakes" with the opening of the St. Lawrence Seaway. Among ore boats, the 729-foot Edmund Fitzgerald will travel from Silver Bay to Toledo carrying taconite, "the latest development in the steel industry, tapping a bountiful supply of raw material for mills faced with depletion of the rich Michigan and Minnesota ores. The rich direct-shipping ores, even including the output of the famous open-pit mine at Hibbing, never amounted to more than 5 percent of the range."

POSITIVELY HOWARD STREET

"I couldn't tell you which phase of housekeeping I like the best," says Mrs. John Oshima, local candidate for Mrs. America. The Japanese-American mother of four, who had lived through World War II in a relocation camp, adds, "Perhaps someday someone of a minority group may represent the United States."

Chiropractors on the Range advise adults to leave hula hoops to their children, having treated numerous back problems since the fad began.—"X-ray" fluoroscope shoe machines are banned because of radiation hazard.—The new beltline highway sees numerous accidents, with drivers turning from wrong lanes and confusing "yield right of way" signs with stop signs.

Contractor Max Gray builds a subdivision on an ore dump. With numerous medical personnel among the early buyers, the elevated plat is dubbed "Pill Hill."—Daylight savings time is voted in by the village council for the first time.—Stone's clothing store, run by Bobby Zimmerman's uncle and grandmother, moves slightly, to 110 E. Howard.—Responding to protests downwind, the village council drops consideration of the gravel pit on Dillon's farm west of the village as a site for garbage disposal.

THE GARMAKER SYNDROME

Hockey: The Russian team plays the U.S. Nationals in the Memorial Building arena.—At Green Bay, Wis., Kleffman Rink brings home Hibbing's second curling championship in the three years of the U.S. tournament.—The Milwaukee Braves reach the World Series for the second year, this time losing to the New York Yankees.

OVER THE RAINBOW

But you are a star...
Yeah, well, I guess so...but I can shine for who I want to shine for. You know what I mean?

<u>Bat Chain Puller</u>, pub. 1990

With the Florian Zabach Variety show is that well-known funny man, Henny Youngman. As he passes through the Androy hotel lobby, Youngman encounters guests from David Zimmerman's bar mitzvah.
"How about coming to our party?"
"If ya wanna pay me, I'll come in," Youngman says.

Now showing. The number of conventional theaters is down nationally, but among more than 4,000 outdoor theaters is the Hibbing Drive-In, showing *Peyton Place, The Bridge on the River Kwai, Vertigo, Man of a Thousand Faces* and *The Sound and the Fury*. Downtown is *The Big Country* with Gregory Peck. *Rio Bravo* with John Wayne, Dean Martin and Ricky Nelson, "the rockin' baby-faced gunfisted kid." *The Girl In the Bikini* with Brigitte Bardot. "You'll see more of Brigitte than ever before." Horror movies: *The Blob, The Fly, The Thing, It Came From Outer Space.*

On *American Bandstand,* a television show hosted by Dick Clark, 29, popular singers pretend to be singing their own records while the teenage audience dances on camera. After what he considers a decade of the new music, Clark produces a documentary.

According to syndicated columnist Gilbert, favorite male singing stars are Ricky Nelson, Pat Boone, Frank Sinatra and Frankie Avalon. Elvis Presley, in serious decline, plunges to sixth place. Most promising new male recording stars: Fabian, Stagger Lee, Johnny Nash, and Earl Grant.

Teen-agers seem to be turning from rock 'n' roll to the Kingston Trio—smooth, witty, young crew-cuts mining the folk idiom: "Hang down your head, Tom Dooley." The folk revival immediately splits between *ethnics*, who prefer ballads by "anonymous," and *popularizers,* who prefer topical songs by college kids in crew cuts and clean cotton shirts. Arthur Ferrante and Louis Teicher, popular duo-pianists, appear in Hibbing, representing a Top 40 already straying from rock 'n' roll. The most popular hit of the year is "Venus" by Frankie Avalon. The favorite all-time song named by teen-agers is "Stardust."

The top-rated TV show, for the second year, is *Gunsmoke*, featuring Matt Dillon. Celebrities on the Range: Hugh Beaumont, TV daddy of "Leave It To Beaver," purchases a 30-acre island in Itasca county. Jerry Mathers, "the Beaver," visits relatives in birch-laden Keewatin.

NORTH COUNTRY FAIR

You're pretty much ruled by nature up there. You might have to sort of fall into line with that, regardless of how you're feeling that day or what you might want to do with your life or what you think about. And it still is like that, I think.

<u>*Playboy,*</u> *1984*

A man driving a 1958 Lincoln Premiere, out on Highway 73, looks up from his rich man's reverie and sees a bull moose standing in the road. Too late. The impact breaks the moose's back and detaches its antlers. The Lincoln is wrecked, the man uninjured.—*January:* Airport temps of minus 35, 43 and 39 are the nation's coldest for those days. *Mid-May:* A heavy gale blows down trees, television aerials and light poles. *June:* "The secret of mosquito extermination is destroying their breeding spots," says the *Tribune,* anticipating another barrage of DDT.

BLACKBOARD JUNGLE

You let that become your story...you sort of covered up your parents, and your old friends...
Did I?
Well, that was the impression it gave...
Jann...you're talking about old friends, and best friends...if you want to go by those standards, I haven't seen my best friends for over 15 years.

<u>Rolling Stone</u>, *1969*

Oh baby, you're terrif, the most, *the utmost,* jazzy, a beaut, dreamy, gone, *real gone,* all gone, cool, *real cool,* swinging, top dog, s'wonderful, dig? Cool caper, *bug the fuzz,* out to lunch, *a blue moon,* a dragger, a cat, a pearl, a neat beat. Square, *harvey,* amoeba, a nose, a brownie, *a drag,* dig? Flaked out, flicks, *gross,* pad, rumble scene, turf.

"But Mommy, I don't want to go to Europe." *Shut up and keep swimming.* "I don't care who you are fat man get those reindeer off my roof." *What weighs 1,000 pounds, has four legs, is yellow and flies?*

Favorite actor for boys: Tony Curtis. For girls: Marlon Brando. Best-liked pictures: *Gigi, The Defiant Ones, Cat on a Hot Tin Roof.* Most promising new actors: Edward (Kookie) Byrnes and David Nelson. Great lovers: Cary Grant, Rock Hudson, Marlon Brando. Kissing and necking (caresses from the head up) are terrif—but most teen-agers deplore petting (caresses from the head down), even for steady sweethearts. Oh baby! Half of boys would not marry a girl who had "gone farther." 32 percent of boys smoke; 30 percent drink beer, 19 percent drink alcohol other than beer; 37 percent want to be famous athletes, 31 percent jet pilots, 26 percent atomic scientists; 33 percent of girls want modeling careers.

What are the three worst sins?
Poison gas used against civilians, deserting a pregnant girlfriend, adultery.
Would you stick out an unhappy marriage?
"No," say 77 percent.
Should Pop do the dishes?
"Yes," say 83 percent of girls.
"No," say 55 percent of boys.

Teens agree the government should *not* pay their college tuition; their *parents* should.

Nuclear energy will destroy mankind, say 90 percent.

In April, Larry Fabbro leads the Catholic Youth Activities campaign asking graduating seniors to pledge not to drink during commencement festivities. "Better than a publicity pamphlet or a million dollars worth of television commercials,

Hibbing High School's students speak for the school, both on and off the campus," heralds the Hibbing High School yearbook, *Hematite*. "More important than winning the game is the town's opinion of us . . . Students can be classified more than one way. Strangers may see them, observe their actions, and shrug, saying, 'Oh, hell, just high school kids.' Or they may say, 'They're from Hibbing High School.'"

"Which one do you like best?" "Don't you think this one's too serious?" "Girls and boys compare graduation photos and labor over that all important decision of which one to add to the Rogues' Gallery of HHS."

Now showing. Movies like *The Blackboard Jungle* and *The Wild One* exploit a popular juvenile image, according to a syndicated column. "The delinquent is black-jacketed and longhaired. He runs around on a bright and noisy motorcycle or in a souped-up hot rod. He is brutal. He is cruel. He is restless. He is dangerously free and uninhibited sexually. He is aggressive. He travels with the pack. He is heartless." But what about the "lost generation" of the 1920s? They became substantial citizens who were, in turn, incensed at their own teen-agers dancing to the wild Benny Goodman swing music of the '30s. "Just so will many of the youngsters now addicted to rock 'n' roll become substantial, although complaining, parents of the next generation."

The decline of the aforementioned Goodman-style swing is attributed to television, which "brought to the small combos of guitar slappers the popularity formerly accorded to the big touring bands."

Also promoting guitar slappers is WHB, Kansas City, the first all-rock radio station, spinning records like "Great Balls of Fire" by Jerry Lee Lewis; "Good Golly, Miss Molly" by Little Richard; "Donna" by Ritchie Valens; "Chantilly Lace" by The Big Bopper; "Rumble" by Link Wray; "Whole Lotta Lovin'" by Fats Domino; "Summertime Blues" by Eddie Cochran; "Witch Doctor" by David Seville and "The Purple People Eater" by Sheb Wooley.

Popular dances tend to one syllable each: *twist, walk, shake* and *fish*. "Stereo" brings to life the 33 rpm record album business. The first transistor radios hit the market. Elvis is drafted.

(Two 500-pound canaries.)

BOBBY

Buddy Holly was a poet, way ahead of his time...I played with Buddy Holly in North Dakota, South Dakota, ballrooms, youth dances...

<u>*No Direction Home*</u>*, pub. 1986*

...Buddy Holly...at the Armory...with Link Wray. I don't remember the Big Bopper...But I saw Ritchie Valens. And Buddy Holly, yeah. He was great. He was incredible. I mean, I'll never forget the image of seeing Buddy Holly up on the bandstand. And he died—it must have been a week after that. It was unbelievable.

<u>*Rolling Stone*</u>*, 1984*

I used to play rock-and-roll...when I was fifteen, fourteen, and by the time I was seventeen you just couldn't make it anymore at all unless you wanted to be a sideman and live forever in carnivals or recording studios.

(1965) <u>The Hollow Horn</u>, pub. 1991

I used to play the rock and roll piano, but I don't want to say who it was for because the cat will try to get hold of me...I did it a long time ago, when I was seventeen years old. I used to play a country piano too.

<u>Bob Dylan: The Early Years: A Retrospective</u>, 1972/90

I played piano when I was seventeen. I played piano for this rock 'n' roll singer. His name is Bobby Vee and he's a big star now, I guess...

That was in Fargo, North Dakota. Then we went all around the midwest. Went to Wisconsin, Iowa, toured around there, and then I left...

I was with him for about, uh, just about every night for about a month or so. And then as soon as I left him he got on another recording label and then I saw his picture in a big picture magazine...

Billy James Interview, 1961

I was playing rock 'n' roll when I was 13 and 14 and 15, but I had to quit when I was 16 or 17 because I couldn't make it that way. The image of the day was Frankie Avalon or Fabian, or this whole athletic supercleanness bit, you know, which if you didn't have that, you couldn't make any friends. I played rock 'n' roll when I was in my teens, yeah, I played semi-professionally piano with rock 'n' roll groups. About 1958 or 1959, I discovered Odetta, Harry Belafonte, that stuff, and I became a folk singer.

<u>Chicago Daily News</u>, 1965

You must've discarded rock 'n' roll around 1960. I did that in 1957. I couldn't make it as a rock 'n' roll singer then. There were too many groups. I used to play piano. I made some records too.

<u>Los Angeles Free Press</u>, 1965

I played rock 'n' roll music, you know, when I was sixteen ...fifteen years old!...I quit doing it because, uh, it just wasn't...I couldn't make it. You know — like, its just too hard...

(1966) <u>Hungry As a Raccoon</u>, pub. 1993

I tried to make it in rock-and-roll when rock-and-roll was a piece of cream...Buddy Holly was dead. Little Richard was becoming a preacher. And Gene Vincent was leaving the country. I wrote the kind of stuff you write when you have no place to live and you're very wrapped up in the fire pump. I nearly killed myself with pity and agony.
  <u>Saturday Evening Post</u>, *1966*

If they had a good time booing, I mean there's just nothing I can say...If they didn't have a good time booing, I gotta...think something's wrong
  Nat Hentoff Interview, 1965

There aren't really any mistakes in life. They might seem to knock you out of proportion at the time; but if you have the courage and the ability and the confidence to go on, well then that failure, you can't look at it as a failure, you just have to look at it as a blessing in a way.
  <u>New Musical Express</u>, *1978*

I was about seventeen, eighteen, and I knew there was nothing I ever wanted, materially, and I just made it from there, from that feeling. But then I realized I couldn't make it with a group...I had to do it alone. So I decided to do it alone through the folk thing.
  (1978) <u>Bob Dylan: The Early Years, A Retrospective</u>, *1990*

I just like the sound. I just like to hear, you know, gospel-type girl sounds
  Toby Cresswell Interview, 1986

And then I had another band with my cousin from Duluth. I played, you know, rock & roll, rhythm & blues. And then that died out, pretty much, in my last year of high school.
  And after that, I remember I heard a record—I think maybe it was the Kingston Trio or Odetta or something like that—and I sorta got into folk music. Rock & roll was pretty much finished. And I traded my stuff for a Martin that they don't sell anymore...the first acoustic guitar I had.
  <u>Rolling Stone</u>, *1984*

The first thing that turned me on to folk singing was Odetta. I heard a record of hers in a record store, back when you could listen to records there in the store. That was in '58 or something like that. Right then and there, I went out and traded my electric guitar and amplifier for an acoustical guitar, a flat-top Gibson...I learned all the

songs on that record. It was her first and the songs were Mule Skinner, Jack of Diamonds, Water Boy, Buked and Scorned.
   Playboy, **1978**

   It's a common thing to change your name...I wouldn't pick a name unless I thought I was that person...Names are labels so we can refer to one another. But deep inside us we don't have a name. I just chose that name and it stuck.
   (1968) *Bob Dylan In His Own Words,* pub. **1978**

Wild Bobby Zimmerman! Starring at the St. Louis County Fair, Hibbing, in early September 1958, "Two combos recently cutting records"—the "Rockettes" and the Satintones. "Giving a wild, 'Elvis' rendition" is "Bobby Zimmerman of the Satintones." Wild Bobby, dressed in jeans and a cowboy shirt, his hair standing straight up like Little Richard. Wild Bobby Zimmerman, backed by his Duluth cousin, Bill Cohen/Morris on drums, Marsh Shamblott on piano and Dennis Nylen on string bass.

   Wild Bobby, playing his heart out, is met with the usual mixture of appreciation, embarrassment, bemusement, befuddlement and boos. *You call that singing? Too damn loud!* He even comes away with some kind of blue ribbon. Benny Orlando, delivery man for the Zimmerman store, kids him, *Boy, you guys are pretty good. You sing and I'll be your manager.*

   In what amounts to a battle of the bands, the Rockets blast off with their Buddy Holly and Elvis favorites. While they play, young fellas from the Reveliers and Teenbeats watch their every move. The Rockets are the band to beat on the Range.

   When Ron Taddei departs for college, a position opens for a rhythm guitar player and vocalist. Bob talks to Monte Edwardson and Monte reports to the others. How about giving Zimmerman another try? LeRoy and Monte had backed him in the Golden Chords. The Rockets are skeptical, knowing Bob is not a big draw. But when Bob arrives at Propotnick's to practice, he seems to fit right in. They get a few gigs, at the Airport Bar, Moose hall, Hibbing youth center. If there's a piano Bob plays it, if not, he brings his guitar.

   Quickly, the problems that broke up the Golden Chords recur. With Taddei, the Rockets had been having fun. Bob is depressingly *serious* about his particular kind of music. *Dig.* His songs are slower, not danceable. *Dig the rebop.* He wants to go off on tangents. *Dig the rebop, daddy-O.* They listen politely, make a few tapes. *See, you guys go 'doo wop.'* They listen; then the Rockets turn on the record player and go back to covering the top hits of the day. *I want you to go 'doo wop doo wop.'*

   The Rockets know that their fans want "Rave On" exactly like the Crickets and "Rock Around the Clock" exactly like the Comets. *Little things you say an' do.* Bob can't or won't cover the numbers faithfully. *Make me wanna be with you.* He wants to play songs no one ever heard of. *Doo woppa doo.* And, looking at it practically, "Little Bobby," with his baby face and pompadour doesn't have a lot of sex appeal.

   After a conference at Propotnick's, the Rockets don't ask Bob back. In his place, they recruit Dave Karakash, whom they've seen at high school talent shows.

He's tall and dark-haired, resembles Elvis, sings like Elvis; and women love him. The Rockets quickly become more popular than ever.

The most prominent local rival to the Rockets are, from nearby Chisholm, the Renowns: Ione Vake, vocals and bass guitar; Tony Tomasetti, guitar; Hibbing High School junior and hockey player Warren Grillo, drums. Like the Rockets, they play teen dances, talent shows and high school programs. When Zimmerman shows up at Italian Hall for a Catholic Youth Association dance and wants to sit in, he is told the band does not need another guitar player or another set of Bob Zimmerman's blues.

Much later in the year, Fran Matosich receives a call from Val Peterson, the Hibbing junior high school music teacher. "I have a young man here who has written some music and would like to perform with backup singers. Rather than asking some high school girls, would you three consider helping out?"

Fran seems to remember the young man from the Itasca county fair the previous autumn, where Fran had performed with two other Hibbing Junior College students, Kathy Dasovic and Mary DeFonso. All were candidates for Queen of the Keewatin Centennial and former members of the Belle Tones. Usually a McGuire Sisters type of group, for the fair, they had performed a rhythm-and-blues song written by a friend.

This is Bob Zimmerman. In the high school music room, he at first appears shy but the young man soon lays out some chording on the piano and the girls catch on to what he wants. As he talks about the music, he acquires the aura of authority. *This is the way it goes.* The girls fill in as they best they can.

With a couple of Bob's friends, they practice at Fran's house in Keewatin on a Sunday afternoon. They also use the empty auditorium in Keewatin school where Kathy Dasovic's dad is the principal.

Bob is not entirely a stranger. Kathy's mom and Bob's mom play bridge together. Fran's mother also knows Beatty from Feldman's clothing store. Fran's mother is impressed: here is this kid who just *knows* he has talent. He's polite but his conversation is limited to the music.

Somebody in Bob's group says, *If we cut a record, would you back us?*

Sure. Well, maybe.

Bob wants the girls to sing background on an R&B song he may or may not have written himself. They are to repeat the phrase: *Drippety drop. Drip drip drippety drop.* Three big college girls backing up a little high school kid, singing—*drippety drop?*

Bob's lead guitarist, John Bucklen, is nervous. He doesn't have to say *drippety drop* but this, his first public performance, takes place before 1,800 students.

This is the Jacket Jamboree, the 1959 school awards assembly, highlighted by the coronation of Queen Jessie "Cookie" Lomoro and King Dick Helstrom. To better cope with the vast arena, Bucklen borrows an amplifier from Jim Propotnick of the Rockets. Old friend Bill Marinac on string bass completes the ensemble. According to the high school newspaper, Bob sings "Time Goes By" and "Swing, Dad, Swing," with vocal assistance from Kathy, Mary and "Franny Kay." The relatively tame performance doesn't attract the controversy of the previous year.

Well, you were okay, Bob tells the girls.

At the Jamboree, Bob's bassist Bill Marinac also joins John Sheppard, Don Koenig and Jerry Scofield for "Night Train" and "When the Saints Come Marching In." Concluding the program are the Rockets: Dave Karakash, Monte Edwardson, LeRoy Hoikkala and Propotnick. They do a number reported as "It," and Eddie Cochran's "Come On Everybody."

Bob continues to perform around town. He rents the Little Theater at the Memorial building with "some guys from out of town." It's more of a practice session than anything; unheated garages can get pretty cold when it's forty-below outside. Only a few invited friends attend.

Her son's budding career also feeling a touch of frost, Bob's mother calls a promoter in Duluth: "Why don't you encourage him?" Bob too looks beyond Hibbing for friends and opportunities. He socializes with summer camp friends and his own relatives in Minneapolis and St. Paul. At parties, he gets out his guitar and sings, to the enjoyment of some and the annoyance of others. A female friend calls him the "Pie-Eyed Piper." He hangs out at the Ten O'Clock Scholar, a beatnik coffee house frequented by University High School and college students. His campus acquaintances believe Bob "hitchhikes down" from Hibbing, although he travels principally with his father's car or by Greyhound bus. He is sitting with Harvey Abrams in the Scholar when he meets Bonnie Beecher, a high school senior who says she likes folk music. "I'm sure you know about folkies," mocks Abrams. "You probably know the Kingston Trio and 'The Blue and the Grey.'"

But she invokes Cat Iron and Sleepy John Estes and people like that.

Oh yeah? Says Bobby. How do you know these people?

"I've got all the records at home."

Oh yeah. Bob concludes the conversation by borrowing her records for a long time.

Echo Helstrom, Bob's Hibbing girlfriend and a kindred spirit for almost a year, can no longer ignore his weekend excursions. It is increasingly apparent that he goes abroad to do more than hear music.

An interest in R&B and a sense of mutual rebellion had brought them together a year previous. Perhaps, it seemed, they would be married. But it is not to be. Echo was born on the wrong side of the beltline; Bobby is the pampered son of a well-off Howard Street businessman and his socialite wife. Echo is a blonde Scandinavian; he is the child of Jews born of Jews who were born of Jews. His forebears, Boruch Edelstein, Shabsie Solemovitz and Zigman Zimmerman, suffered at the whim of Russian czars and Christians. Tradition, born of trial, dictates Bob's children will also be born of Jews.

Not long after their senior year begins, Echo finds Bob in the high school hallway, boasting about the fun he's been having in the Cities. She thrusts his I.D. bracelet into his hand.

"You might as well have this."

He pushes her against the lockers and whispers.

Not here!

That night at Echo's place out by Maple Hill, his tears fall like rain.

What do you think you're doing?

They talk desperately in the car. He plays dumb.

"You *know* what's wrong."

But he just wants to be melodramatic. She jumps out of the car and runs in the house. It's over.

On weekends, Bobby sometimes hangs around Duluth. Much larger and more lively than Hibbing, the Lake Superior port is the place Bobby was born, where his father was born, and where his shoe-man grandfather landed from Russia less than fifty years earlier. Sometimes he meets Judy Rubin, up from the Cities to stay with a friend. Since Camp Herzl, she and Bob have had a friendly relationship, although her parents object. To them, Bobby looks suspiciously like some kind of rebel, especially when he shows up on a motorcycle.

Bobby's Duluth buddies include Steve Friedman from Camp Herzl, and Steve's non-Jewish buddy, Jim Beron, a high-school dropout who has actually "done time" at Red Wing reformatory—if only for truancy. Although the three are heavily into rhythm-and-blues, they also tune into WLS-Chicago, Nashville or Duluth's own "Pat the Cat" Cadigan. When there's a rock 'n' roll band playing, they find it. Sometimes, while cruising Superior Street, they stop at Coney Island for hot dogs or at Sammy's for pizza. Their ever-present cigarette smoke is accompanied by a cloud of sarcastic remarks. Duluth is bad news; Hibbing is worse. The Superior Street late night raconteurs are somehow above all that. *Dig the rebop, bongs.*

One night, they pick up three girls, who sit in the back seat—until Bob grosses them out and the girls jump off at a red light. When a fourth buddy insults "niggers," Bob gets hot and threatens to run him out of town.

Sometimes they drive up to Hibbing, where it's always quiet. One night, Bobby claims he has to find a bald-headed girl. *You gotta see her.* Friedman and Beron and Zimmerman run around Howard Street like the Marx brothers, ducking into little shops and hamburger joints. *You gotta see this bald-headed girl.* They do not find her.

Zimmerman takes them to the Virginia radio station, WHLB, to meet the disc jockey, Jim Dandy. A black guy on the Range—with a million jazz records. A real gone cat. Somewhere in the midst of the enormous Mesabi winter, they have a snowball fight.

To Beron, Zimmerman seems bright, creative, funny, light-hearted and serious—pretty hip for the times. He will make a good lawyer some day.

Other kids in Hibbing get drunk more often than Bob and John do but they too drink on occasion. Sometimes, they go down to the basement rec room and sample shots of Scotch from Abe's bar. Sometimes, they find their way to a house party. They show up at Linda's, wearing black leather jackets. Somebody brings beer in and Linda's father throws them all out. Other times, Bob is evicted for making a racket when a racket is not wanted. In Virginia, there's a party upstairs with plenty of guitars and girls around. They put the beer and whiskey away when they find out Dad is coming. He goes back to work and they get out the booze.

One night, Bob calls John Bucklen.
I'm gonna beat the shit outa you.
You're going to beat the shit out of me? Okay, I'll meet you on the corner.
Along the placid sidewalks of Hibbing hobbles the chubby little high school kid—the loner, the juvenile delinquent, the rebel without a cause—spotlighted by one street light, then another. *Bucklen!* As he approaches, you can hear him cussing. He teeters into each light, resembling Jett Rink, about to give his *Giant*

speech. *Yer not firin' me. I quit.* He staggers up to Bucklen and takes a swing. Completely misses and falls down.
Boy howdy!
The confrontation is terminated when Bobby barfs in Bucklen's doorway.

Dick Kangas, a 1957 Hibbing High School graduate and Elvis enthusiast, operates a truck for Kelly's Furniture, waiting for a chance to get out of Hibbing. With Bob, he usually finds himself driving—and footing the bill.

Kangas takes Bob and John cruising along the Range in his 1953 Ford, looking for dances. They're leaving Calumet when they see three girls walking on the road.
Wanna ride?
A typical conference is held inside the car. *Who gets the chubby blonde?* A parallel parley takes place on the road. *Who gets the chubby little curly-head?*

Since Kangas owns the car, he gets first choice and picks Judy, the best looking of the three; John gets the other one; Bob—the blonde. After a party at Snowball Lake, they're cruising through Calumet when some old guy comes running toward the car and the girls sound a warning, *Beat it, here comes a cop!*
It's just an old guy. He can't catch me.
But the cop runs in front of the car, waving.
Shut it off! Shut the car off!
While the cop is writing down the license number, Kangas starts the car again. The cop jumps up and starts yelling. *Never do that again!*
The girls are laughing. John and Bob, too, like it's a big joke. *Bug the fuzz!*
The same night, Kangas appears in Calumet to pay his fine for reckless driving. It's a little gimmick they have. Give you a ticket and send you right over to the justice of the peace. *Har dee har har.*

On Saturday, January 31, the Winter Dance Party comes to the Duluth Armory: Mexican-American singer/songwriter Ritchie Valens ("La Bamba," "Donna," "Come On, Let's Go"), disc jockey The Big Bopper ("Chantilly Lace"), Dion and the Belmonts ("I Wonder Why," "Don't Pity Me") and singer Frankie Sardo, all assisted by Waylon Jennings ("Jolé Blon") on backup guitar. Perhaps the most popular is Buddy Holly, 22, a Lubbock, Texas, native. Holly is usually pictured wearing thick dark-framed eyeglasses under a bountiful mop of curly locks. For many, he's a model—an ordinary but soulful young man, standing out front of his band, singing songs he has written. You can't go to a dance without hearing "Rave On," "Maybe Baby" and "That'll Be The Day."

Some of the Rockets—LeRoy, Monte and Jim—go up together to see Holly. Their former associate, Zimmerman, according to his account, also attends, though he doesn't say with whom. It's a brisk night, even for the north country. The temperature at the ice-racked shore of Lake Superior is -25 degrees Fahrenheit with 15 mph northwest winds. *Oh baby!*

During the concert, a replacement school bus is shuttled in to take the musicians the seven hour drive to Green Bay, Wis. But the bus heater isn't working and a.m. temperatures are still 25 below or worse. When the bus breaks down in northern Wisconsin, Charles Bunch, the drummer of the stranded company, gets frostbite.

Reaching Green Bay finally, the troupe plays the Riverside Ballroom and moves on to Iowa, for a concert at Clear Lake, near Mason City. As soon as he can, supposedly to gain time to launder some shirts, but most likely, to avoid another cold overland ordeal, Holly charters a plane.

It's a shocker. "3 Nationally Known Singers Die In Crash." At 12:30 a.m., February 3, after the Clear Lake performance, the Beechcraft Bonanza carrying Ritchie Valens, Jiles Perry Richardson, a.k.a. The Big Bopper, and Buddy Holly, crashes in a snowy corn field, killing all aboard. *Three new stars in Heaven.*

"A year at Hibbing High without a talent show would be like Christmas without snow," says the school newspaper. The ten featured acts of March 1959, do not include Bob Zimmerman nor is he mentioned at the College Capers talent show, where the "top-notch" Rockets present their rock 'n' roll singing and dancing to great acclaim.

In May 1959, Bob and Dick Kangas get together in Kangas' bedroom, where Kangas has a recording setup, complete with microphone. They tape one song Dick has written and three that Bob may or may not have written. "I got a baby," "I got a new girl," "I got a something else." You might call it rhythm-and-blues. Bob's voice is smooth and melodic—for him.

As a high school scholar, Bob burns hot and cold. In crabby, "old" Miss Barron's English 12, oral reports are required. But he will not, or cannot, get up in front of the class. Without a guitar or piano, his speaking is nothing more than a fedora of mumbles. He even pulls his desk away from the others, to the great irritation of Miss Barron. Receiving unsatisfactory evaluations, they say he composes a petition in study hall. *Ya gotta sign this. Get her out of this school.* With Bob, you can't take him too serious.

Seniors receive a dose of liberal thinking in Charlie Miller's Social Studies 12. Union president and Democratic Farm Labor Party captain Miller talks about the strikes on the Range and berates mining company "goons."

In "dramatics," Bob is for the moment more attuned to the milieu; he grabs a guitar, mounts a platform and imitates Elvis. A sophomore girl is amazed to hear wild singing coming from a quiet boy who usually keeps to himself. She finds Bob witty and hilarious. One of the class skits involves only the two of them and they have to rehearse together "upstairs." Bob writes in her yearbook that she should have won an Academy Award for her performance.

After school, Bob gives a classmate and her cousin a ride—and embarrasses them with off-color jokes.

As graduation approaches, the Senior Class Banquet is planned. On the entertainment committee are Keith Johnson, chairman; Peg Teske; Bonnie Marinac; and Bob Zimmerman.

The high school newspaper, *Hi-Times*, reminisces: "Midnight serenades, Rock an' Roll at the Youth Center, Junior-Senior Prom, class plays, someone to talk to at the next locker—these have been the most fondly remembered associations . . . that delicious mixture of excitement, maturity, pleasure, and fear that you felt when you were first introduced to high school life and its changing classes every hour? . . . Perhaps after these ceremonies there will be many fellow seniors whom you shall never see again, for each senior will follow the trail which both he and destiny have carved out."

The high school yearbook, *Hematite*, as is the custom, characterizes each senior with a few words under his photo. Bob Zimmerman, credited with a nominal connection with Latin Club and Social Studies Club, aspires, according to the editors, "To join Little Richard."

At Baccalaureate, 425 graduates are told by Rev. Edward S. Marti, "Life is so arranged so as to oscillate between the hammer and the anvil." Graduates, he says, have more advantages than ever before. "They must use these advantages to hammer away at injustices, to preserve religion and the laws of God, and to work for the unfortunate and the underprivileged."

The 1959 class motto: *"I am a part of all that I have met."*
The class flower is the forget-me-not.

The senior honor roll reiterates a familiar sequence: "Dennis Wichman, Laura Wilcox, Robert Zimmerman." Wichman is named 1959 Merit Scholar. Wichman and Wilcox are recognized with gold "Hibbing" honor pins. Though he has achieved the honor roll off and on throughout his high school years, Bobby does not receive a pin, which requires four appearances in a single year.

Abe and Beatty throw a big graduation party but Bob says he won't be there. *Can't you just come for a few minutes?* Bob makes the scene, and stays longer than expected.

At midnight, he takes a long walk, perhaps beginning at the beginning: the edge of the mine—returning through the lightless ghost town of his mother's youth to the mercury vapors of Howard Street. Now past curfew age, he can relax over a last cherry pie *a la mode* at the L&B cafe. In the early morning, he heads toward home, past the Androy Hotel, where dim lights within suggest visitors from another planet—one that he now anticipates traveling to. At the high school, the American flag flaps and snaps in the chill wind and the boy of the north country pulls his collar up around his ears.

At 2 a.m., he returns to the 7th Avenue house, where Beatty and a cleaning woman are finishing their work. *It was all right*, he admits. On the table is a pile of gifts, including a set of Leadbelly 78s from one of his relatives. It was better than all right.

The next day, Bob almost shouts over the phone to John Bucklen, *I've discovered something great!*

Bucklen listens to the record. It's an old thirties guy singing "The Rock Island Line," "Midnight Special," and "Goodnight Irene." John thinks, *this isn't great, it's okay*. Bobby thinks it's great.

The night after commencement, a Saturday, Crippa music brings pop singer and Elvis imitator, Harold Jenkins, a.k.a. Conway Twitty, to the Memorial building. A guy with a number one top-forty rock 'n' roll hit, "It's Only Make Believe," coming to Hibbing! *People see us everywhere, they think you really care—*

Bob and John join several hundred others in a hall that has held many thousands. *But it's o-only make bele-e-eve.* After the concert, Twitty signs autographs. Kangas takes the pen and jokes, "Where do you want me to sign?" Twitty's guitar players set down their instruments and glare. *Wise guy.*

Sorry there were so few people, Kangas says.

It doesn't matter, I get paid the same, retorts Twitty.

Enthralled by Twitty's Gretsch-wielding guitar player, Bob and John tell him, "Boy, you're really good."

"Next time, maybe I'll take my gloves off." *Har dee har har.*

Twitty stands outside by his white Cadillac convertible and signs more autographs. When he drives off, a bunch of bongs follow him.

A few days later, Bob borrows his dad's car and heads down to St. Paul with Bucklen. On the way, they visit Bill Morris, who plays "Topsy" for them. They stop at Camp Herzl to visit a girl counselor from Highland Park.

In St. Paul, Bucklen stays at his aunt's house, Bob with more cousins. As they travel around the Twin Cities, Bob tells anyone who will listen that he is down to cut a record and Bucklen is his bass player. At parties, Bob plays piano, impressing people with how *talented* he is.

Later that summer, Bucklen is working for the Green Giant canning company at LeSueur, Minn. After work, he watches a dance party on Minneapolis Channel 11. To his amazement, he sees Bob with some Jewish kids, including his drummer cousin, playing rock 'n' roll. John notes that the lead guitarist wields an impressive Stratocaster guitar. These would seem, John thinks, to be the Satintones. John calls the television station and leaves a message. Bob calls back and drives out to LeSueur with two other guys.

A little later, in Fargo, North Dakota, Bobby Shane and the Poor Boys want a piano player for Jerry Lee Lewis tunes. Ron Joelson, a friend, knows such a cat. He had met Elston Gunnn at a summer camp. Gunnn had come to stay at Joelson's house until Ron's mother could no longer tolerate his "singing" and Gunnn moved to an apartment in town, supported by a job busing tables at the Red Apple Cafe.

The Poor Boys take Gunnn to a few jobs but he can only play if there's a piano available and only in the key of C. The Poor Boys prefer to limit Gunnn's singing, which to them sounds like an inferior version of Ernest Tubb. Gunnn starts above the note, slides down through it and winds up somewhere in the subterranean. Furthermore, Gunnn's ragamuffin look does not match the glowing white socks and slick ducktails of the Poor Boys. When the manager of the popular Crystal Ballroom says *that guy's gotta go* —Elston Gunnn is gone, but not forgotten.

Another young man in Fargo wants to be a singer in a rock 'n' roll band. When Robert Velline saves enough paper-route money for a $30 guitar, he is allowed to join big brother Bill's jam sessions.

The Vellines' big chance comes unexpectedly when Buddy Holly, Ritchie Valens and The Big Bopper, beginning a flight to a Fargo concert, crash in Iowa. The Fargo radio station promoting the show asks for local acts to fill in and the now-named *Shadows* are ready to oblige. High school sophomore Robert becomes *Bobby Vee*.

After the show, a local talent agent signs them up. On June 1, with their own $500, *Bobby Vee and the Shadows* record "Suzie Baby," at Soma records in Minneapolis. "Suzie Baby" hits number one in Fargo, Duluth, Minneapolis, Hibbing and Eau Claire, Wis.

In August 1959, the Shadows want to add a saxophonist or piano player to their three guitarists and drummer. What luck, when an 18-year-old piano-playing dishwasher introduces himself to Bill Velline in Sam Paper's Recordland. He says his name is Elston Gunn (soon dropping one of the superfluous "N"s) and he has recently played piano with Conway Twitty.

Bill auditions "Gunn" at Fargo radio station KFGO, the only place he can think of that has a piano. Finding the newcomer plays pretty well in the key of C, the Shadows buy him a black shirt to match theirs.

Bobby Vee knows that Gunn is really Bob Zimmerman from Hibbing. When Zimmerman tells them he has written some songs, the *Shadows* aren't real impressed; everybody is writing songs. But they like him all right—kind of a scruffy little guy, limited by what he can play, but who really loves to rock 'n' roll.

When the Vellines pick Bob up for a Friday night job at Gwinner, N.D., they belatedly confront the fact that he doesn't have a piano. In the church basement "ballroom" venue, a turn-of-century upright is found, far out of tune.

Never mind. They are finally playing "Whole Lotta Shakin' Goin' On" *with* a piano player. On Gene Vincent's "Lotta Lovin'," Vee is bemused to find Zimmerman has left the piano and come to the microphone, where he sings background and does Blue Caps-style hand claps.

After a second night, at a small pavilion near Fargo, Zimmerman is told he will have to buy a piano if he wants to continue with the band. That being out of the question, he is paid $15 for each of his two nights as a Shadow.

On a rainy night in August, Zimmerman returns to Hibbing on a bus. He tells no one but his family the big gig has fallen through. To Bucklen, he spins a "Suzie Baby" 45 and a yarn. *Yeah, I went out and cut a record and changed my name to Bobby Vee.*

On Howard Street, when he runs into Sharon LeVoir Taddei, Zimmerman says he is now known as Bobby Vee. Sharon calls a friend in Fargo to find out if it's true. The friend says it's not.

Trying out a new identity is a family tradition. Zimmerman's grandfather, Benjamin Solemovitz, remade himself as Ben Stone. A stage name is also a Mesabi tradition. *Frances Gumm* became Judy Garland. *Helen Naeseth* became Kirsten Kenyon. *Arvo Halberg* became Gus Hall. It's show biz. Roy *Leonard Slye* Rogers; Robert *Walden Cassotto* Darin; Conway *Harold Jenkins* Twitty; Harry *Erich Weiss* Houdini; Ethel *ZimMerman*. Who knows who or what Bobby will become, once he shakes off his heritage and the red dust of a bong town?

As "going away to college" becomes imminent, Bobby drops in at the Minneapolis house of the Jewish fraternity rush chairman, who happens to be writing a pledge skit, "Annie Get Your Buns," with three fraternity brothers. Bobby sits down at the piano and knocks off several songs, claiming he is Bobby Vee and has played with Buddy Holly and Little Richard.

He is still signing himself Robert A. Zimmerman when he enrolls in the University for what his parents see as an uncertain future. *Don't keep writing poetry, please don't.* Apparently, he's dead set against returning to the family business. *Promise you'll study something practical.* An autumnal chill blows in early from the borderline. *I am an orphan.* The troubadour shivers and checks his pocket for Luckies. *I got my first guitar off Big Joe Williams in Chicago.* He bids adieu forever to the north country fair.

IRRC

I Shall Be Free

Above: Hibbing house owned by Abe and Beatty Zimmerman. *RCMM, 1995* •
Below: The Zimmermans rented the upstairs of this Duluth duplex. *RCMM, 1995*

BIBLIOGRAPHY

Primary Biographies: Scaduto, Anthony. *Bob Dylan: An Intimate Biography.* New York: Grosset & Dunlap, 1971. • Shelton, Robert. *No Direction Home: The Life and Music of Bob Dylan.* New York: Morrow, 1986. • Spitz, Bob. *Dylan: A Biography.* New York: McGraw Hill, 1989. • Thompson, Toby. *Positively Main Street: An Unorthodox View of Bob Dylan.* New York: Coward-McCann, Inc., 1971.

JUDAISM: Ausubel, Nathan. *A Pictorial History of the Jewish People.* New York: Crown, 1983. • Cohen, Chester G. *Shtetl Finder.* Los Angeles: Periday, 1980. • de Lange, Nicholas. *Atlas of the Jewish World.* New York: Facts on File, 1984. • Dubnow, S.M. *History of the Jews in Russia and Poland, Vol. II.* Philadelphia: Jewish Publ. Soc. of America, 1918. • *Encyclopaedia Judaica.* • *Encyclopedia Lithuania.* • Finkelstein, Louis. *The Jews, Their History.* New York: Schocken, 1974. • Joseph, Samuel. *Jewish Immigration to the United States from 1881-1910.* New York: Arno, 1914/1969. • Lamm, Maurice. *The Jewish Way in Death and Mourning.* New York: Jonathan David, 1969. • McGoldrick, Monica, et al., *Ethnicity and Family Therapy.* New York: Guilford, 1982. • Reiss, Ira. *Family Systems In America.* Hinsdale, Ill.: Dryden, 1976. • Rottenberg, Dan. *Finding Our Fathers: A Guidebook to Jewish Genealogy.* New York: Random House, 1977. • Sachar, Abram. *A History of the Jews.* New York: Knopf, 1968. • Schoenburg, Nancy and Stuart. *Lithuanian Jewish Communities.* New York: Garland, 1991. • Sorin, Gerald. *A Time for Building: The Third Migration 1880-1920.* Baltimore: Johns Hopkins, 1992. • Zipperstein, Steven J. *The Jews of Odessa: A Cultural History, 1794-1881.* Stanford, Cal.: Stanford University, 1985.

DULUTH/SUPERIOR: "125 Years," Duluth *News-Tribune*, July 3, 1994. • Auerbach, Selig. *History of the Jews of Superior, Wisconsin.* Typescript. • Covner, Thelma C. *Shabsie Karon, Patriarch: 1865-1966.* Unpublished, 1975.—*The New Wilderness: Building the Jewish Community in Duluth, Minnesota, 1870-1975.* UM-Duluth, 1975. • Dorn, Mary. *This Is Duluth.* Duluth, 1950. • *Duluth's Legacy, Vol. 1, Architecture.* Duluth: City of Duluth, 1974. • Eldot, Walter. *Jews of Duluth, Minnesota.* Unpublished, 1955.—"'Little Jerusalem' gone but Jewish life stays strong." Duluth *News*, Aug. 24, 1985.—"Everything you always wanted to know about Bob Dylan's life in Duluth but were afraid to ask," Duluth *News-Tribune*, January 27, 1974.—"My Son, the Folknik," Duluth *Sunday News-Tribune*, Oct. 20, 1963. • Frommer, Myrna Katz and Harvey. *Growing Up Jewish In America: An Oral History.* New York: Harcourt Brace, 1995 • Goldish, Mrs. S.L. *Background and Summary of Early Settlers in Duluth.* • *Jewish Fellowship News Jubilee Edition.* Duluth, 1995. • "Jews Role in Area," Duluth *News Tribune*, March 2, 1955. • Kobs, Peter. "Bob Dylan's boyhood home draws few tourists to Duluth," Duluth *News-Tribune & Herald*, Aug. 29, 1983. • Lydecker, Ryck. *Duluth: Sketches of the Past, A Bicentennial Collection.* Duluth: American Revolution Centennial Comm, 1976. • Olkon, Sandy. *Berkowitz etc. family history.* • Papo, Joseph M. *A Study of the Jewish Community of Duluth.* Duluth: Jewish Welfare Federation, 1941. • Peterson, Merton B. "WPA Church Records Survey, Agudas Achim and Superior Synagogue," Superior, 1940. • Plaut, W. Gunther. *The Jews in Minnesota: The First Seventy-five Years.* New York: American Jewish Historical Society, 1959. • Sandvik, Glenn N. *Duluth: An Illustrated History of the Zenith City.* Woodland Hills, CA: Windsor, 1983. • Singer, Bertha. *Highlights: A Short History of the Duluth Jewish Community.* Duluth: 1976. • Singer-Miller, Lael. *Rachel.* 1976. • Tarlowe, Laurie J. Interviews with Superior Jews. SHSW-Superior, Public Library, 1977. • Thompson, Lester. *WPA Church Records Study.* St. Louis County, 1938. • Van Brunt, Walter. *Duluth and St. Louis County*, 1921. • Woodbridge, Dwight and John S. Pardee. *History of Duluth and St. Louis County Past and Present Vol. II.* Chicago: C.F. Cooper & Co., 1910. • WPA Writers Project. *Minnesota: A State Guide.* New York: Hastings House, 1938/1954. • WPA Writers Project. *Wisconsin: A Guide to the Badger State.* New York: Wisconsin Library Association, 1941. • *Zenith*, Duluth Central High School yearbook, 1926-29. • Yudelson, Larry. "Tangled Up in Jews," from *Washington Jewish Week*, 1991.

HIBBING: Ackerson, Bert E., "This 'n That," in Hibbing *Tribune*, 1971. • "Bob Dylan and Jesus: The Scratching of Heads in Hibbing," Minneapolis *Tribune*, Dec. 7, 1979. • Alexander, Paul. *Boulevard of Broken Dreams: The Life, Times and Legend of James Dean.* New York: Viking, 1994. • Anderson, Chester G. *Growing Up in Minnesota: Ten Writers Remember Their Childhoods.* Minneapolis: University of Minnesota Press, 1976. • Ashenmacher, Bob. "Dylan's feelings for native North deep but mixed," Duluth *News-Tribune & Herald*, June 26, 1986.— "Dylan Talks: His Images of the North are faint but fond," Duluth *News-Tribune*, June 29, 1986.—"Looking back on Bobby," Duluth *News-Tribune* (?)• Berg, Steve. "In Dylan's Home Town They Remember Bobby," Minneapolis *Star*, Nov. 18, 1979.—"Dylan and Jesus. The scratching of heads in Hibbing," Minneapolis *Star*, Dec. 7, 1979. • Blegen, Theodore C. *Minnesota: A History of the State.* St. Paul: U. of Minn. Press, 1963. • Bream, Jon. "Minnesota, myth and movie?" Minneapolis *Star*, Feb. 3, 1978. • (Dylan's Hibbing home for sale), Chisholm *Free Press-Tribune*, Oct. 6, 1988. • Chmielewski, Florian. *Mixing Polkas with Politics.* Sturgeon Lake, Minn.: Chmielewski, 1992. • Du Kruif, Paul. *Seven Iron Men.* Harcourt, Brace & Co., 1929. • Filth, Dr. *The fiddler now upspoke: A collection of Bob Dylan interviews and press conferences,* Vols. I and II, England, 1996? • Furst, J.P. "Dylan's Hibbing home sold," Duluth *News-Tribune*, August 24, 1990.—"Noting Dylan's 50th: All quiet in Duluth," Duluth *News-Tribune*, May 24, 1991• *Giant.* Warner Brothers, 1956. • Greenberg, Mrs. Morris. Paper to St. Louis County Historical Society. Eveleth, Minn.: March 1, 1955. • Guello, Dr. Samuel. *Hibbing: The Man and the Village.* Hibbing: Hibbing Historical Soc., 1957. • Hall, Gus. *Working Class USA: The Power and the Movement.* New York: International, 1987. • Halberstam, David. *The Fifties.* New York: Villard, 1993. • *Hematite.* Hibbing High School yearbook, 1932, 1956-59. • Hibbing Centennial Committee. *The Sleeping Giant: Hibbing, Minnesota, The Beginning.* Hibbing: *Manney's Shopper*, 1993. • Hibbing *Daily Tribune* 1947-59. • *Hi-Times,* Hibbing High School, 1955-59. • Howard, Sandford A. *Hibbing, The Old and The New,* 1921. • Coyle, Pam. "HIGH TIMES Exclusive: An Interview With Bob Dylan," *Hi-Times*, Oct. 18, 1978. • Holmquist, June. *They Chose Minnesota: A Survey of the State's Ethnic Groups.* St. Paul: Minnesota Historical Society, 1981. • Karni, Michael G. *Entrepreneurs and Immigrants: Life on the Industrial Frontier of Northeastern Minnesota.* Chisholm, Minn.: IRRC, 1975. • Kaufman, Joanne. "The House of the Rising Son: Bob Dylan's Boyhood Home Goes on the Block in Hibbing," *People*, Oct. 17, 1988. • Kitchen, Robert *et al. Hibbing, Minnesota: On the Move Since 1893.* Hibbing, 1993. • Landis, Paul Henry. *Three Iron Mining Towns.* New York: Arno Press, 1970. • Lemmons, Michael. "Dylan fans coming to Hibbing," Hibbing *Daily Tribune*, Oct. 4, 1989. • Lockwood, Sarah. *The Man from Mesabi: A Novel of Iron, Money and Love.* New York: Doubleday, 1955. • Longyear, Edmund J. *Mesabi Pioneer: Reminiscences of Edmund J. Longyear.* St. Paul: Minnesota Historical Soc., 1951. • Maier, Dr. R. *History of Congregation Agudath Achim.* Hibbing: Unpublished, 1956 • McCuistion, Laurie. "An Exclusive 'On the Tracks' Interview with Bill Marinac," *On the Tracks*, Vol. 4, No. 2, 1996. • *The R&B Box: 30 Years of Rhythm, & Blues.* Los Angeles: Rhino Records, 1994. • Rank, Perry R. "How to Invest in Your Child's Soul," *Series of Dreams* 32, 1996. • Shaw, Arnold. *Honkers and Shouters: The Golden Years of Rhythm and Blues.* New York: Macmillan, 1978. • Stong, Phil. "Minnesota's

Iron Giant," *Holiday*, July, 1950. • Thompson, Lester. *History of Agudes Achen (Hibbing)*. WPA, 1936. • Tourville, Tom. *Minnesota Rocked!! The 1960's: A Discography & Guide To The Music & People of Minnesota from the 1960s*. Spirit Lake, Iowa, 1983. • Steuer, Mark. "A Night Before the Music Died." *Voyageur*, Brown County Hist. Soc., Winter/Spring 1993. • Worthington, Rogers. "The town of Bob Dylan's youth leaves his past blowing in the wind," Chicago *Tribune*, July 13, 1988.—"No sign of Dylan legacy in Hibbing," Duluth *News-Tribune*, Aug. 17, 1988.

BOB DYLAN: Aaseng, Nathan. *Bob Dylan: Spellbinding Songwriter*. Minneapolis: Lerner Press, 1987. • Anderson, Dennis. *The Hollow Horn: Bob Dylan's Reception in the United States and Germany*. Munich: Hobo Press, 1981. • "Angry Young Folk Singer," *Life*, April 10, 1964. • Baez, Joan. *And a Voice to Sing With*. New York: Summit Books, 1987. • Bauldie, John. *Wanted Man: In Search of Bob Dylan*. New York: Citadel Press, 1991. • BBC TV, *Highway 61 Revisited*, 1993. • Beal, Kathleen. *Bob Dylan*. Mankato, Minn.: Creative Education, 1975. • Bowden, Betsy. *Performed Literature: Words and Music by Bob Dylan*. Bloomington: Indiana U., 1982. • Braun, Jonathan. "Is Bob Zimmerman Really Jewish?" *Rolling Stone*, July 8, 1971. • *Changin'* (magazine). • Clepper, P.M. "Mr. Tambourine Man, Play a Song for Me," St. Paul *Pioneer Press*, October 31, 1965.—"Dylan's Fortune," Hibbing library file. • Cohen, John and Happy Traum, "Conversations with Bob Dylan," *Sing Out!*, Oct./Nov. 1968. • Cohen, Scott. "Don't Ask Me Nothin' About Nothin' I Might Just Tell You The Truth: Bob Dylan Revisited." *Spin*, December 1985. • Cott, Jonathan. *Dylan*. Garden City, N.Y.: Doubleday & Co., 1984. • Colón, Carlos. "Stan's Record Shop," *The Telegraph*, Summer, 1988. • "The Cracklin', Shakin', Breakin' Sounds," *New Yorker*, Oct. 24, 1964. • Diddle, Gavin. *Images and Assorted Facts: A Peek Behind the Picture Frame*. Manchester: Printe Centre, 1983. • Dolen, John. "A Recent Interview with Bob Dylan." *On the Tracks*, July, 1995. • Dunn, Timm. *Look Back*. Chardon, Ohio (magazine). • Dylan, Bob. *Biograph*. New York: CBS, 1985—*Bob Dylan*. New York: Columbia Records, 1962.—*Lyrics: 1962-1985*. New York: Knopf, 1985—*Planet Waves*. New York: Asylum Records, 1974.—*Tarantula*. New York: McMillan, 1971.—*Writings and Drawings by Bob Dylan*. New York: Knopf, 1973. • Carman, John. "Dylan rumors blow in wind; he's not here," Minneapolis *Star*, Nov. 11, 1974. • Eliot, Marc. *Death of a Rebel: A Biography of Phil Ochs*. New York: Franklin Watts, 1979/89. • Elrod, Bruce C. *Your Hit Parade & American Top Ten Hits: A Week-by-Week Guide to the Nation's Favorite Music, 1935-1994*. Ann Arbor, Mich.: Popular Culture, Ink, 1994. • Federal Bureau of Investigation. Bob Dylan file. • Gilmore, Mikal. "Bob Dylan at Fifty." *Rolling Stone*, May 30, 1991. • Gleason, Ralph. *Rolling Stone Interviews #2*. New York: Warner, 1973. • Gray, Michael. *All Across the Telegraph: A Bob Dylan Handbook*. London: Sidgwick and Jackson, 1987.—*Song and Dance Man: The Art of Bob Dylan*. New York: Dutton, 1973. • Green Bay Packers. • Gross, Michael. *Bob Dylan: An Illustrated History*. New York: Grosset and Dunlap, 1978. • Guralnik, Peter. *Last Train to Memphis: The Rise of Elvis Presley*. New York: Little, Brown & Co., 1994. • Hendler, Herb. *Year By Year In the Rock Era*. Westport, Conn.: Greenwood Press, 1983. • Heylin, Clinton. *Bob Dylan: Behind the Shades*. New York: Summit Books, 1991. • Hickey, Neil. *TV Guide*, Sept. 11, 1976. • Hilburn, Robert. *Los Angeles Times*, Oct. 30, 1983, and Feb. 9, 1992. • Hirsch, Chuck. "Tom Paxton on Dylan: An Interview." • Humphries, Patrick. *Absolutely Dylan*. New York: Viking Penguin, 1991. • "I Am My Words," *Newsweek*, Nov. 4, 1963. • *Isis* (magazine), England • "Julie Znidar," *Isis 45*, Oct.-Nov., 1992. • Keller, Martin. "50 Years of Bob Dylan," *Minnesota Monthly*, May, 1991. • *Knockin' on Dylan's Door: On the Road in '74*. New York: Pocket Books, 1974. • Kooper, Al. *Backstage Passes: Rock 'n' roll Life in the Sixties*. New York: Stein and Day, 1977. • Kramer, Daniel. *Bob Dylan*. New Jersey: Castle, 1967. • Krogsgaard, Michael. *Positively Bob Dylan: A Thirty-Year Discography, Concert and Recording Session Guide*. Ann

Arbor, Mich.: Popular Culture, Ink, 1991. • Landy, Elliott. *Woodstock Vision: The Spirit of a Generation.* New York: Continuum, 1994. • Ledeen, Jenny. *Prophecy in the Christian Era.* St. Louis: Peaceberry Press of Webster Groves, 1995. • "Let Us Now Praise Little Men," *Time,* May 31, 1963. • *Little Richard: the Specialty Sessions.* Ace Records, 1985. • Loder, Kurt. *Bat Chain Puller: Rock & Roll in the Age of Celebrity.* New York: St. Martin's Press, 1990.—"The RS Interview: Bob Dylan," *Rolling Stone,* July 21, 1984. • *Lost & Found,* Eden Prairie, Minn., Dec. 1995. • McGregor, Craig. *Bob Dylan: The Early Years: A Retrospective.* New York: Da Capo, 1972/1990. • McKeen, William. *Bob Dylan: A Bio-Bibliography.* Westport, Conn.: Greenwood Press, 1993. • Mellers, Wilfred. *A Darker Shade of Pale: A Backdrop to Bob Dylan.* New York: Oxford U. Press, 1985. • Meyer, Mike. "Bob Dylan: Bringing It All Back Home," *Wisconsin State Journal,* Oct. 14, 1994. • Miles, Barry. *Bob Dylan In His Own Words.* New York: Quick Fox, 1978. • Miller, Jim. *The Rolling Stone Illustrated History of Rock & Roll.* New York: Random House, 1976. • *Minnesota Daily,* Feb. 17, 1978. • *On the Tracks* (magazine). Grand Junction CO. • Pagel, William. *Archives.* Pickering, Stephen. *Bob Dylan Approximately, A Midrash: a Portrait of the Jewish Poet in Search of God.* New York: David McKay Co., 1975. • Riley, Tim. *Hard Rain: A Dylan Commentary.* New York: Knopf, 1992. • Rinzler, Alan. *Bob Dylan: The Illustrated Record.* New York: Harmony Books, 1978. • Robbins, Paul J. "Bob Dylan as Bob Dylan," Los Angeles *Free Press,* 1965. • Romanowski, Patricia. *The New Rolling Stone Encyclopedia of Rock & Roll.* Rolling Stone, 1995. • Rosenbaum, Ron. "Bob Dylan: *Playboy* Interview." *Playboy,* March 1978. • Rowley, Chris. *Blood on the Tracks: The Story of Bob Dylan.* London/New York: Proteus Books, 1984. • Scobie, Steven. *Alias Bob Dylan.* Red Deer, Alberta: Red Deer College Press, 1991. • Shepard, Sam. "Bob Dylan: A one-act play, as it really happened one afternoon in California," *Esquire,* July 1987.—Shepard, Sam. *Rolling Thunder Logbook.* New York: Penguin, 1977. • Siegel, Jules, "Well, What Have We Here?" *Saturday Evening Post,* July 30, 1966. • Sirak, Ron. "Dylan: Can he be 50?" Duluth *News-Tribune,* May 19, 1991. • Sloman, Larry. *On the Road with Bob Dylan: Rolling with the Thunder.* New York: Bantam, 1978. • "Tangled Up In Bob," *Entertainment Weekly,* March 29, 1991. • *The Telegraph* (magazine), England. • Thomson, Elizabeth and David Gutman. *The Dylan Companion: A Collection of Essential Writings About Bob Dylan.* New York: Delta, 1990. • Thomson, Elizabeth. *Conclusions on the Wall: New Essays on Bob Dylan.* Manchester: Thin Man, 1980. • Tosches, Nick. *Unsung Heroes of Rock 'n' roll.* New York: Scribners, 1984. • Tuttle, John. *In His Own Write, Vol. II.* Mash Prod., 1990. • 20/20 interview, Oct. 10, 1985. • *Twenty Years of Rolling Stone: What a Long Strange Trip It's Been.* New York: Straight Arrow Press, 1987. • Von Schmidt, Eric. *Baby, Let Me Follow You Down: The Illustrated Story of the Cambridge Folk Years.* Garden City. N.Y.: Anchor/Doubleday, 1979. • Ward, Ed, Geoffrey Stokes and Ken Rucker. *The Rolling Stone History of Rock & Roll.* New York: Rolling Stone Press, 1986. • Way, John B. *Hungry as a Raccoon: Bob Dylan talks to his fans and other strangers...1966 and 1986.* England: 1993. • Weberman, A.J. *My Life in Garbology.* New York: Stonehill, 1980. • Wenner, Jann S. *20 Years of Rolling Stone.* New York: Straight Arrow, 1987. • Williams, Chris. *Bob Dylan In His Own Words.* London: Omnibus Press, 1993. • Williams, Paul. *Dylan: What Happened?* Glen Ellen, Cal.: Entwhistle Books, 1979. • Williams, Richard. *Dylan: A Man Called Alias.* New York: Henry Holt, 1992. • Wissolik, Richard. *Bob Dylan: American Poet and Singer: An Annotated Bibliography and Study Guide.* Greensburg, Penn.: Eadmer Press, 1991. • *Bob Dylan's Words—A Critical Dictionary and Commentary.* Greensburg, Penn.: Eadmer Press, 1994. Worrell, Denise. *Icons: Intimate Portraits.* New York: Atlantic Monthly Press, 1989. • *Zimmerman Blues* (magazine).

Index

—A—

A&W, 176
AAA travel notes, 116
Aanes, Nancy, 88, 156
Abrams, Harvey, 202
Abramson, 29
Accentuate the Positive, 38
Acknowledgments, 4
Adas Israel synagogue, 30, 35
Adas Israel, Duluth, photo, 41
Agnew, 20
Agranoff, Jeanette, 108, 109
Agudas Achim, 17
Ahlden, Dietrich Heinrich, 13
Airport Bar, 200
Aladdin Record Co., 181
Albany, 20
Alice, 51
Alice School, 56, 121
All-Nations bsktbl tourn. 60
Along the Iron Range, 72
Altman, Gerald, 74
Alto, Marilyn, 63
Alto, Roger, 63
American Legion, 15
American Zionist Assoc. 33
Anderson, Bus Andy, 52
Androy, 74, 86
Androy Hotel, 52, 55, 61, 109, 110, 133, 149, 195, 206
Androy Hotel, photos, 25, 58, 66, 112, 160, 186
Annie Get Your Buns, 208
Anti-Defamation League, 55
Antonelli girls, 56
Aristocrats, 79
Armory, Duluth, 37, 39, 191
Armory, Hibbing, 180, 190
Arrowhead Furniture, 148
Arrowhead Furn., photo, 186
Arthur Godfrey Hour, 53
Ashtabula, 31
Asian Flu, 164
Auditor's Addition, 62
Autry, Gene, 118
Avalon, Frankie, 198
Averbrook, Azriel, 17, 18
Aviators Addition, 78
AZA basketball, 33
AZA basketball team, photo, 45

—B—

B'nai B'rith, 33,55, 62, 74, 119
B'nai B'rith convention, 55
Baccalaureate, 205
Band, High School, photo, 158, 184
Banen finance, 54
Banen, Bernice, 88, 110
Banen, Marsha, 110
Banen, Maury, 110
Barbara, 154, 156
Bardot, Brigitte, 108, 176, 195
Barg, 31
Barron, Miss, 205

Baseball, High School, photo, 140
Bauldrica, Jim, 79
Beat Generation, 116, 181
Beat Generation, cartoon, 190
Beatniks, 167
Beatty's aunt, 33
Beaumont, Hugh, 195
Becker, Barbara, 106
Beecher, Bonnie, 202
Belafonte, Harry, 153, 198
Belle Tones, 181, 201
Beltline highway, 194
Bemidji, 150
Bennett Pk, 15, 49, 61, 104, 117
Bentnix, Mickey, 79
Berkovitz, Rachel, 13
Berkovitz, Yehuda Aren, 13
Beron, Jim, 203
Bessemer, Michigan, 14
Beverly Hills, Calif., 79
Bianchini, Barbara, 131
Big Black Train, 179, 181
Big Bopper, The 148, 179, 181, 197, 205, 207
Big Sandy Lake, 176
Bijou Theatre, 15
Birdie, R.D., 15
Black Hills Passion Play, 132
Black Rebels Motorcycle Club, 120, 173
Blackboard Jungle, 120
Blatnick, John, 50, 103
Blessed Sacrament, 56, 130
Bloom, Hyman, 62
Bloomquist, Gerald, 80
Boat Club ballroom, 33
Boone, Wild Bill, 132
Boston Celtics, 117
Boston Store, 62
Boutang, Dale, 174
Bovey, 143, 177
Bowling, 130
Bowling champs, photo, 137
Bowling League, 135
Boy Scouts, 15, 75, 135
BPOE, 14
Brando, Marlon, 118, 120, 121, 171, 196
Bridge, Aerial Lift, 39
Bridgeman Dairy Store, 60
Brooklyn, 20, 54, 74, 156
Brooklyn, N.Y., 107
Bucklen, John, 88, 110, 111, 136, 152-156, 171, 172, 178-182, 201, 203-208
Bucklen, John, photo, 185, 189
Bucklen, Ruth, 177
Bugliosi, Ray, 72
Bugliosi, Vince, 56, 72, 79, 130
Buhl, 156
Bunch, Charles, 204
Bunyan, Paul, 51, 135

—C—

Cadigan, Pat, 148, 203
Calumet, 86, 177, 204

Camp Herzl, 75, 135, 156, 182, 203, 207
Camp Herzl, photo, 114
Camp Rucker, 77
Cansona, Salvator, 72
Carlson, John Verne, 62
Carnival Talent Contest, 180
Carson Lake, 20, 78
Carstens, Dr. Fred, 51
Caruso, 79, 80
Catholic Youth Association, 196, 201
Caulfield, Holden, 131
Central Addition, 15
Central H School, 30, 32, 35, 39
C of C Winter Frolic, 180
Charles, Ray, 155, 180
Charm (magazine), 50
Checco, Tom, 154
Cheever Stadium, 97, 104
Cherson, James, photo, 45
Cherson, Max, photo, 45
Chez, Bert, 166
Chez, Dennis, 87
Chez, Dennis, photo, 91
Chez, Harriet, 166
Chez, Mrs. Bert, 166
Chicago, 17, 34
Chisholm, 16, 85, 116, 132, 144, 145, 148, 173, 193
Chmielewski "Polka Hour", 181
Christ Memorial Church, 52
Chun King, 85, 104
Churches, Hibbing, 15
CIO, 34
CIO Local 1663, 143
Cippelones Rhythmaires, 61
Cippeloni, Joe, 79
City directory, Hibbing, 104
Clark, 20
Class flower, 206
Class motto, 206
Clear Lake, 204
Cleveland, 17, 20
Clevenstine, Shelby, 179
Clooney, Rosemary, 131
Club Band Box, Leetonia, 61
Clyde Beatty's circus, 53
Clydesdales, photo, 126
Cobb-Cook school, 117
Cohan, Robert, 63
Cohen, 17, 30
Cohen, Bill, 196
Coleraine High School, 173
College All-Stars, 105
College Capers, 131, 152, 205
Collier's Bar-B-Cue, 178
Collier's Bar-B-Q, photo, 126, 127
Collins, Dorothy, 131
Come On Everybody, 201
Comfort Station, 15
Coney Island, 203
Connors Pt, 18, 20, 21, 34, 38
Connors Point schoolhouse, 17
Cook American Legion, 103
Coolidge, Calvin, 104
Corner Bar, photo, 82

Corrigan and McKinney, 20
Costello, John, 63
Council of Jewish Women, 74, 99, 119
Court House addition, 164
Courthouse, new, 130, 164
Courthouse, old, 52, 104, 144
Courthouse, old, photo, 90
Cousy, Bob, 117
Covenant Club, 37, 38
Crests, 153
Crewcuts, 149
Crickets, 200
Crippa music store, 99, 106, 122, 147, 153, 175, 206
Crippa music store, photo, 141, 188
Crippa, Chet, 79
Crippa, Chet, photo, 76
Crystal Ballroom, 207
Crystal's Corner Deli, 32
Crystal, Isadore, photo, 45
Crystal, Jacob, 32
Curtis Hotel, 117
Czar Alexander II, 12
Czar Alexander III, 12

—D—

Dairy Queen, 60
Dall, Jimmy, 79
Dandy, Jim (Reese, James), 171, 178, 203
Daneiko office supplies, 54
Darin, Bobby, 153
Dark, Johnny, 173
Dark, Johnny, photo, 185
Dasovic, Kathy, 201
Davidson, Harry, 72
Dean, James, 118, 120, 131, 136, 145, 150, 153, 155, 165, 171, 174
Delvic Hotel, photo, 112, 188
Dempsey, Jack, 61
Denfeld, 85
Detroit, 107
Deutsch, Mrs. Louis, 38
Diachok, Leo, 63
Diamonds, 149, 155, 168
Diarrhea Blues, 153
Dickens, Little Jimmy, 118
Dillon Road, 54
Dillon's farm, 194
Dillon, Bobby, 97,131, 145, 164
Dillon, George, 130, 143
Dillon, James, 15
Dillon, Joseph, 193
Dillon, Matt, 132, 145, 195
Dillon, Merritt, 78
Dillon, Mrs. Gerald, 117
Dillon, Mrs. Mary, 85
Dillon, Mrs. Robert, 105
Dion & the Belmonts, 191, 204
Dion, photo, 191
Dominoes, 153
Dougherty, Mrs., 55
Drunkard's Son, The, 111
Dubnow, S.M., 12

Duluth all-Negro Travelers, 79
Duluth Herald, 32
Duluth, photos, 42, 46, 47
Duluth, bird's eye, 8, 9
Dupont highway, 87
Dupont Lake, 110, 132, 182
Dupont Lake road, 53, 167
Dyer-Bennet, Richard, 165
Dylan, Dave, 24

—E—

Eddy, Nelson, 86
Edelman, 29
Edelstein Amusement Co., 53
Edelstein theaters, 54
Edelstein, "Chuck", 85
Edelstein, Ann (Chana), 13
Edelstein, B.H., 12, 13, 16, 20, 37, 40, 149, 166, 202
Edelstein, Barbara, 63, 122
Edelstein, David, 13, 21
Edelstein, Ethel, 16, 34
Edelstein, Etta, 13
Edelstein, Florence, 12, 16, 20, 40
Edelstein, Goldie, 16, 20
Edelstein, Ida, 21
Edelstein, Ida Berkovitz, 13
Edelstein, Jean, 63
Edelstein, Jennie, 16, 20
Edelstein, Julian, 20
Edelstein, Julius, 16, 38, 106
Edelstein, Lena, 13
Edelstein, Lybba, 13, 17, 20, 37, 40, 53, 110
Edelstein, Max, 16, 38, 60, 74, 85
Edelstein, Maxie, 20
Edelstein, Mike, 16, 20
Edelstein, Morris, 13
Edelstein, Mrs. Max, 99
Edelstein, Robert H., 59
Edelstein, Rosa, 20
Edelstein, Rose, 13, 16
Edelstein, Roy, 13, 21
Edelstein, Samuel, 13, 20, 16, 38
Edelstein, Sarah, 13
Edelstein, Sylvia, 16, 34
Edmund Fitzgerald, 194
Edwardson, Monte, 155, 156, 178, 180, 181, 183, 201, 204
Einstein, Albert, 115
Ekola, Gustie, 74
el MOTEL COURT, 71
Elephant Lake, 166
Ellington, Duke, 131
Ellis Island, 31
Ellis, E., 116
Elstad, R.J., 51
Elvis, 118, 131, 136, 147, 151, 153, 154, 155, 167, 168, 170, 173, 197, 199, 200, 205
Elvis, photo, 141
Emerg. Civil Lib. Com., 16, 95
Engel, Dave, 2
Enger park, 33, 39
Erickson, David, 121
Eveleth, 16, 119

—F—

Fabbro, Larry, 56, 151, 152, 196
Fabbro, Larry, photo, 140, 157
Fabian, 198
Fair Store, Duluth, 32
Fairview Add., 57, 58, 88 172
Fargo, N.D., 109, 145, 198, 207, 208
Father's Day, 81
Feldman's, 153
Feldman's, 54, 56, 78, 109, 155, 201
Feldman's, photo, 101
Feldman, Herman, 55, 166
Feldman, Mrs. Herm., 132, 166
Feldman, Shirley, 63, 132
Fergus Falls, 150
Ferrante and Teicher, 195
Fiedler, Arthur, 106
Fifth Ave. W., photo, 4
Finn, 20
Fire Tower Road, 176
First Ave., photo, 138, 139, 188
First Settlers of Hibbing, 143
Fischman, Ben, photo, 45
Fisher, George, 53, 71, 72, 77, 78, 80, 81, 84, 85, 86, 104, 109, 166
Fitzgerald, F. Scott, 134
Florian Zabach show, 195
Flying saucers, 50, 84, 105, 147
Flynn, 116
Fontigrossi, Jenny, 173
Football, B squad, photo, 140
Ford, 176
Forest Hills cem., Duluth, 14
Forest Lake Lodge, 148
Forrest, Helen, 38
Four Naturals, 61
Four Sharps, 61
Fran Matosich, 201
Fraser mine, 116
Frazer, 20
Freberg, Stan, 153
Free, I Shall Be, photo, 209
Freeman, Bobby, 171
Freeman, Orville, 50
French, 20
Friedman Clothier, photo, 188
Friedman's clothing store, 54
Friedman, Samuel, 31, 33
Friedman, Steve, 136, 203
Friends of the Wilderness, 132
Fudge bar recipe, Beatty's, 110

—G—

Gabardi, Gene, 63
Gabrielson, Conrad, 172
Garland, Judy, 86, 98, 118, 132, 146, 208
Garmaker, Dick, 85, 105, 117, 130
Gaskins, J., 103
Genealogy table, 40
General Appliance Co, 34
Ghandi, Mohandes K., 50
Giant, 150
Gilbert football team, 117
Gilmore, Ethel Milne, 98
Girls Athletic Association, 164
Gitlis, Ivry, 131
Glass schoolhouse, 51
Glen, 20
Godfrey mine, 116
Gogebic, 17
Goldberg, Stevie, 136, 155
Goldberg, Sylvia Edelstein, 109
Golden, 29
Golden Chords, 178, 179, 181, 200
Golden Circle, 34
Golden Gloves, 173
Goldfarb, Norman, 33
Goldfine, Henry, 81
Goldfine, Irene, 166
Goldfine, Joseph, 33
Goldfines, 35
Goldish, 29
Goldman, Ben, 55
Goldman, Ronald, 132
Goldstein, 30
Goldstein, Marvin, photo, 45
Gopher Theatre, 53, 71, 96
Grammy Award, 134
Grand Rapids, 61, 86, 146, 172, 201
Gray, Max, 60, 130, 194
Graysher, 96, 164
Graysher Shopping Center, 130
Green Bay Packers, 97
Green Bay, Wis., 204
Greenberg, Barbara, 119
Greenblatt, Max, 16
Greenhaven, 78, 96, 164
Greenhaven school, 117
Greenstein, Anna (Chana), 40, 110
Grey, Arvella, 108
Greyhound bus line, 52
Grillo, Warren, 200
Gumm Sisters, 98
Gumm, Frances, 98, 208
Gumm, Frank, 98
Gumm, Suzanne, 98
Gumm, Virginia, 98
Gunn(n), Elston, 207
Gurley, 116
Gusse, Charlotte, 34
Gusse, Rabbi, 34
Gutter Boys, 135
Gutter Boys, photo, 137
Gwinner, N.D., 208

—H—

Hadassah, 36, 74, 81, 99, 119, 122, 132
Haidos family, 56
Haidos, George, 56, 174
Halberg, Arvo, 50
Hall, Gus, 50, 77
Hallock's, 54
Hallock, Charles, 16
Hallock, Lester, 166
Hallock, Naomi, 63
Hallock, Norman, 87
Hallock, Norman, photo, 91
Hallock, Sara, 55
Hammel, 29
Harlem Globetrotters, 130
Harold, 20

Hartley, 20
Hautala, Mr., 179
Haymes, Dick, 38
Haywood, 116
Hebrew Brotherhood, 17
Hebrew cemetery, Superior, 38
Helstrom, Dick, 201
Helstrom, Echo, 11, 110, 152, 170, 173, 175, 176, 178, 180, 181, 202
Helstrom, Echo, photo, 185
Helstrom, Martha, 177
Herald Mine, miners, photo, 68
Herberger's Carnival Days, 72
Herberger's dept. store, 54
Herzl, Camp see Camp Herzl,
Hibbing aerial photo, 124, 125, 158
Hibbing Greyhounds, 79
Hibbing High School, description, 52, 121, 164
Hibbing High School, photos, 25, 127, 140, 184
Hibbing Hospital, photo, 91
Hibbing Hotel, photo, 24
Hibbing Jr Col. talent show, 118
Hibbing map, 1955, 123, 159
Hibbing Pol. Relief Assoc., 131
Hibbing Rotary club, 164
Hibbing, 1893 photo, 22
Hibbing, Anna Marie, 14
Hibbing, Capt., 14
Hibbing, Catherine, 13
Hibbing, Diederich, 13
Hibbing, Frank, 13
Hibbing, Frank, photo, 65
Hibbing, H.D., 13
Hibbing, old, photo, 65
Hickman, Ken, 146
High School singers, photo, 82
High School talent show, 131, 133
Highland Park, 182, 207
Highway 169, 87, 97, 130, 175, 177
Highway 5, 167
Highway 61, 116
Highway 61 Revisited, 220
Highway 73, 195
Hildegarde, 79, 119
Hilingoss Chevrolet, 73
Hilstein, 17
Himons, Rabbi Herman, 99
Hoikkala, LeRoy, 106, 121, 135, 136, 144, 153, 155, 156, 171, 174, 178, 180, 181, 183, 201, 204
Holbrook, Stewart, 50
Holiday magazine, 69, 71
Holly, Buddy, 148, 153, 168, 179, 181, 191, 197, 200, 204, 205, 207, 208
Holly, Buddy, photo, 191
Holzberg, 17
Home Acres, 78, 172
Homer Theatre, 53
Hooker, John Lee, 149, 153
Howard Gnesen Road, 34
Howard Street, photos, 26, 66, 67, 92, 102, 112, 113, 126, 160, 161, 186, 187, 188
Howard, Sandford, 15

Index

Howlin' Wolf, 153
Hughes, R.H., 96
Hull-Rust-mine, photo, 65
Hultstrand, John, 154
Humphrey, Hubert, 50, 59, 103
Huttonen, Paul, 144

— I —

I.W.W., 50, 77, 116
I.W.W., photo, 22
Immigrants, 15, 17, 39, 60, 110
Indianapolis Olympians, 85
Ink Spots, 53
International Falls, 167
Interstate Bridge, 34, 38
Iron lung, photo, 91
Iron Range Exec. Club, 129
Island Farm Creamery, 56
It, 201
Italian Hall, 61, 201
Itasca County, 134
Itasca county fair, 201
Ives, Burl, 165

— J —

Jacket Jamboree, 169, 179, 180, 201
Jaffe, Aaron, 12
Jaffe, Fannie, 12
Jaffe, Lybba, 12, 40
Jaffe, Sam, 20
James, Harry, 53, 106
Jay Lurye's Winter Theatre, 145
Jeanne Mitchell concert, 86
Jefferson school, 96
Jenkins, Harold, 206
Jennings, Waylon, 204
Jenny Jenny, 152, 154
Jewish Center of Superior, 149
Jewish center, Duluth, 156
Jewish Welfare Fed. campaign, 37
Jive Tones' *Flirty Gerty*, 155
Joe Mlaker's Polkatiers;, 61
Joelson, Ron, 207
Johnson, Keith, 205
Johnson, Roberta, 131
Jolowsky's junkyard, 54
Jolowsky, Sally Mae, 63
Jones, Spike, 131
Josephs, 29
Judaism, throughout
Junior C of C Teen-Age Canteen, 52

— K —

Kamman, Janey Lee, 63
Kaner, 29
Kaner, Kate, 18
Kaner, Oser Shabsie, 18
Kaner, Samuel, 18
Kaner, Shabsie (Solomon), 17
Kangas, Dick, 144, 155, 172, 173, 177, 204, 205, 206
Kangas, Dick, photo, 189
Kangas, Jeff, 156
Kansas, 108

Karakash, Dave, 131, 133, 200, 201
Karon, 17, 29
Karon (& Mark), 18
Karon, Shabsie, 29, 30
Kasonavarich, William W., 117
Kay Bank studio, 181
Kay Hotel, 56
KDAL, 106, 132
Keegan, Larry, 136
Keewatin, 103, 156, 177, 181, 195, 201
Keewatin Queen, 201
Kefauver, Estes, 84, 129, 145
Kelly Lake, 174
Kelly Lake road, 167
Kelly's furniture, 99, 172, 204
Kemp, Louis, 136
Kenner, 29
Kenner, Gerald, 33
Kenyon, Kirsten, 51, 72
Kerouac, Jack, 167
Kerr, 20
KFGO, Fargo, 207
King Hematite honorarium, 61
King Hematite Jubilee, 50
King, Louis, photo, 45
King, Wayne, 106
Kingston Trio, 195, 202
Kinsley Apartments, 34
Kirchboitzen, Germany, 13
Kitchen's Kitchenette, 175
Kitz, Jacob, 16
Kitzville, 20, 146
Kitzville Location, 16
Klatzky, 29
Kleffman Rink, 194
Klein, 29
Knevevitch, 117
Knezelvitz, 117
Knezovich, Milan, 53, 105, 118
Koenig, Don, 201
Kopstein, Rabbi Milton, 87
Kossoff, Dan, 155
Kossoff, Harry, 33
Krause apartment building, 33
Krznarich, William John, 173
KTHS, Little Rock, Ark, 153
Ku Klux Klan, 95
Kuntara, William, 73

— L —

L&B Cafe, 56, 110, 133, 152, 156, 173, 174, 175, 178, 206
L&B Cafe, photo, 126, 141, 186
La Pizzeria, 119, 133
Labovitz, Froike (Frank), 32
Ladin Nash Sales, photo, 102
Ladin, Barbara, 63
Ladin, Rochell, 63
Ladin, Sharon, 63
LaFreniere, Mary Louise, 86
Laine, Frankie, 131
Lake Superior Iron Co., 14
Lasky, 17
Last Chance Int. Bonspiel, 145
Latin Club, 150
Latin Club, photo, 137
Latto, Lew, 148, 191
Laura, 20

Lavina, 20
Leadbelly, 206
Leave It To Beaver, 195
Lebanon addition, 164
Lebedoff, Mrs. Martin, 132
Ledbetter, Huddie (Leadbelly), 118
Lee, Peggy, 131
Leetonia, 20, 21, 78
LeSueur, Minn., 207
Let Me Know, 181
Letter to a Teen-ager, 168
Levant, Edwin, 20
Levinson, Bennie, 21
Levinson, May, 21
Levinson, Rabbi Burton E., 37
Levinson, Roy, 21
Levinson, Sam, 21
LeVoir, Sharon, 56
Lewis, Jerry Lee, 118, 148, 154, 168, 169, 197, 207, 208
Lewis, Sarah, 74
Lewis, Stan, 153
Liberty School, 32
Library, new, 11, 96, 104, 118, 119, 164, 166
Library, old, 15, 52, 104, 129, 144
Lincoln High School, 144
Lincoln Jr High School, 96, 130
Lincoln School, photo, 90
Lippman Department Store, 54
Lithuania, 12, 13, 17, 18, 30, 35, 37, 62
Little Richard, 133, 147, 149, 151, 152, 154, 155, 165, 168, 173, 175, 179, 180, 181, 197, 199, 200, 208
Little Theater, 51, 63, 180, 202
Liverpool, England, 13
Lockhart, Dee Dee, 175, 176, 181, 182
Lockhart, Joey, 176
Locklin, Hank, 165
Loeb, 29
Lomax, Alan, 118
Lombardo, Guy, 131, 135
Lomoro, Jessie "Cookie", 201
London Opera Company, 86
Lubbock, Texas, 204
Lurye, 17
Lutz, Barbara, 13
Lutz, Michael, 14
Lybba, 175
Lybba Theatre, 53, 60, 71, 80, 106
Lyceum Building, Duluth, 14
Lyric Theatre, 15

— M —

Mackinac bridge, 164
Mackoff insurance, 54
Mackoff, Fredda, 63
Madden, Exhilda, 57
Madden, Timothy, 57
Maier, Dr. Joseph, 99
Maier, Rabbi R., 99, 107, 110, 146
Maki, Arnie, 176
Mal-Rad's, 152, 153
Man In the Little White Coat, 131
Man of the North Country, 165

Manhattan Woolen Mills, 32
Mankato, 118
Manley, Dr. James R., 36
Manoloff, Nick, book, 100, 108
Maple Hill, 54, 60, 176, 177, 202
Maple Hill Cemetery, 50, 87
March of Dimes, 53, 60
Margulis, Betty Ann, 55
Marinac, Bonnie, 205
Marinac, William, 105, 110, 135, 136, 151, 152, 156, 201
Marinac, William, photo, 157
Marinelli, Ron, 171, 172
Maris, Roger, 145
Mark & Karon, 18
Marti, Rev. Edward S., 205
Martin, Russell, 85
Mason City, 204
Mathers, Jerry, 195
McCarthy Beach, 104, 166
McDonald, May, 19
McGowan, Barbara, 38
McHale, Kevin, 165
McKinley, 20
McKinnon, Police Chief, 19
McNeill, Don, 37
McPhatter, Clyde, 155
McReddy, Terrance, 72
Meadowlands, 173
Meanest person, 104
Mehle, Stanley, 54
Memorial Building, 51, 52, 63, 72, 73, 78, 79, 84, 85, 95, 96, 103, 105, 106, 111, 117, 120, 130, 131, 133, 135, 145, 180, 194, 202, 206. See
Memorial Building, photo, 158
Mercer, Johnny, 38
Merritt, Dan, 14
Merryview addition, 96, 164
Mesaba camp, 50
Mesaba Civic Music Assoc., 131, 145
Mesaba clinics, 70
Mesaba Country Club, 55, 79
Mesaba Finance Co., 110
Mesabi Range, map, 64
Mesabi—Arrows To Atoms, 181
Micka Electric, 37, 49, 54, 56, 62, 71, 99, 130, 147, 148, 149, 157
Micka Electric, photo, 102
Micka, Ed, 37
Mikan, George, 85, 130
Milkes, Lori, 63
Milkovich, Cpl. Michael, 103
Miller, Charlie, 121, 180, 205
Mills Brothers, 131
Milwaukee Braves, 194
Minkler, Betty Lou, 53
Mpls Lakers, 85, 105, 117, 130
Mpls Star and Tribune, 105
Minn. Historical Society, 84
Minn. Northwestern Bell, 85
Minnesota, 1950 map, 6
Minors Club, 96, 120, 133, 200, 205
Mitchell bridge, 144
Molohon, Jim, 72
Monroe, 20
Monroe, Vaughn, 98
Montreal, Quebec, 13

Moose Lodge, 99, 155, 156, 175, 178, 200
Moose Lodge, photo, 102
Morris, 20
Morris, Bill, 196
Morton, 20
Morton mine, 144
Motherway, James B., 95
Mountain Iron, Minn., 13
Mrkonjich, Joe, 54
Murray, Don, 145

—N—

Naeseth, Chester, 95
Naeseth, George, 72
Naeseth, Helen, 72
Naeseth, Marius, 72
Nagurski, Bronko, 61
Nara, Chuck, 150, 151, 152
Nara, Chuck, photo, 140, 157, 184
Nashwauk, 63, 96, 117, 177
Nassau, 20
National Broth. Week, 119
National Geographic, 194
National Guard, 15, 77
National Tea store, 78
NBC Breakfast Club, 37
Nehiba, Jim, 122
Nelson, 20
Nelson, Ricky, 149, 154, 195
Nettleton school, 35, 40
New Brighton, 156
New Holstein, Wis., 79
New York, 35
NY and Missabe Iron Co., 14
New York City, 12, 31, 33
Newman the Great, 72
Newman, Jimmy, 165
Nicholas II, 13, 31
Nickoloff, Mrs. C.A., 118
Nides, 17
Nides, Nathan, 16
No Name Jive, 151, 153, 155, 175
North Central Air Lines, 104
North Dakota, 51
North Hibbing bridge fatalities, 105
North Hibbing, see King Hematite
North Street riot, 116
Novak, Vern, 50
Nu-Epsilon Phi, 33
Nylen, Dennis, 196

—O—

Oberlander, Col. Ted, 77
Odessa, 30
Odetta, 198, 199
Olson, Sigurd F., 132, 166
Oreckovsky, 29, 30
Orlando, Benedict, 150, 174, 200
Oshima, Mrs. John, 194
Oswald, 29
Our Savior's Luth. Church, 119
Overmans, 35

—P—

Panter, 116
Paper, Sam, 207
Papo, Joseph, 35
Parilli, Babe, 97
Parking meters, 60, 75, 97, 105
Paul, Les, 155
Paulucci, Jeno, 85, 104, 164
Paulucci, Michelina, 56, 85, 164
Pavich, Pete, 177
Pederson, Kenneth, 85, 121, 167, 180
Pengilly, 96, 177
Penobscot, 20
Penobscot Hill, 20
Peoples' Theatre, 15
Perella, Sam, 104, 119
Perpich, Rudy
Peterson, Donald, 145, 165
Peterson, Val, 121, 135, 201, 180
Pie-Eyed Piper, 202
Piggly Wiggly, 130
Pill Hill, 194
Pillsbury, 20
Pittsburgh, 17
Pizza, 96, 104, 119, 133, 147
Plant Towns magazine, 71
Pogroms, 12, 31
Pogue, George, 178
Polinsky, 29, 30
Polio, 40, 49, 60, 109, 117
Pool, 20
Popkin, 17
Pound, Ezra, 163
Power Field, 53
Power's theater, 15
Presbyterian church, 96
Pribich, Mike, 50
Prom, 178
Prom, photo, 184
Propotnick, 200
Propotnick, Jim, 181, 183, 201, 204
Propotnick, Louis, 181, 183
Prudential Life Ins. Co., 32, 34
Purity Baking Co., 57

—R—

Rabinovitch, Dr. Ralph D., 134
Radio City, Minneapolis, 72
Radovich, Bill, 105
Randy, James, 63
Randy, Lynette, 63
Ray, Johnnie, 86, 109, 122, 131
Rebel Without A Cause, 136
Recordland, 207
Red Apple Cafe, 207
Reed, Jimmy, 149
Reese, James (Dandy, Jim), 172
Retica, Mario, 53, 105
Retica, Mike, photo, 140
Rex Hotel, photo, 126
Rhythm- and-blues, 61, 100, 106, 107, 118, 135, 147, 149, 151-155, 173, 182, 199, 201, 202, 205
Rich, Buddy, 106

Richardson, Jiles Perry, 205
Riverside Ballroom, 204
Rochester, 150
Rockets, 181, 200, 204, 205
Rockets, The, photo, 183, 188
Rogalsky, Max, 16
Romberg, Sigmund, 72
Rood hospital, 15
Rote, Tobin, 97
Roth, Michael, 63
Roth, Mrs., 132
Round Table, 74
Rowan, Carl, 96
Rubin, Judy, 203
Rutstein, Harriet, 81
Rutstein, Les, 132
Rutstein, Mrs. Goldie, 38

—S—

Sach's, 54
Sachs brothers' Fair Store, 16
Sachs, Dr. Bertram, 62, 74, 146
Sachs, Thomas, 74
Salk, Jonas, 117
Salks, 29
Salnovitz, 29
Sammy's Pizza, 180, 203 206
Sammy's Pizza, photo, 188
Sanborn, Sgt. Donald, 84
Sapero clothing store, 54, 155
Sapero, Abe, 16
Sapero, Moe, 16
Sapero, Simon, 16
Sardo, Frankie, 204
Sardo, Frankie, photo, 191
Satintones, 200
Satisfied Mind, 177
Sault St. Marie, Michigan, 13
Schmidt, Alfred, 80
Schreiber, Marcelaine, 105
Schubert Chorus, 79
Scofield, Jerry, 201
Security bank, 116
Sellers, 20
Servicemen's Club, 61
Shabsie by the Bridge, 29
Shabsie Collis-Pointee, 18
Shabsie Connors Point, 17
Shabsie Downtown, 17
Shabsie the Geller, 29
Shabsie the Sam Kaner, 17
Shabsie the Schwartzer, 29
Shabtai Zisel ben Avraham, 37
Shadows, 207
Shamblott, Marsh, 196
Shane, 99, 100
Shane, Bobby and the Poor Boys, 207
Shapiro, 29, 30
Shapiro drug store, 54
Shari Ann, 181
Sheppard, John, 201
Sher insurance, 54
Sher, Diane, 63
Sher, I.R., 130, 119
Sher, James, 63
Sher, Mrs., 99
Sholom nursing home, 122
Shreveport, 149
Shriner, Samuel, 119
Shuirman, Thomas, 63

Shul, 4th Street, 30
Side Lake, 147, 182
Siegel, 17
Siegel, Mike, 87
Sills, Beverly, 145
Silver Bay, 194
Sinatra, Frank, 131
Singing Wilderness, The, 132, 166
Sioux City, Iowa, 109
Sioux Falls, South Dakota, 108
Skyline Parkway, 39
Smoltz, Frankie and orchestra, 61
Snow, Hank, 176
Soap Box Derby, 96
Solberg, Chuckie, 56
Solemovitz, Abraham, 18
Solemovitz, Ben, 18, 20, 208
Solemovitz, Bessie, 18, 20, 40
Solemovitz, Chana, 18
Solemovitz, Eddy, 18
Solemovitz, Ida, 18, 19
Solemovitz, Kate, 18
Solemovitz, Mary, 18
Solemovitz, Rosy, 18
Solemovitz, Sam, 19, 34
Solemovitz, Shabsie, 18, 21, 40, 110, 202
Solemovitz, Shabtai, 37
Solidaires, 53
Soma records, 207
Some Sunday Morning, 38
Song of Norway, 51
Sons of Italy Hall, 53, 95
Sorci's Market, photo, 138
Spector, Allen, 63
Spector, Mrs. Edward, 132
Sportsmen's Cafe, 175
St. James Church, 107
St. John, New Brunswick, 13
St. Lawrence Seaway, 194
St. Louis County Centennial Talent Show, 181
St. Louis County Fair, 52, 104, 200
St. Mary's Hospital, 35, 36
St. Paul Bible Inst. Choral Club, 86
Stan's Rockin' Record Review, 153
Standard Oil, 33, 34, 37, 40
Stark, Jim, 136
Starkweather, Charles, 163
State Theatre, 53, 71, 80, 96
State Theatre, photo, 141, 160
Stein drug, 54
Stein law office, 54
Stein, Leone Rae, 74
Stein, Louis, 55, 62, 74
Steinbeck, John, 118, 172, 177
Stern, Isaac, 53
Stevens Point, Wis., 13
Stevenson, 20, 21, 149
Stevenson, Adlai, 129
Stevenson, road to, photo, 23
Stolee, Rev., 119
Stone's clothing, 54, 56
Stone, Beatrice, 20, 33, 40, 56
Stone, Beatrice, photo, 1932, 28
Stone, Benjamin D., 20, 21, 34, 38, 40, 208
Stone, Benjamin (II), 87
Stone, Benjamin, photo, 91

Index

Stone, Florence, 11, 12, 20, 21, 34, 38, 40, 53, 56, 81
Stone, Florence, photo, 94
Stone, Irene, 20, 38, 56
Stone, Lewis, 20, 38, 55, 56, 81
Stone, Mrs. Ben, 38
Stone, Nancy, 63
Stone, Vernon, 20, 38, 170
Stong, Phil, 69
Strand, Al, 74
Strick, Thom, 181
Strikes, 50, 70, 84, 96, 130, 149, 194
Sturgeon Lake bridge, 144
Sturgeon River, 73
Sunrise Bakery, 57, 110
Superior, bird's eye, 8, 9, 10
Superior, Wis., 19
Surovsky, 30
Suzie Baby, 207, 208
Swandale road, 87
Swedish Lutheran church, 54
Sweet Shop, Chisholm, 144, 147, 173
Sweet Shop, Deluxe, 133, 174, 175
Swing Low, Sweet Chariot, 177
Swing, Dad, Swing, 201
Synagogue, 4th Av. West, 111

— T —

Taddei, Ron, 181, 183, 200
Taddei, Sharon LeVoir, 208
Tannenbaum, Abraham, 87
Temple Emanuel, 37
Temple Men's Club, 36
Ten O'Clock Scholar, 202
Tent Caterpillar Control, 87
Tent caterpillars, 86, 87, 98
Teske, Peg, 205
Thomas, Dylan, 78, 98
Thomas, Dylan, photo, 48
Thomas, Norman, 129
Tibroc, 132, 148
Tifereth Israel, 30- 36, 74, 122
Tifereth Israel Cemetery, 34
Time Goes By, 201
Toledo, 194
Tolstoy, Leo, 146
Tomasetti, Tony, 200
Tourist Court school, 117, 130

Tower, 16
Town line road, 87
Travis, Merle, 155
Trimble, A.S., 14
Triple Digits, 133, 135
True Fine Mama, 152
Truman, Bess, photo, 89
Truman, Harry, 59, 69, 77, 95
Truman, Margaret, 86
Tubb, Ernest, 207
Tunisia, 13
Turbins, 153
Twitty, Conway, 206, 207
Two Harbors, 73

— U —

U.S. Nationals, 194
University High School, 202
Upper Michigan, 85
Utica, 20

— V —

Vake, Ione, 200
Valens, Ritchie, 197, 204, 205, 207
Vallee, Rudy, 106
Van Feldt, Jerry, 178
Vandalism, 71, 85, 133
Vaudeville house, 15
Vecchi's Market, 147
Vee, Bobby, 197, 208
Vee, Bobby, photo, 191
Velline, Bill, 207
Velline, Robert, 207
Vendetti's grocery, 56
Venditto, Leonard R., 144
Vermilion, 17
Victory Theatre, 15, 16
Vilkomir, Lithuania, 12, 13 17
Vincent, Gene, 133, 147, 149, 151, 153, 168, 199, 208
Virginia, MN 16, 33, 38, 72, 98, 103, 171, 172, 178, 203
Virginia, Minn., photo, 189
von Ahlen, Franz Dietrich, 13

— W —

Waring, Fred, 118
Warren, Gov. Earl, 95
Washington Jr High, 32, 35, 39
Washington School, 96, 130
Water & Light, 135
Wayne King's orchestra, 86
WDSM, 106
Webb, 20
Webster, Wis., 75, 135
West Superior, 13, 19
What's-His-Name, 13
WHB, Kansas City, 197
Whitaker's, 120
WHLB, 171, 203
Wichman, Dennis, 110, 121, 150, 206
Wiesenberg, Rabbi Joseph, 62, 74, 80
Wilbur, 108
Wilcox, Laura, 110, 121, 150, 206
Wild One, The, photo, 185
Wild Bill Boone, 147, 148
Williams, 98, 151
Williams, Big Joe, 107
Williams, Bob, 130
Williams, Hank, 86, 97, 109, 122
Windom, 105
Winter Dance Party, 204
WLAC Nashville, 148
WLS, 203
WMFG, 52, 132, 135
Woman of North Country, 87
Workers Hall, 54
Workman, David Tice, 121
Workmen's Circle, 33
World Jewish Child's Day, 80
WPA guide to Hibbing, 52
WPA handbook, Duluth, 35
Wray, Link, 197
Wright, Jean, 119

— Y —

Yankovich, Frank, 73
Yiddish, 36
Yiddish theater, 33
YMCA, 33

Young Judea, 75
Young, John, 19
Youngman, Henny, 195
Young-Town Clothing Store, 109
Your Hit Parade, 131
Youth Center, see Minors Club
YWCA, 15

— Z —

Zimmerman house, Duluth, photo, 210
Zimmerman house, Hibbing, photo, 210
Zimmerman, Abe, photo, 45, 157
Zimmerman, Amy, 166
Zimmerman, Anna, 34, 122
Zimmerman, Anna Greenstein, 31, 32
Zimmerman, Beatrice, photo, 48
Zimmerman, Beth, 166
Zimmerman, David, 38, 56, 83, 87, 110, 134, 135, 146, 166, 195
Zimmerman, David, photo, 91
Zimmerman, Gary, 166
Zimmerman, Harry, 116
Zimmerman, Jake, 31, 32
Zimmerman, Joseph, 31
Zimmerman, Laura, 166
Zimmerman, Marion (Minnie), 31, 32
Zimmerman, Maurice, 31, 34, 37, 49, 62, 74, 81, 99, 109, 122
Zimmerman, Max, 32, 34, 63
Zimmerman, Morris, 32
Zimmerman, Paul, 31, 32, 33, 34, 37, 49, 99
Zimmerman, Paul, photo, 45
Zimmerman, Samuel, 31
Zimmerman, Wolfe, 32
Zimmerman, Zigman, 30, 32, 34, 37, 40, 110, 122, 202
Zimmerman, Zigman, photo, 44
Zim-Sax-Meadowlands, 104
Zionism, 36, 50, 62, 63, 74, 136
Zionist picnic, 33

Just Like Bob Dylan's Blues

When he left Hibbing for the University of Minnesota after his 1959 high school graduation, Bob Zimmerman was 18. His parents hoped he would study something useful but, during his one school year plus a quarter, his main preoccupation was learning to play folk music, meanwhile assuming a new identity. He left for New York in the winter of 1960-61 and, shortly before his 21st birthday, recorded his first album: *Bob Dylan*. The next few years provided a display of charismatic brilliance, culminating in *Bringing It All Back Home, Blonde on Blonde* and *Highway 61 Revisited*, a nod to U.S. Highway 61, which connects Duluth and Minneapolis. "Like a Rolling Stone"; "Tombstone Blues"; "It Takes a Lot to Laugh, It Takes a Train to Cry"; "Ballad of a Thin Man"; "Queen Jane Approximately"; "Desolation Row"; "Just Like Tom Thumb's Blues." *Well Abe says, 'Where do you want this killin' done?' God says, 'Out on Highway 61.'*

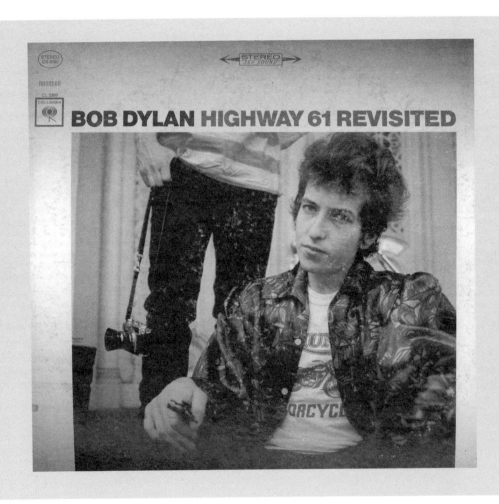

Author's 32-year-old album cover

an' I know I shall meet the snowy North again...
t' walk lazily down its streets...
find old friends if they're still around
<u>**11 Outlined Epitaphs**</u>**, 1964**